VOLUNTEER ACES OF CHURCHILL'S FEW

VOLUNTEER ACES OF CHURCHILL'S FEW

THE PART-TIME PILOTS AND THEIR AUXILIARY SQUADRONS WHICH HELPED WIN THE BATTLE OF BRITAIN

MARTIN WADE

AIR WORLD

VOLUNTEER ACES OF CHURCHILL'S FEW
The Part-Time Pilots and their Auxiliary Squadrons which Helped win the Battle of Britain

First published in Great Britain in 2025 by
Air World
An imprint of
Pen & Sword Books Ltd
Yorkshire – Philadelphia

Copyright © Martin Wade, 2025

ISBN 978 1 03612 169 3

The right of Martin Wade to be identified as Author of this work has been asserted by him in accordance with the Copyright, Designs and Patents Act 1988.

A CIP catalogue record for this book is available from the British Library.

All rights reserved. No part of this book may be reproduced, transmitted, downloaded, decompiled or reverse engineered in any form or by any means, electronic or mechanical including photocopying, recording or by any information storage and retrieval system, without permission from the Publisher in writing. NO AI TRAINING: Without in any way limiting the Author's and Publisher's exclusive rights under copyright, any use of this publication to "train" generative artificial intelligence (AI) technologies to generate text is expressly prohibited. The Author and Publisher reserve all rights to license uses of this work for generative AI training and development of machine learning language models.

Typeset by SJmagic DESIGN SERVICES, India.

Printed and bound in the UK by CPI Group (UK) Ltd.

The Publisher's authorised representative in the EU for product safety is Authorised Rep Compliance Ltd., Ground Floor, 71 Lower Baggot Street,
Dublin D02 P593, Ireland.
www.arccompliance.com

For a complete list of Pen & Sword titles please contact:

PEN & SWORD BOOKS LIMITED
George House, Units 12 & 13, Beevor Street, Off Pontefract Road,
Barnsley, South Yorkshire, S71 1HN, England
E-mail: enquiries@pen-and-sword.co.uk
Website: www.pen-and-sword.co.uk

or
PEN AND SWORD BOOKS
1950 Lawrence Rd, Havertown, PA 19083, USA
E-mail: uspen-and-sword@casematepublishers.com
Website: www.penandswordbooks.com

CONTENTS

Acknowledgements vi
Foreword ix
Introduction xi
Prologue xv

Chapter 1   The AAF, the RAFVR and the Coming of War 1
Chapter 2   Phoney War and the Battle of France 29
Chapter 3   Prelude and First Attacks, 26 June – 16 July 66
Chapter 4   Channel Battles, 17 July – 12 August 85
Chapter 5   The Hardest Days, 13 August – 6 September 112
Chapter 6   Beginning of the Blitz, 7 September – 2 October 161
Chapter 7   Fighter-bomber Autumn, 3 – 31 October 188

Epilogue 202
Endnotes 213
Bibliography 236
Index 241

ACKNOWLEDGEMENTS

I am very grateful to Group Captain Richard Mighall OBE (Retd) for writing the foreword to this book.

As chairman of the Trustees of the Royal Auxiliary Air Force Foundation, he works tirelessly in support of the Foundation's mission to provide a focal point for researching, recording and promoting the history and achievements of the Royal Auxiliary Air Force (RAuxAF) from its formation in 1924 up to the present day.

This includes the maintenance of, and organisation of events relating to, the RAuxAF Memorial at the National Memorial Arboretum, the RAuxAF Roll of Honour in St Clement Danes Church, the RAuxAF Archives and the Foundation's website. Alongside these monuments and memorials, I hope that this book can play its part in telling the story of the Royal Auxiliary Air Force squadrons, its pre-war part-time members, the RAFVR and their pivotal role in the Battle of Britain.

I thank him also for his advice, guidance and encouragement in the writing of this book.

I thank also the following whose help in researching and compiling this book has been essential and much appreciated. They are Carolyn Horton, Aldon Ferguson, Bob Kemp, David Ross, Bill Simpson, Roddy MacGrgor, Ian MacDonald, Dougal McIntire, Edward McManus and Christopher Shores. The Royal Auxiliary Air Force Foundation as a body has been most helpful, as have the Air Historical Branch and The National Archives.

ACKNOWLEDGEMENTS

I also want to give particular thanks to Dilip Sarkar MBE from whom I was lucky to have advice and guidance. Coming from someone who has written so many works on the Battle of Britain – this help was precious indeed.

I'm grateful also to my own squadron of the Royal Auxiliary Air Force – No. 614 (County of Glamorgan). While sadly missing from these pages, as one of the auxiliary squadrons not to serve in the Battle of Britain, it is my privilege to be the squadron's historian (among my official duties). I'm very grateful to the support given by them under the leadership of our commanding officer, Wg Cdr Lee Matthews, not least in the publication of my first book – *On Dragons' Wings* – the first published history of Wales' only auxiliary squadron. It is my privilege to serve alongside all of you.

As the members of today's Royal Auxiliary Air Force, we walk in the footsteps of those reservists who served before us and whose exploits fill these pages. I salute them all and the sacrifices they made. It is to their memories that this book is dedicated.

I thank also my wife Su and daughter Carys. You have supported this labour of love and your support is repaid with love from me.

This book is dedicated to my Mum, Jackie who passed away during its final production stages. She was a businesswoman, politician and activist who did much to make our town of Peel in the Isle of Man a better place. A woman of boundless energy, heart and love, I owe her a debt for her kindness and generosity of spirit. I'm grateful for the values she gave and inspired in me of service, of energy, of commitment and of striving for the common good.

Mum never knew her father John. He joined the RAF in 1925 and served in India and the Middle East in the 1920s and 30s and through the war when he was a founder member of the RAF Regiment. He was tragically killed at RAF Cranwell in August 1946, just five weeks before his daughter was born. After his death, the Royal Air Force Association gave my grandmother a grant which enabled her to set up a hairdressing salon. This was where Mum learned her trade which was her profession for most of her life. As I owe her, she felt she owed the Royal Air Force a lot – as we all do; not least for the actions described in these pages over those desperate months in 1940.

Martin Wade

FOREWORD

Many books have been written about the Battle of Britain and its Aces. However, none have concentrated on the 'part-time' Aces of the pre-war Auxiliary Air Force and Royal Air Force Volunteer Reserve who, along with their regular colleagues, contributed so much to the successful outcome of the Battle.

Part-timers like Archie McKellar and James 'Ginger' Lacey were among the highest-scoring aces of the battle. Moreover, of the 60 RAF squadrons that took part in the Battle, 14 were from the Auxiliary Air Force, and they accounted for a disproportionately high number of enemy aircraft shot down.

This extensively researched, detailed and very readable book by Martin Wade, addresses for the first time the exceptional performance of these pilots and why it was they were able to punch above their weight. He has drawn heavily on primary sources including interviews and memoirs, squadron operations records and histories, combat reports and press releases. He has also examined the all-important role that former part-time pilots played, and experience gained, in the months leading up to the Battle including their downing of the first enemy aircraft over both land and sea in Britain. Moreover, as becomes any in-depth review of a major battle, he has woven into his narrative the prevailing political agenda and the concomitant tactical and strategic military priorities and objectives both in the United Kingdom and overseas.

What is particularly significant is that the author has also captured the very essence of being a reservist and the wish, alongside like-minded fellows, to serve one's country as a part-timer to the best of one's ability – and which was so clearly evidenced during the Battle of Britain.

This excellent book fills an important gap in our understanding and appreciation of the achievements of these remarkable reservist pilots. It reminds us of their commitment, skill and bravery. Inasmuch, it serves as a tribute not only to them but also to all reservists who have so effectively supported – and continue to support – their regular colleagues in both peace and war. It deserves a place on every military aficionado's bookshelf.

Tradition does not die in the ashes but is carried forward in the flames.

Richard Mighall
Group Captain RAF/RAuxAF (Retd)
Royal Auxiliary Air Force Foundation

INTRODUCTION

The inspiration for this book came in 2020 with the 80th anniversary of the Battle of Britain. I was tasked with researching content for five videos on reservist pilots from the Battle of Britain. That research introduced me to the pilots who served with the RAF in their spare time during the 1930s and learned to fly with the Auxiliary Air Force (AAF) and RAF Volunteer Reserve (RAFVR). When war came they well-practiced pilots who had honed their craft at weekends and on summer camps. I learned of names like Archie McKellar, a plasterer, James 'Ginger' Lacey, a chemist, John Dundas, a journalist, and Raymond Davis, a mining engineer.

I was struck by the wide variety of their backgrounds, their reasons for joining and their Auxiliary squadrons which represented places they often were from – like No. 602 (City of Glasgow) Squadron. They decided to join as reservists when tensions across Europe were rising as Hitler came to power. In those years, as the drumbeat of war became louder, they honed their craft as fighter pilots at weekends and on annual, two-week summer camps.

By the time war did come in September 1939, they had gained much vital experience which would pay dividends as the war grew more intense over France and then exploded in those frantic months of 1940. I decided that I wanted to tell their stories and those of other reservists more fully, and to honour the distinct contribution of those Battle of Britain pilots who joined as part-time members of the AAF and RAFVR.

VOLUNTEER ACES OF CHURCHILL'S FEW

As an RAF reservist I am a proud member of the Royal Auxiliary Air Force, and my main role is as a Media Operations Officer. Recruitment of media specialists by the RAF began in the Second World War when journalists were trained and commissioned as officers so that the RAF could have uniformed reporters on the front line. The unit operating them became No. 7644 (VR) Squadron, and it recruited journalists, photographers and videographers from civilian life to be trained and deployed to cover RAF operations wherever they may be. My unit, No. 614 (County of Glamorgan) Squadron has a Media Flight which is part of RAF Media Reserves, which is centred on No. 7644 Squadron.

As a Media Officer, it's been my privilege to report from around the world on the people who serve in the RAF today – from pilots to chefs and to ensure their voices are heard. I did a similar job working as a journalist in civilian life, with my daily paper, the *South Wales Argus*, often writing on military themes. It was a privilege then in connecting with the past, to remind people of extraordinary stories. I feel privileged too in writing this book and it is my hope that it tells the stories of those reservists who fought in the Battle of Britain and honours their memories.

To do that, this book deliberately draws heavily on primary sources: squadron diaries, combat reports, memoirs, logbooks and interviews. I wanted to capture the first-hand accounts and experiences of those reservist pilots. It is a story often told in their words and through their eyes – about their background, their training, the aircraft they flew and the battles they fought. I hope those voices I have chosen represent the story of this 'few' within 'The Few'.

This is complemented by crucial events referenced with key characters who decided those pivotal moments of the battle – Churchill, Hitler, Fighter Command Chief, Air Chief Marshal Hugh Dowding and his German counterpart Reichsmarschall Hermann Goering in particular. Alongside this, published squadron histories were most useful in fleshing out the individual's accounts.

INTRODUCTION

I have used the definitions of phases of the Battle of Britain as set out by the RAF Museum and those definitions mark the beginning of each chapter. Their definition divides the battle into five phases and has the first stretching from the 26 June to 16 July. Explaining the thinking behind that definition the RAF Museum stated, 'In the United Kingdom the Battle of Britain is recognised officially as having taken place between 10th July and 31st October 1940. Different historians have described the progress of the Battle in different ways, but it is possible to identify five main phases, which started soon after the Luftwaffe had regrouped and consolidated its position following the defeat of France. Although they have been given precise dates one phase often drifted into the next and they should not be treated as hard and fast.[1]

Using this as the opening phase allows the build up to 10 July after the fall of France to more logically included, in my view, with the narrative of the Battle of Britain proper. Also whenever a pilot's Battle of Britain tally is mentioned, the date range is that from the official beginning and end of the Battle of Britain, ie 10 July – 31 October.

I deliberately had a chapter to cover the part-time volunteer services – Auxiliary Air Force (AAF) and RAF Volunteer Reserve (RAFVR) – their founding principles, the thinking behind them and their formative years. I wanted to establish the achievements, valour and elan of the reservists – as the sub-title has it, 'the part-time pilots and their Auxiliary squadrons which helped win the Battle of Britain'. As such it pays regard to both the AAF and the RAFVR. Although the AAF of course features heavily, through its members and the squadron identities – the 'Volunteer' in the title refers to those who served in their spare-time pre-war and then made a great contribution in Auxiliary squadrons when war came.

While the focus is on those pilots who joined as part-timers before the war and who then served in Auxiliary squadrons, due regard is also paid to those members of the RAFVR who went on to fight with spectacular success in regular RAF squadrons, like Eric Lock and Bob Doe.

Additionally, not all pilots mentioned in this book are 'aces', in that not all of them were credited with five enemy aircraft destroyed, the customary yardstick in qualifying to be an 'ace'. However, it would have been a grave omission to not tell the stories like that of Ray Holmes, who exemplified the volunteer spirit of those part-timers in the 1930s and the Auxiliary ethos of his squadron and other auxiliary units. He showed the determination to balance his day job with reservist service and would travel hundreds of miles across the country after work on a Friday to learn to fly. That commitment saw him score his famous victory – the dramatic downing of a Do 17 bomber as it flew towards Buckingham Palace. Similarly, in telling the stories of these aces, it is necessary (and right) to tell the story of the wider squadron at the same time. The accounts and the voices recounted here are intended to give an insight into the part-timers' experience both before the war and during the battle. Similarly Hugh Dundas of No. 616 (South Yorkshire) Squadron, while also not an ace, gives great insight into the motivation, training and combat from an Auxiliary perspective that is hugely valuable.

The Royal Auxiliary Air Force (RAuxAF) and the RAF Volunteer Reserve (RAFVR) were merged in 1997 and many of the squadrons mentioned in this book still operate today. Their members fulfil several roles in support of RAF operations in the UK and across the world.

The year 2024 marked the centenary of the RAuxAF and the following year the centenary year of four other squadrons mentioned in these pages – Numbers 600, 601, 602 and 603 – all of which were formed in 1925.

The RAuxAF's members serve as Intelligence Analysts, RAF Regiment Gunners (the air force's soldiers), Drivers, Chefs, Photographers, Logistics specialists, RAF Police, Cyber Experts, Human Resources specialists, musicians and more.

They inherit the proud tradition of those part-timers, who, just 85 years ago fought in the skies over southern Britain which were alive with the sound and fury of battle – a battle for Britain's very survival.

PROLOGUE

It was 27 September 1940. Pilots of No. 609 (West Riding) Squadron were patrolling over the Dorset coast. They saw the Me 110s circling over Swanage at 25,000 feet to protect their bombers. The Spitfires immediately turned towards the enemy fighters and started to climb above them.

'We were very close to them now and we started to dive', Pilot Officer David Crook remembered. His anticipation grew. 'I think that these moments just before the clash are the most gloriously exciting moments of life. You sit there behind a great engine that seems as vibrant and alive as you are yourself, your thumb waits expectantly on the trigger, and your eyes watch the gun sights through which in a few seconds an enemy will be flying in a veritable hail of fire. And all round you, in front and behind, there are your friends too, all eager and excited, all thundering down together into the attack. The memory of such moments is burnt into my mind for ever'.

He turned right in order to get on to the tail of a 'Hun'. 'My Spitfire immediately went into a very vicious right-hand spin – the atmosphere at these great altitudes is so rarefied that machines are very much more difficult to manoeuvre – and when I recovered, I had lost my German. The whole enemy circle had been broken up by our attack, and various Messerschmitts were streaming out to sea with our people chasing after them. I saw an Me 110 about half a mile ahead and went after him on full throttle. He also was going flat out and diving to get extra speed, but my beloved Spitfire rose nobly to the occasion and worked up to over 400 mph, and I caught him fairly easily, though we were about 20 miles out to sea by this time.

'The enemy rear gunner, who obviously had wind up, opened fire at me at rather long range, though I could see his tracer bullets flicking past me'. Crook dived slightly to get underneath his tail, as he could not fire at him in that position, and when in range he opened fire. 'I must have killed the gunner, he recalled, 'because he never fired again, though I must have been visible to him at times and at very close range'. He fired into the fuselage and port engine which started to smoke furiously.

He pressed the trigger to fire a final burst but his ammunition had gone. Just then a voice said on the R/T 'OK, OK, help coming,' and John 'Bishop' Bisdee gradually overtook him and finished off the Me 110, which fell into the sea. Bishop and Crook were credited with a half share each in the Me 110's destruction.

Six enemy aircraft had been destroyed and one or two more were probable 'kills'. He thought that the German squadron wouldn't look forward to their next trip over England. 'I know what we should feel like if we were attacked by an equal number of Messerschmitts and half our squadron was destroyed in four minutes'.[1]

Before the war, No. 609 (West Riding) Squadron, Auxiliary Air Force (AAF) was based at Yeadon at what is now Leeds Bradford Airport. David joined 609 Squadron in August 1938 and learnt to fly with them while working in the family sporting equipment business.

His wing-mate John Bisdee became a fighter pilot via a slightly different route – but still as a part-timer. He joined the RAF Volunteer Reserve (RAFVR) in July 1937 while working as a management trainee with Unilever. Called up on 1 September 1939, he joined 609 Squadron on Boxing Day that year.[2]

In that brief and violent encounter – typical of many which happened during those desperate months in the summer and autumn

PROLOGUE

of 1940, Crook, Bisdee and thousands of other RAF reservists who had been called up would show similar skill and killer instinct. They were highly capable pilots, capable of manoeuvring their powerful Spitfires and Hurricanes into a position where they could shoot German bombers and fighters out of the sky. The moments when this was possible were brief and extremely fleeting. It would take enormous experience and skill to master the art of the dogfighter, but former reservists like Crook and Bisdee showed again and again that summer that they were more than equal to the task.

Crook saw that as reservists they had shown real commitment to give up their spare time to train to defend their country. 'As we did our peace-time training at weekends and in the evenings during the week, this meant that we had to give up almost all our normal pursuits and spare time pleasures'. As training increased with growing tensions across Europe that year, so did the demands on their lives – with one foot in the miliary camp and the other in civilian life. 'It seemed only just possible to find time to carry on one's normal civilian job, and in addition, to do the flying and ground training in the squadron. Tennis, golf, rugger, going away for weekend – we had to cut these out almost entirely and concentrate instead on loops and rolls, formation flying and fighter tactics, armament and engines.'[3]

But this is essentially what he and thousands of other reservists in the RAFVR and AAF squadrons set up in the cities and counties across the UK would do. Alongside No. 609 (West Riding) Squadron, there was No. 504 (County of Nottingham); No. 600 (City of London); No. 603 (City of Edinburgh) and more. Together with these there were 'Town Centres' in cities and towns across the country where RAFVR reservists would gather and from where their flying training was often organised.

By September 1939, there were 20 AAF flying squadrons from No. 612 (County of Aberdeen) in the north to No. 501 (County of Gloucester) at Bristol in the south-west with RAFVR town centres across the country. The RAF went to war with just under 200,000 personnel, of whom 20,000 were RAFVR. Of its 12,600 officers, 3,000 were from the AAF.[4]

Of the 62 squadrons involved in the Battle of Britain, 14 would be from the Auxiliary Air Force and they accounted for approximately 30% of the accredited enemy kills.[5] Of the fourteen most successful squadrons, six would be from the AAF.[6]

'Everybody', Crook remembered 'was extraordinarily keen, from the CO down to the groundcrews, and we all realized the urgency of the situation and the great part that fighter squadrons would play in the event of war'.[7] They sometimes had to convince sceptical regulars of their worth. Station commander of RAF Hornchurch, Group Captain C.A. Bouchier, was one of them.

He recalled vividly his thoughts on the arrival of 603 Squadron at his fighter station on the front line of the Battle of Britain in August 1940. 'I shall never forget them coming! Could this really be a squadron, I thought as I went out to meet them on the tarmac on their arrival? The CO on getting out of his Spitfire had his little side hat perched on the back of his head and meandering towards the control tower with bent shoulders, hands in pockets, followed by the motliest collection of unmilitary-looking young men that he'd seen for a very long time. I was not impressed!' Bouchier remembered that No. 603 was an auxiliary squadron. 'That explained it' he thought, 'but why should they be unloaded on me?'

More used to 'regular' fighter squadrons, like Nos. 54, 65 and 74, he wondered how could an auxiliary squadron expect to acquit themselves in the manner of these renowned regular squadrons? 'How wrong I was! How I was made to eat my unspoken words – literally made to eat them for did I not attend the dinner given by the CO of 603 Squadron to celebrate the shooting down of their 100th Hun from Hornchurch?'

He continued: 'They were, I think, the greatest Squadron of them all. Within an hour of their arrival at Hornchurch, they were in the air

PROLOGUE

again to give battle to the Hun over Kent and the English Channel, charging through the smoke and the haze of the Hornchurch area and the hazards of the London balloon defences. From that moment until the Battle of Britain had been won, 603 stayed with me at Hornchurch'.[8]

There were some other things which marked them out. No. 601 Squadron enlivened their powder-blue uniforms with scarlet linings, and sported blue ties because the RAF's black depressed them. Edinburgh-based 603 Squadron boasted their own pipe-band.[9]

This book pays tribute to some important concepts and groups. The reservist principle and how effective it was enabled, in the words of Trenchard (Marshal of the Royal Air Force Hugh Trenchard, known as the 'Father of the RAF'), to help build the foundations of a castle, ready for when the castle had to be quickly built. The members of the AAF and RAFVR were part of those foundations.

As the numbers of pre-war part-timers thinned during the battle, the ethos that they had built continued through the remaining keepers of the often mentioned 'auxiliary spirit' and the group and squadron identity that had been built in those pre-war part-time years.

Additionally, with their regional identity, distinctive culture and ethos, the AAF squadrons were the places where training and learning was done and comradeship built and cemented. That was to pay dividends when war came.

Lastly, both RAFVR and AAF personnel showed the commitment which drives someone to give up their free time to serve their country.

The other part of this book's title, is of course, Winston Churchill. Through much of his career, he played an important role in the birth and the development of air power, the RAF and the AAF.

But it is through his war leadership that he is of course best remembered. Having come to power at a pivotal moment in May 1940, his leadership and in particular his speeches would frame this momentous battle.

In the dark days when Britain's weapons were few, Churchill mobilised the English language, using words instead.

The speeches he delivered then are among the most powerful ever given in English. His words were defiant, heroic and human, lightened by flashes of humour. As journalist Beverley Nichols wrote, 'He took the English language and sent it into battle.'

The phrases that he uttered in those frantic months have become part of the national story – a kind of shorthand for that struggle and for many more to come:

'We shall fight them on the beaches...'
'Their finest Hour.'
'Never in the field of human conflict has so much been owed by so many to so few.'

Of all those words, perhaps those which resonate – and particularly for this book are those on 'The Few'.

Churchill had long been a supporter of aviation. As Secretary of State for War and Air in the early 1920s, he did much to defend the infant RAF from the unfriendly attacks from the Army and Royal Navy who saw no reason for the independent upstart to survive the coming of peace. Through the 1930s he was a constant voice urging Britain to bring attention and money to its air defence and make the RAF strong enough to resist an onslaught from Hitler's Luftwaffe.

But perhaps the most obvious connection between the AAF and Churchill was through No. 615 (County of Surrey) Squadron. He was made their Honorary Air Commodore in April 1939 and wore his RAF uniform with pride on notable occasions such as meeting Stalin and Roosevelt at the pivotal Tehran conference in 1943. He took flying lessons before the First World War and 29 years after his first solo flight, he was awarded his RAF wings.

Additionally, a quote often attributed to Churchill encapsulates some powerful ideas about the place of reservists in a democratic

PROLOGUE

society and the contribution they make to that society. The line 'The Reservist is Twice the Citizen' frames a profound idea about the role of individuals within a society, particularly around their commitment to both civilian and military duties. By volunteering to become a reservist, they take on further responsibilities and commitment to their nation's defence.

As David Crook observed, reservists must balance their civilian lives with military service. The fact that they have a foot in each camp emphasises their versatility and adaptability in charting a course between the demands of military duty and their civilian lives.

That sense of living across two worlds extended to the fight in the Battle of Britain. Fought over the home counties, their battles took place over Surrey, Sussex and Kent – often over their piers and golf courses. They sometimes ended in relief at the club house bar having baled out or in tragedy having crashed to their death on the links. The pubs they frequented, with thatched roofs and tankards of warm beer – all were suddenly part of the front line as Britain entered this time of total war. During air raids on their stations, they would sometimes shelter with families in nearby houses and share meals with them. What exemplified this engagement of all the population in total war more than a cadre who had one foot in both camps already? The reservists already knew and lived in both worlds – civilian and military – now the rest of the country was learning how to do this too.

This book is not intended to be a comprehensive history of the Battle of Britain nor can it be an exhaustive survey of every action involving AAF and RAFVR reservists. Rather it is an attempt to tell the story of the vital contribution of these pre-war part-timers to eventual victory in the world's first battle conducted entirely in the air.

It is an attempt to gather those disparate accounts and voices into a whole which tells the story of those part-timers. Who they were, where they came from and what their contribution was to eventual victory.

David Crook summed up what he saw as the motivation those reservists had before the war and how they unleashed the skills they had gathered into the face of a merciless assault from Hitler's Luftwaffe.

'I think that to most of us flying was the dominating interest in our lives – I know that it has always been so to me – and therefore the more flying we did, the better we were pleased. The experience we gained stood us in good stead in the future, and when the war came, and our training was put to the sternest tests of all, 609 and the other auxiliary squadrons came through with flying colours and a record which equalled that of the very best regular squadrons.'[10]

Another auxiliary pilot who would fly with distinction in the Battle of Britain was Hugh Dundas. The pilot with No. 616 (South Yorkshire) Squadron was in no doubt about what made them special.

> We wore big brass 'A's on the lapels of our tunics and no amount of official pressure could persuade us to remove them. The regulars insisted that those 'A's stood for 'Amateur Airmen' or even 'Argue and Answer back'. To us they were the symbols of our membership of a very special club. The members had two things in common – a passion for flying and a fierce determination that anything the regulars could do, the auxiliaries could do better. In order to implement this determination a very high standard of flying had to be achieved, as every auxiliary pilot secretly appreciated, in spite of the assumed contempt for regulars and all their ways.
>
> In every auxiliary squadron I ever knew there was an exceptional spirit of enthusiasm and joie de vivre.[11]

THE AAF, THE RAFVR AND THE COMING OF WAR

The concept of reserves, or a part-time military force had long existed in Britain, but a modern incarnation came in 1907 when a system of territorial regiments raised by County Associations was set up. This was the system which some of the squadrons who would play a central role in the Battle of Britain would later be based on.[1]

The founding document of the RAF, the Air Force Constitution Act 1917, was put before Parliament on 29 November 1917 and led to the RAF's foundation on 1 April 1918. It included the right to 'maintain an Air Force Reserve and an Auxiliary Air Force'.

That right was left unused until March 1924 with the Auxiliary Air Force (AAF) and Air Force Reserve Bill which heralded the formation of the AAF. The Air Estimate, effectively the budget for the RAF, then allowed for a reserve capacity of 700 pilots and 12,000 airmen in five auxiliary squadrons.[2]

Some people linked with a future squadron had a seminal influence in the formation of the Auxiliary Air Force. One well-connected man in particular was determined to be at the forefront of this new force.

Lord Edward Arthur Grosvenor was an adventurer. After leaving Eton he had joined the French Foreign Legion, later joining the Royal Horse Guards.

But from an early age he had been fascinated by flight. Following Blériot's crossing of the Channel in 1909, there was the realisation that, as in the famous headline that 'Britain an island no more'. The nightmare possibility of attack by continental enemies from across the Channel was a fantasy no more. Grosvenor realised the value of aeroplanes and obtained his licence – No. 607. He was 'intoxicated by the miracle of flight in an open-cockpit stick and rudder aeroplane. He thrilled at the roar of the engine at full throttle, the sight of the ground falling away and the horizon unrolling infinitely, the fantastic downward view of earth and the tops of clouds'.[3]

His club – White's in fashionable St James' Street, Mayfair, effectively became the HQ for Lord Grosvenor's nascent squadron.

There he'd gathered a group of friends who shared his passion for flying. Following the First World War and service with the Royal Naval Air Service (RNAS), Grosvenor strived to make private aviation popular and endowed an air racing award, the Grosvenor Challenge Cup. He saw in those air-minded friends at White's – and those who competed for his cup – the kernel of a part-time air force.

The then Secretary of State for Air, Sir Samuel Hoare recalled in his work, 'Empire of the Air': 'Trenchard envisaged the Auxiliary as a *corps d'elite* comprised of the kind of young men who earlier would have been interested in horses, but who now wished to serve their country in machines. He conceived the new mechanical yeomanry with its aeroplanes based on the great centres of industry. Trenchard realised that a fighting service must possess a non-regular branch with its roots firmly set in the civil life of the country.' Sharing Trenchard's vision, this was exactly what Grosvenor was asking for.[4]

By 1923, with plans being set out for this citizen air force, Grosvenor gathered his chosen few for dinner at White's. 'It will happen', he assured them, 'so let us together form the first squadron of the "territorial air force"', and it went without saying that he would command it.

No legislation had been passed by that point but the spirit of the squadron was in being.

Returned to power as Secretary of State for Air in 1924, Hoare oversaw the creation of the Auxiliary Air Force. Although it wasn't

Grosvenor who conceived and delivered the AAF, his influence was significant having offered and then provided a ready-made flying unit of pilots and a commanding officer. Grosvenor never doubted that he was the Auxiliaries' father. In his own words he had 'sat on the doorstep of "Sammy" Hoare and "Boom" Trenchard until he had his way. Hoare expressed his own delight by becoming the first Honorary Air Commodore of Grosvenor's squadron'.

That squadron would be formed in 1925 and as it turned out, Grosvenor's band of flyers would not be the first but his unit of this part-time air force would not be far behind.

The first squadron was formed on 15 May 1925 when No. 502 (Ulster) Squadron became the first of the reserve units to be set up. This was followed that year by No. 602 (City of Glasgow) on 15 September. On 14 October a further three were formed: Nos. 603 (City of Edinburgh) at Turnhouse, 600 (City of London) and Grosvenor's No. 601 (County of London) – both at Northolt.

The different numbering reveals how the reserves were organised at the beginning. The '500' squadrons, like the Ulster unit were so-called 'Special Reserve' while the '600' squadrons like County of London were 'Auxiliary'.

While Auxiliary squadrons were recruited and administered by the County Associations, Special Reserve squadrons were recruited directly by the unit. Also, one-third of their strength were regulars and were administered directly by the RAF. The Auxiliary squadrons had a higher proportion of locally-recruited volunteers.

Also for the Auxiliary units, pilots were expected to be already qualified while airmen were trained by the squadron. For the Special Reserve units, the reverse was true.

The two families of reserve squadrons continued to grow. Four more Special Reserve units were formed: 503 (City of Lincoln) in 1926, 504 (County of Nottingham) in 1928, 501 (County of Gloucester) in 1929, and 500 (County of Kent) in 1931. Auxiliary squadrons formed as day-bomber units were 605 (County of Warwick) in 1926, and 604 (County of Middlesex), 607 (County of Durham) and 608 (North Riding) all in 1930.

The Auxiliaries – at least the officers – at this time came from a particular social background which can be seen by the leaders of the squadrons already formed. We've already met the commanding officer of No. 601 (County of London) Lord Edward Grosvenor. Other distinguished members including Sir Philip Sassoon, later to become Under-Secretary of State for Air, were too at the heart of the establishment and led to 601 becoming known as the 'Millionaries' Squadron'. Other Auxiliary squadrons counted nobles and notables in their numbers. The Marquis of Clydesdale flew with No. 602 and Lord Willoughby de Broke with 605.

As well as Grosvenor of 601, there was another driving force in those formative years of the AAF. Hugh Dundas, who would later join 616 Squadron, saw how the first commanding officer of No. 600 (City of London), also formed in 1925, the Right Honourable Edward Guest, was 'quite unlike Grosvenor in character and habit'. Dundas told how 'He was a most serious-minded man, who had given all his life to public service.' Already 51 years old when he formed 600 Squadron, he had first fought for his country on the White Nile and in South Africa at the turn the century. After the First World War he turned to politics. The personalities of Guest and Grosvenor shaped their squadrons, which later shared the same airfield at Hendon and set the pattern for the whole Auxiliary Air Force. Guest looked for solid, worthy and conventional qualities in his officers. Grosvenor wanted mercurial men around him and he did not care in the least whether they were conventional. 'Thus, in an atmosphere combining light-heartedness and an underlying determination to excel at operational flying, the "auxiliary spirit" was born and developed. And it flourished strongly as new units were formed up and down the country between that first beginning and the outbreak of war fourteen years later'.

THE AAF, THE RAFVR AND THE COMING OF WAR

Recruitment practices ensured that 'the right sort' was welcomed into the fold. Wg Cdr Dore, CO of 604 (County of Middlesex) Squadron noted that:

> The intention was to ensure that 604 got the best material possible for its officer candidates, and this inevitably meant recruitment came from the upper echelons of 1930s society: the public schools, with Malvern being to the fore, the universities, Oxford and Cambridge, the legal profession, the Stock Exchange and the City. I gave each applicant marks for his school record in scholarship and athletics; and if he could ride a horse, or drive a car or a motorcycle, or sail a boat, or ski or play the piano, I gave him extra marks.[5]

The Auxiliaries counted many from exotic backgrounds in their numbers too. One of 601's 'Millionaires' Raymond Davis, although born in South Africa of American parents, was sent to Sherborne College in Britain at the age of 13. After studying at Trinity College, Cambridge and McGill University, Montreal, he qualified as a mining engineer. He took flying lessons in New Jersey before becoming a British citizen in 1932 and returning to the United Kingdom in 1935. He joined 601 Squadron at Hendon while living in London and was commissioned in August 1936.

An incident the following summer exemplified the rarefied social strata in which 601 existed. His widowed father lived at Fryern Hall in Sussex. In July 1937 he invited the squadron to fly to a social event there where they could land their Hawker Demons in the estate grounds. A fellow-pilot of Davis had a lucky escape when his aircraft caught fire and he had to crash-land at Parham airfield near Storrington and Davis rescued him from the burning wreckage.[6]

This focus on recruitment from a certain section of society was just one of the ways a distinctive ethos and *esprit de corps* was instilled and which would serve the squadrons well as they grew and eventually to fight in the Battle of Britain.

Northern squadrons, although not quite as starred as the 'Millionaires' of 601 Squadron, still had their fair share of members drawn from the upper echelons of society.

One pilot of No. 610 (County of Chester) Squadron recalled at flying training he'd 'never seen so many Rolls-Royce cars in one spot at the same time.'[7]

No. 607 (County of Durham) Squadron meanwhile, counted the Eton and Cambridge educated Leslie Runciman, the eldest son of Viscount Runciman among its officers.

Among those minor nobles there were many from the upper middle-classes. In the same squadron was Joseph Kayll was born in Sunderland in 1914 and attended Stowe School but, after failing all exams, he started work at 16 in the family's sawmill firm in the city. In 1934 he obtained his 'A' flying licence and joined 607 Squadron. While by no means working-class, they were not part of the landed gentry and came from commercial and industrial backgrounds.

Recruits for No. 603 (City of Edinburgh) Squadron came from a mix of backgrounds and professions. 'These were professional businessmen from Edinburgh and its environs.' Some were wealthy young professionals and students, 'young tearaways' of who could afford to pay for flying lessons.[8]

George Denholm partly fitted this profile. Born in 1908 in Bo'ness, West Lothian, his father's company imported props for coal mines. Educated at Cargifield Prep School, the city's prestigious Fettes School and Cambridge, he took flying lessons at Edinburgh Flying Club and was commissioned with 603 Squadron in June 1933.

As well as class, there were other features of the AAF which gave its character and shape and which enabled it to construct an ethos of its own. Robert Dixon, in his history of 607 Squadron, observed too how critical was the squadrons' local recruitment and identity in the Auxiliaries' *esprit de corps*: 'Most of the men on the squadrons, groundcrew as well as aircrew, would have a shared identity. They may not have exactly known each and every other person on the squadron but they would be aware of their background. A strong sense of community spirit would survive among the Auxiliary squadrons'. This 'shared past' he saw would see these men through hardship and conflict that lay in the future. 'The squadron', he observed 'apart from being a military fighting unit, was almost a family.'

Alongside this strong local identity, units would have their own well-equipped headquarters, mess, and distinctive life of its own and social meetings were encouraged.[9]

At 616 (South Yorkshire) Squadron the young Hugh Dundas, a newly-recruited pilot found the clubbable atmosphere of the Officers' Mess at Doncaster an introduction to another, more confident world.

'There I was emancipated as I started living, for the first time, with grown-up men quite unconnected with my family or its immediate circle. They were in the habit of living their lives at a brisk pace. It was an exciting novelty for me to be able to press a bell at any time and order a whiskey and soda or a cocktail'.

It was while ordering his drink that he acquired his nickname. An older pilot, Teddy St Aubyn, shouted 'Hey, you – Cocky – press the bell'. The young Dundas did so. 'But why had he described me as "Cocky"?' 'Because I couldn't remember your name and because you look like bloody great Rhode Island Red,' he said.[10]

Aside from this exclusive atmosphere, the Auxiliaries' conditions of service were designed to strengthen their attachment to the squadron, in contrast to their regular RAF counterparts. Once the recruit signed on with the AAF, he could not be posted to another squadron without his consent. This gave members of the squadron a sense of stability and security. Alongside this was the shared sense of place, of belonging to the city or county on which the squadron's identity was based.[11]

An insight to the self-perception of some in the AAF was given by Dr Tony Mansell who has written widely on the history of the various RAF Reserves arms.

> In all the history of arms, there can seldom have been a body of men more outwardly confident and pleased with themselves than the pilots of the Auxiliary Air Force – amongst them were lawyers and farmers, stockbrokers and journalists, landowners, accountants and playboys. They represented par excellence, that powerful amateur tradition which characterised so much of British life before the war.[12]

One episode in the 1930s clearly demonstrated that spirit of adventure which Trenchard and others had identified as central to the ethos of the auxiliaries.

In 1933, two pilots from No. 602 (City of Glasgow) Squadron, Commanding Officer Squadron Leader Douglas Douglas-Hamilton (Lord Clydesdale) and his number two, Flt Lt David MacIntyre; became the first men to fly over Mount Everest. The objective was to survey and map the area which was, until then, largely uncharted.

Clydesdale described the risks as 'no more than walking across Hampstead Heath on a foggy night…it's the highest mountain in the world, it's true there must be some risk but isn't it a risk well worthwhile?'

Flying in Westland Wallaces, a development of the Westland Wapiti biplane which 602 Squadron flew, they managed the feat of flying at 34,000 feet above Everest twice. As well as over-flying and photographing the world's highest mountain, the expedition gave valuable lessons in flying clothing, oxygen, engineering, and aerial photography.[13]

Sometimes the boisterousness found outlet in what might be described as 'japes'. After winning the coveted Esher trophy for

Auxiliary Efficiency in 1934, there were exuberant celebrations in the Officers' Mess of No. 604 (County of Middlesex) Squadron. As the news of the victory was telephoned by the CO 'There was a whoop of joy from the boys. I ordered half a dozen Verve Cliquot and when I left discreetly, the celebrations had reached the stage of nose-diving over the sofas and chairs'.[14]

From the derring-do and spirit of adventure to the tom-foolery – they would all play a part in honing the ethos and spirit which would be vital when war came.

By the mid-1930s the expectations of people like Trenchard in recruiting and training a reserve were not fully being met. There seemed to be a problem with how the Auxiliary Air Force had been set up. The division between special reserve squadrons and auxiliary – while seeming quite logical was not producing results.[15]

During 1936, the five SR squadrons – 500, 501, 502, 503 and 504 – were merged into the AAF and the two reserves became one.[16]

As the Auxiliary and Special Reserve squadrons merged, the AAF as a whole was about to get bigger. With the worsening political situation in Europe in the mid-1930s, expansion of the RAF accelerated, and there began a programme which resulted in a further eight AAF squadrons being established.

Of those new squadrons, three formed in February 1936; 609 (West Riding) Squadron formed at Yeadon, 610 (County of Chester) formed at Hooton and 611 (West Lancashire) formed at Hendon and moved to Speke on 6 May 1936. Three more formed in 1937 as army co-operation units; 612 (County of Aberdeen), 615 (County of Surrey) and 614 (County of Glamorgan).

No. 503 (City of Lincoln) Squadron was disbanded, to re-form at Doncaster on 1 November 1938, as 616 (South Yorkshire) Squadron. The final squadron, No. 613 (City of Manchester) was formed in 1939. Of these 609, 610, 611, 615 and 616 would become fighter units and would fight with distinction in the Battle of Britain alongside the older squadrons of the AAF.

Further development of the reserves was to come. In part this was a recognition that Britain was a changing society. As a highly technical service the RAF depended on the outputs of the public and other secondary schools but the AAF was not attracting enough of them.

In July 1936, the RAF Volunteer Reserve (RAFVR) was formed in answer to this challenge. It was intended to provide a reservoir of trained aircrew to support the regular and auxiliary squadrons. Pupil pilots would learn to fly at weekends at civilian-run flying schools and attended classes in the evenings for their ground based tuition.[17]

Air Chief Marshal Lord Tedder intended that the RAFVR should not be linked to the County Associations to which the AAF was connected and largely controlled. He intended to recruit from a wide range, including poorer secondary school boys as well as boys from the more expensive public schools, since these young men from contrasting social backgrounds would have to be able to work together both in the air and on the ground. Subsequently the idea was that the RAFVR would be more accessible to local people because regulations surrounding entry were less rigid. Members of the RAFVR did not need to be officers to fly and it also allowed men without a trade to become serving members enabling them to train on entry.

Entry was to be in the rank of AC2 with promotion to sergeant on the following day. Commissions were to be available to all who subsequently proved their worth, and on entry for some with appropriate aptitudes and previous flying experience, such as former and current UAS (University Air Squadron) members.[18]

It was later unkindly, said that there were three sorts of Air Force pilot:

> The Regular, who is an Officer trying to become a Gentleman.
> The Auxiliary, who is a Gentleman trying to become an Officer.
> Then there is the RAFVR, who is neither, would like to become to become both.[19]

This maxim didn't include a further category. Following continued pressure on recruitment of aircrew, the AAF reluctantly allowed NCOs to be trained as pilots in 1939.

In January 1938 the AAF was running at only 51% of its peacetime establishment of pilots and it was forced to begin – in the face of opposition from among its squadrons – to train some of its own non-commissioned ground and aircrew members as pilots to compensate for the shortfall in its officer numbers.[20]

One of those NCO pilots from the AAF, was Horatio Chandler. Born in 1916 in Bexhill-on-Sea. He joined No. 610 (County of Chester) Squadron on 10 March 1936 as an Aircrafthand while working as a compositor on the *Birkenhead News and Wirral General Advertiser*. In April 1939 he joined this new NCO pilot-training scheme and had already carried out some flying training before being called up on 24 August 1939.[21]

The motivations for those becoming reservists varied, but many of course, yearned to fly. One of them was Jim Lacey. He was 16 when he told his father that he wanted to enter the RAF Apprentices' School at Halton. He was against it. The RAF was a short way to suicide, he said. It was no use pointing out that aeroplanes were becoming safer every day – that was final. His father hoped he would follow him into farming.

Jim recalled realising what that future would have meant for him. 'Just before I was due to leave school, I suddenly realized for the first time that being a farmer was a life sentence! It's a seven day a week job, twenty-four hours a day.'[22] James became an apprentice chemist on leaving school in 1933 and the same year, his father died. He half-heartedly went on with his pharmaceutical studies but still dreamed of a career in the RAF.

Working in a chemist's shop, he discovered was mainly a matter of selling perfumes. He pored over books on aviation, talked about aeroplanes with air-minded friends.

'But,' as Lacey's biographer told, 'Jim Lacey's bondage ended. He took his exams but turned his back on pharmacy for ever. Standing on the pavement, with the shop door shut for the last time behind him, he heard a drone overhead and looked up. Moving across the darkening sky, a pair of bright lights – one red, the other green – brightly symbolised the far horizons that beckoned to him'.[23]

Ray Holmes long had a fascination for speed and all things mechanical. Racing driver E.B. Ware, who broke the 100mph barrier for a three-wheeled car in 1926 at the Brooklands racing circuit, was the boyfriend of his aunt. He quickly became close to Holmes' family. 'He taught me about engines and had me riding his motorbike and driving his cars before I reached my teens,' Ray recalled.

In September 1936, Ware told Ray, who was working as working as a junior reporter on the *Birkenhead Advertiser*, a competitor with Horatio Chandler's newspaper in the same town, about a new scheme the RAF was starting to train pilots – the RAFVR and thought it ideal for the young Holmes. Pilots under training would sign on for five years and start with a 10-week intensive course of theory and flying to then carry on flying at weekends at airfields near their homes. Travelling costs would be met and a £25 bonus would be paid annually. Ray recalled, 'It was possible to buy a second-hand car for £25 in those days. To learn to fly and be paid enough to buy a car for doing so, sounded too good to be true.'

There was a catch. All entrants, who were given the rank of Sergeant Pilot, would in the event of war, be mobilised into the regular RAF. But, Ray recalled, 'In those carefree days – the thought of war, though stirring and exciting, was quite remote.'

Soon a letter arrived in a manila envelope summoning Holmes to the Air Ministry for an interview and medical. He recalled: 'For six hours, with an hour's break for lunch, we were pummelled, interrogated, observed and sounded by five different specialists in their own field. We jumped on and off chairs, balanced rods on rulers, did handstands, head-stands and press-ups. We had knee jerks, pulse readings, breath holdings. We blew columns of mercury up tubes.'

A week after he arrived home, 'pummelled but proud', another manila envelope arrived. It was addressed to Sergeant Holmes, R.T., RAFVR. 'I was in,' he said.[24]

THE AAF, THE RAFVR AND THE COMING OF WAR

Now free of his father's disapproval and his humdrum job, Lacey too applied to join the RAFVR. The 19-year-old, had two friends in his local rugby club – both strapping forwards – who had already tried and both were turned down. But Lacey passed both the medical and interview.

Some weeks later he joined 29 other student pilots for his flying training at Scone in Scotland. Within four hours of arriving there, he was strapped into the rear cockpit of a Tiger Moth a 1,000 feet above the Perthshire hills. His eyes darted from the gently jiggling joystick to the rudder bar which moved this way and that as his instructor, Nick Lawson, turned.

Through the Gosport tube came Lawson's voice, telling him to touch the controls gently and follow their movements. Eagerly he put his hand on the stick and his feet on the rudder bar.

A gruff command told him not to hold 'so damned tight' and to put less pressure on the rudder controls with his clumsy feet. He didn't mind. He didn't mind what anybody said to him, as long as he could stay there and enjoy the wonderful sensation of flight. Lacey took naturally to flying. At the end of the course, he was graded 'Above Average' and was the first to fly solo, after just 6 hours 55 minutes' instruction.[25]

In 1938, Lacey then took an instructor's course at Grimsby, and having passed the Guild of Air Pilots and Navigators exam, obtained an instructor's endorsement on his pilot's licence. He then got a job as an instructor at the Yorkshire Aeroplane Club. There then followed a happy 12 months when he recalled he could be instructing one day, the next flying by day or night around the Territorial Army gun sites to give the soldiers aiming practice; the following day, he might fly a club member down to London for a few hours' business, the day after give joy-rides to cash customers at five shilling for ten minutes. 'Flying at its best,' he called it, 'none of this bus-driving like an airline pilot has to do. Just the kind of flying I like.' He spent his annual holiday flying too, on attachment to a regular RAF squadron for training. On completing 250 hours' flying, all Volunteer Reserve pilots were invited to carry out these periods of duty. All too soon, the experience he was building as a pilot would pay dividends when war came.[26]

Ray Holmes too would be bound for Scotland. Another early recruit, he received a letter on 1 February 1937 stating: 'You are instructed to report to the Reserve Flying School of Scottish Aviation Ltd, Prestwick, Scotland at 0900 hrs on 8/2/37 to commence ground and flying training.' His number on the Volunteer Reserve was 740055 – 55th to join the RAFVR.

'I boarded the train at Liverpool Exchange a week later with my Notice Paper for the Flying School safely in my wallet, and mixed feelings in my mind. It was hard to believe that next time I arrived home at West Kirby I would be a pilot.'

He wore his regulation RAFVR uniform for the journey. Navy blue double-breasted blazer, with flat silver buttons embossed with RAF wings, a VR tie, blue shirt and collar, grey flannels and black shoes. On the train, he wondered: 'What lay ahead? How would I cope? What would it feel like to look down from the air?' By the time he got to Prestwick aerodrome it was dark. He was delivered in front of a sandstone hotel, looking grim and forbidding with its towers on each corner.

The hotel proved to be half-residential, half RAF mess and he quickly met his fellow-pupils. The next morning, they began the day on the airfield with PT, shivering in rugby shorts, shirt and gym shoes and a biting Highland wind. He was later kitted out with a Sidcot flying suit with a fur-fabric collar and lining, a helmet with earphone, fur-lined flying boots, and leather gauntlet gloves with silk inners.

He was told he must complete fifty hours' flying each, 25 dual and 25 solo, including five hours' instrument or cloud flying. His instructor was Douglas Shields, a former pilot with No. 603 (City of Edinburgh) Squadron and now a civilian flying instructor. He explained the petrol system, the effect of the control column on elevators and ailerons, and the foot pedals on the rudder. Shields showed Holmes the throttle and mixture control, and explained the dashboard dials and blind flying instruments. Then giving him a leg up into the rear cockpit checked his Sutton harness was correctly fastened and climbed into the front.

Shields plugged in his headset and his voice came down the speaking tube, loud and metallic. 'Can you hear me, Holmes?' he said 'Yes, sir.' 'Good. Let's go flying.'

With a shout of 'Contact', from Shields to the fitter, who heaved the prop and stepped back clear of the airscrew, the engine fired. The whole aircraft trembled to life; Holmes recalled. 'Wings, fuselage, and cockpit instruments all vibrated so violently that I felt sure the engine was ready to jump out of its cradle and the airframe collapse in a heap'.

Having taxied out across the airfield, the moment of truth had come. 'He opened the throttle fully. The engine roared, and the airscrew spun itself invisible. In a cloud of exhaust smoke and flying grass our tail went up and our Tiger Moth, triggered by its 120hp Gipsy Major engine, was away. This was it. This was the moment at which for the first time I said farewell to Mother Earth'.

Ray Holmes' school was at one of the 56 Elementary and Reserve Flying Training Schools across the UK. Formed from 1935, they expanded rapidly following the formation of the RAFVR, and would train the part-time pilots of this new arm. From Prestwick and Scone in Scotland to Exeter in Devon with Doncaster, Cambridge and Gatwick among those in between – the schools churned out thousands of pilots for the RAFVR who would prove vital when war and then the Battle of Britain came.

Soaring upwards, the acceleration forced his back against the seat, Holmes looked out from the cockpit:

> Fields became pocket handkerchiefs. The engine quietened as Shields eased back the throttle and stopped climbing.

The altimeter read 2,000 feet. Sheep were just dots, hedges lines, roads ribbons. The clouds seemed close enough to touch. The land was a map of roads, railways and coastline. In front the leather-coated shoulders of my instructor moved forward as he reached for his speaking tube.
'All right, Holmes?'
'Fine sir, thank you.'

Shields pointed out the aerodrome as he dipped the port wing. 'Always know where you are, to find your way back.' Shields taught him much about flying and the dangers he would face, but the final lesson would be a painful one.

Later four trainee navigators were killed alongside their pilot, Douglas Shields when their Anson crashed. Holmes recalled 'He was the first of many good friends I was to lose, and one of the best'.

'From that day', Holmes said, 'I realised what insecurity was. If the ever-reliable Shields could not protect you, who could? From now on only one person could protect me in an aeroplane'. 'God helps those who help themselves,' he decided.[27]

For flyers in the AAF, although many of its pilots were trained on the squadron or had learned to fly before joining – the thrill of learning to fly was just as powerful.

Hugh Dundas was born in Doncaster in 1920. He attended Aysgarth School in Yorkshire and Stowe School. After leaving he worked as a trainee solicitor and joined No. 616 (South Yorkshire) Squadron at Doncaster in May 1939. While fellow-Yorkshireman and farmer's son Jim Lacey joined the RAFVR, the public schoolboy Dundas opted for the AAF and 616 Squadron.

Flying in an Avro Tutor biplane – the standard training machine for AAF squadrons, Dundas spent as much time as he could that June and July in the air.

He pestered Flt Lt Dudley Radford, their Chief Flying Instructor, to take him flying. 'He was a fine instructor, very firm, very fair. He got through to me at an early stage the need to combine delicacy with strength and decisiveness in handling an aircraft. Everything he did in the air was done with a sense of deliberation and firm purpose but yet with a gentle hand.

'I quickly mastered loops and turns, but slow rolls I hated and had great difficulty in achieving. I felt quite helpless when the machine was upside-down and I was hanging on my straps, dust and grit from the bottom of the cockpit falling around me. Again and again Radford went through it, patiently and firmly, until at last I got it.'

Instructors like Shields, Radford and Lawson would not have known precisely the stern test which awaited Lacey, Holmes, Dundas and hundreds of other pilots who made up the few, but their wisdom and skill put their pupils on the road to becoming deadly fighter pilots of the future.[28]

The rise of Nazi Germany from 1933 had prompted much of the expansion of the RAF, the AAF and the RAFVR.

Following the birth of the RAFVR in July 1936, geo-political omens continued to worsen, with Germany making ever more war-like moves in Europe. One of these came in March 1938 with the annexation of Austria by Nazi Germany. The union between the two German-speaking countries had been forbidden by the peace treaties at the end of the First World War and was seen as another sign of German territorial ambitions in Europe. In September of 1938, the tensions heightened further with the crisis over the Czech Sudetenland and its disputed German population. Nazi Germany demanded that it should be able to annex this region of Czechoslovakia which bordered Germany and was home to 3 million ethnic Germans. Hitler threatened to march his forces across the frontier and seize the territory.

In the UK, the tension grew as German demands escalated and the prospect of war looked very real. From the weekend of 24–25 September, the country as a whole began to prepare for a new conflict in Europe.

Across the country that weekend, Air Raid Precautions stations opened, gas masks were given out and Sunday, 25 September 1938 was nicknamed 'Gas Mask Sunday' in parts of the press. On the morning of Monday, 26 September, war, to many, seemed certain.[29]

In this climate of crisis, the UK's armed forces were put on alert. Many of the gleaming silver aircraft of the RAF were hurriedly painted in camouflage.[30]

When 607 Squadron returned from its annual camp at Warmwell in Dorset that summer, the crisis was growing. Finally, from 0200 on 27 September, the squadron was duly embodied – that is incorporated into the full-time service. This was a first step to full mobilisation.

All airmen were to be billeted in the station and the whole embodiment was completed with the squadron ready for action by 30 September.

However, no further order was given to mobilise, and all training was carried out as normal. With the international situation calming down once more, the squadron was once more disembodied as from 11 October.

Coincidentally, Walter Runciman, First Viscount Runciman of Doxford, ex-government minister and father of Leslie Runciman, CO of 607 Squadron, headed a mission to Czechoslovakia aimed at resolving the crisis. Prime Minister Neville Chamberlain was intent on averting war and between 15 and 30 September he made three trips to Germany to see Hitler.[31]

At Munich on 29 September, Chamberlain agreed to the incorporation of the Sudetenland into the Reich while securing Hitler's recognition of the independence of the rest of the Czech state. The Prime Minister hoped this would mark the dawn of a new era of European stability. He returned to the UK to wave his famous 'Piece of Paper' – an agreement signed by Hitler which he believed would guarantee 'Peace for our time'. History, of course, would prove him to be wrong, but war would not come to Britain – for now.

Intriguingly, an auxiliary pilot would play a small role in these negotiations.

John Dundas, the brother of Hugh, joined 609 Squadron at Yeadon in May 1938, just months before the crisis broke out. Their father was a Colliery Director and the family related to Lord Halifax and the Marquis of Zetland (the Zetland fortunes being founded by businessman Sir John Dundas in the eighteenth century). Dundas was also a cousin of Harald Peake, 609's first Commanding Officer. He won a scholarship to Stowe and followed this by going to Christchurch College, Oxford aged 17, taking a First in Modern Greats. He then went to France to study at the Sorbonne before finishing his education at Heidelberg.[32]

Returning to England, he became a journalist on the *Yorkshire Post*. In 1938 as a foreign correspondent specialising in European international affairs he travelled to Czechoslovakia during the Munich crisis to report on the international response, before accompanying Neville Chamberlain and Lord Halifax to Rome to meet Mussolini. He would go on to become one of the highest-scoring auxiliary aces of the Battle of Britain.[33] While at Yeadon he experienced a crash which would build his experience as one of the pre-eminent AAF fighter pilots.

On 18 June 1939, when taking off the engine cut out and his Hawker Hind crashed into the side of a house in Victoria Avenue nearby. Neither Dundas nor his passenger, Harrogate man, LAC Hunter were injured. The Yorkshire tones of F/S Cloves provided a record: 'It was left to Pilot Officer Dundas to provide us with a real pile up. The occasion was the first squadron formation take-off. The aircraft concerned, Hind 6848, happened to be the CO's aircraft, but that,' Cloves recalled, 'was no deterrent', adding, 'Human ballast was LAC Hunter'. It took some time for all twelve aircraft to form up. 'The word "Go" came, and bang went the throttles, and the squadron became almost airborne, but the engine in K6848 decided to cut at the crucial moment'. Dundas throttled back to nurse the engine, but, as Cloves described, 'he decided he couldn't clear the houses in Victoria Avenue so put the aircraft earthwards'. The Hawker Hind touched down, but was 'still doing some considerable speed'. Dundas applied the brakes but the wheels skidded on the damp ground and the aircraft carried on 'unperturbed'. Cloves continued: 'It burst through the aerodrome fence, chopped down a windsock, which fell on a boy on a pushbike, and conveniently turned on its nose in the back garden of one of the houses'. The stricken biplane leant nicely on a well-placed tree and gently rested its rudder on the house roof. 'A lady occupant of the house had hysterics but was restored with the aid of brandy. The brandy was passed on to the pilot and passenger who didn't really require it. It was then handed to some unidentified airman to look after; he did, by drinking the lot. He calmly handed over the empty bottle when the aforementioned lady had further hysterics and quietly vanished'. The aircraft was a complete write-off. To ensure his confidence was not broken, Dundas was quickly sent aloft again for 'a short flip at dual in the Hind trainer, then was sent off solo'. 'This time' it was noted, 'he cleared the houses this time with plenty to spare'.[34]

Other auxiliary pilots in 609 included solicitor Stephen Beaumont; Alexander Edge, who worked for IG Dyestuffs (and was known as 'Grandpa' because he was 32); Michael Appleby; Geoffrey Gaunt, who worked at a Huddersfield cigar manufacturers; and David Crook. John Dundas was known as 'Scruffy' or 'Dogs'. Crook and Gaunt had known each other all their lives, had been at school together and were together again in the same squadron.[35]

After Munich, some RAFVR aircrew who had reached an appropriate stage of training were required to spend a period of attachment to an RAF squadron – which in practice ranged from a few weeks to as long as six months. This practice would continue until the outbreak of war.

In the spring, the situation in Europe deteriorated further. On 15 March, Nazi Germany invaded the remaining part of Czechoslovakia, breaking the Munich Agreement. Within a week Hitler made new demands – this time that the Free City of Danzig must be returned to Germany. On 31 March, France and Britain pledged to guarantee Poland's security and independence.

Meanwhile, the RAF's expansion plans continued apace. In the years following the First World War there was a strong belief that another major war was unlikely. Based on the so-called 'Ten-Year Rule' (the assumption from 1919 that Britain would not be engaged in any great war during the next ten years) it saw the RAF shrink dramatically to just 371 first line aircraft in 1923.

With the coming to power of the Nazis in 1933, it became clear that Germany had started an ambitious rearmament scheme and Britain needed to respond to this threat. The RAF then began a series of expansion plans, each given a letter. There were so many that before war broke out, Scheme 'M' was set out to incorporate all the features from previous schemes which had not been implemented.

In 1934, 42 squadrons existed providing a first line strength of some 800 aircraft. By 1939 this had grown to 157 squadrons and 3,700 aircraft. Alongside this there was an increase in aircraft and engine production and an expansion of training for air and groundcrews.[36]

Following the Munich crisis – and in line with RAF expansion plans – many AAF squadrons re-equipped. Although their machines were more advanced – they still weren't the latest, such as the Hurricane, with which some regular squadrons were starting to receive. From the Gloster stable – the Gauntlet and the Gladiator, although biplanes, were of superior performance to the Hawker Demons they replaced. Some squadrons like 603, were redesignated as fighter units (in their case in October 1938) and flew Hinds until the arrival of Gladiators at the end of March 1939. No. 504 got the Gauntlet to replace their Hinds in November, which were an improvement, giving around 40mph increase in speed, greater armament and agility, and in the case of the Gladiator an enclosed cockpit. However, they were not as capable as the monoplanes then beginning to equip some regular units – with 111 Squadron receiving the first eight-gun Hawker Hurricane Mk1s in January 1938.

But further improvements would come. In March 1939, No. 501 (County of Gloucester) Squadron started to receive Hurricanes, while No. 602 (City of Glasgow) Squadron began to exchange their Gloster Gauntlets for the Spitfire Mk1 in May 1939.

One way in which this new equipment could be shown off was the Empire Air Day. An annual event, it featured air shows at Royal Air Force stations in the United Kingdom with the first held in 1934. The idea was that the public 'should be enabled to see the Royal Air Force at its everyday work. As many stations as possible... are opened to the public on payment of a small charge for admission.'[37]

AAF squadrons, with their strong regional identity, were ideally placed to do this at the local Empire Air Day display.

Programmes included displays of dive-bombing, aerobatics, formation flying, blind flying, artillery observation, air combats between bombers and fighters, attacks on towed targets and machine-gun attacks on ground targets.

The day featured flying displays at RAF stations across the UK but also during the preceding week, flypasts over major centres of population by large formations of aircraft.

The Empire Air Day that year would take place beneath the darkening shadow of war in Europe and would take on a more purposeful tone. The aircraft, many now in camouflage rather than gleaming silver, would demonstrate the capability of the RAF to friend and potential foe alike. The drumbeat of war was quickening across Europe and the show would be more than just a pleasant day out.

The tensions and portents of future conflict could be seen in other ways. Richard Hillary had joined the Oxford University Air Squadron early in 1939 – which, along with all University Air Squadrons, became part of the RAFVR, thanks to the Military Training Act of May 1939,[38] and would go on to join No. 603 (City of Edinburgh)

Squadron. An accomplished rower, he went to Germany to compete in the 'General Goering Prize Fours' in July 1938. His time there taught him much about the mentality and ethos that Nazi Germany was cultivating.

The German rowers came with 'car-loads of supporters', he recalled and 'set, determined faces'. Shortly before the race they walked to the changing-rooms to get ready. An impressive spectacle greeted him. 'All five German crews were lying flat on their backs on mattresses, great brown stupid-looking giants, taking deep breaths.' One of them came up and spoke to Hillary 'or rather harangued me'. He had been watching the English rowers, he said, and 'could only come to the conclusion that we were thoroughly representative of a decadent race. No German crew would dream of appearing so lackadaisical if rowing in England: they would train and they would win'. He added that losing this race might not appear very important to the English, 'but I could rest assured that the German people would not fail to notice and learn from our defeat'.

In retrospect, Hillary saw that this foretold the next few years very well. 'This race was really a surprisingly accurate pointer to the course of the war. We were quite untrained, lacked any form of organization, and were really quite hopelessly casual. We even arrived late at the start, where all five German crews were lined up, eager to go'.

As the German supporters yelled out encouragement to their crews in a regulated chant, the English rowed in silence. Then somebody from the bank spat on them. 'It was a tactical error' Hillary recalled. Goaded, their cox urged them on and they won the race by two-fifths of a second. 'General Goering had to surrender his cup' and the gold shell-case mounted with the German eagle was taken back to Oxford. Hillary saw that their victory and their nonchalance had got under the Germans' skin. 'Had we shown any sort of enthusiasm or given any impression that we had trained they would have tolerated it, but as it was, they showed merely a sullen resentment'.[39]

In the coming months the crisis in Europe continued to build. On 10 July, Prime Minister Neville Chamberlain reaffirmed his support for Poland over the Danzig claim, and would intervene on behalf of Poland if hostilities broke out between the two countries.

Meanwhile, troubling news came from the Continent. After Germany's invasion of Czechoslovakia in March, thereby reneging on the Munich Agreement, Chamberlain hoped to strengthen ties with the Soviet Union and form an alliance between themselves and France to guard against further German aggression. There was no longer any illusion of German good faith as there had been the previous autumn.

As always, many squadrons held their annual camps that August, but this year they would come together as storm clouds gathered over Europe.

No. 605 (County of Warwick) Squadron took their Gladiators and four new Hurricanes to Tangmere where they practiced interception and exercised with the French Air Force. No. 607 (County of Durham) Squadron took their Gladiators to Abbotsinch in Scotland. As war loomed on the Continent, a small group from this unit who would soon be fighting for their lives in the skies over southern England, were intent on a wholesome and healthy pursuit. Pilots Joe Kayll, Jim Bazin, Peter Dixon, Will Gore, Alan Glover and Dudley Craig decided to climb up Ben Lomond. Like excited schoolboys Alan Glover and Jim Bazin raced to the last few hundred yards to the summit. On the way back down they swam in the ice cool waters of a pool they'd spotted on the way up. The trip was rounded off with a stop at the Buchanan Arms at Drymen.[40]

Amid such a display of innocent enjoyment and friendship, the simmering tensions of Europe must have seemed a world away. But that robust camaraderie and spirit would hold them in good stead when war came.

Hugh Dundas recalled very clearly that summer. 'In the middle of August the squadron went to Manston, a big grass airfield on the eastern tip of Kent, for annual camp. Those were magic days, the very last of peace'. The newly-joined Dundas saw it all with 'tremendous excitement', recalling, 'it seems almost unbelievable, looking back, that I had never even seen the English Channel before then and the south coast was quite unknown to me. The very fact of being able to climb up to a few hundred feet and thence to look across to France was a thrill. That was "abroad" where I had never been.'

They lived in tents at Manston, and in the mornings got up at dawn and took off against the low sun and with mist still lying in the valleys.

As well as seeing France across the Channel, there were other portents of the future; a future that was nearer than he knew. 'I was to be up at dawn more often than not in the course of the next six years – until I hated the sound of the word. But I learned then, with wonder and delight, the magic of taking off into the sky when the air was crisp and new and the young day sparkled'. He remembered 'It was a magic that never failed to uplift me a little, even in the darkest days to come, when fatigue and fear were overpowering'.

That final time of innocence played out in the afternoons when flying had ceased. 'The weather was fine and warm and we sat outside the mess tent drinking our gins or pints of beer'.[41]

The desperate hope that war could be avoided was fading. But in the last week of August, that hope seemed to vanish completely. The overtures to the Soviets were still being made when news came on Tuesday, 22 August which rocked Britain and France.

Newspapers reported that a pact between Nazi Germany and the Soviet Union was about to be signed. This had seemed impossible as Hitler had made it clear his hatred of Communist Russia. Nazi Foreign Minister Joachim von Ribbentrop was reported to be flying to Moscow to sign the deal. Headlines read: 'Russia and Germany: non-aggression treaty to be signed – Ribbentrop flying to Moscow tomorrow'.[42]

The next day it was confirmed, the two sworn enemies had forged an agreement which committed both countries not to attack each other and which sealed the fate of Europe. For the Germans it meant they could avoid a war on two fronts in the East and the West, and have access to much-needed raw materials. For the Soviets, it gave them vital breathing space to rebuild her armed forces following the purges of the mid-1930s and allowed continued access to arms and machinery from Germany.

Britain's attempts to create an alliance with the Soviets had failed – the British and French strategy lay in tatters. Parliament was recalled the next day to urgently debate the next course of action. On Thursday, 24 August, Parliament passed the Emergency Powers (Defence) Act, giving the government broad powers in order to conduct war effectively.[43] The same day, the Reserve Forces were 'embodied' – just as some had been in 1938. But this time there was to be no going back.

Still at Manston, Hugh Dundas remembered this moment as clearly as those flights in the clear morning sky over Kent and the Channel.

> We knew that we would not be going back to our civilian jobs when camp came to an end. I remember the exact moment when this fact became clear to me. We had been flying all morning, as usual, and were just beginning lunch. Someone came into the mess tent and announced the news of the infamous pact between Russia and Germany. Teddy St Aubyn, who was sitting opposite me, put down his soup spoon and said in a clear voice: 'Well that's f****d it. That's the start of the f*****g war.'

He knew that the moment had come at last. 'Teddy', he recalled 'was not noted as a political pundit or a serious student of international affairs. But I heard his words and I knew they were true'. As if to emphasise the gravity of the news, a steward was entering their mess with a tray at that moment. 'He stopped dead in his tracks. He turned his head to listen to the man who brought the news. He turned it the other way to listen to Teddy's succinct interpretation of that news. Simultaneously his mouth fell open and the tray dropped from his hands'.

The camp ended abruptly on a sombre note he recalled. 'The Auxiliary Air Force was being embodied into the Royal Air Force. The next day we were told to fly back to Doncaster'.[44]

Some had further to travel back from then Kent to Yorkshire. After attending Eton and Oxford, William 'Billy' Clyde spent three years in Switzerland and became a proficient skier, representing the United Kingdom and winning the World University Championship in 1935. The year later he joined 601 Squadron along with his friend Max Aitken, the son of Lord Beaverbrook.

Clyde was working for a London firm of stockbrokers in early 1937 when he left to serve a six-month attachment as aide to Sir Bede Clifford, Governor of the Bahamas. He later took a job with Johnson & Johnson Surgical Dressings in the USA and went onto the Reserve of RAF Officers in February 1938.

Another famous 601 Squadron figure, Roger Bushell, was able to contact Clyde and alert him to return to the UK. Clyde travelled to New York and booked a passage on the *Aquitania*. He sailed on 30 August, arriving at Southampton on 5 September.[45]

On Friday, 25 August, just two days after the Nazi-Soviet Pact, the Agreement of Mutual Assistance between the United Kingdom and Poland was signed. The treaty promised military aid if either was attacked by some 'European country'.[46]

In the last few days of August, the Nazis stepped up their demands. On Wednesday, 30 August, Hitler issued an ultimatum to Poland demanding that she give up the Polish Corridor and the Free City of Danzig. Germany was on a collision course with Britain and France who were committed to helping their Polish ally.

Two days later, on Friday, 1 September, Germany invaded Poland. Although the UK was not yet at war, on this day evacuation of civilians in large cities began, Air Raid Precautions introduced and blackout enforced from sunset to sunrise.

The next day, Prime Minister Neville Chamberlain and French Prime Minister Édouard Daladier issued a joint ultimatum to Germany, demanding the withdrawal of troops from Poland within 12 hours.

On Sunday, 3 September, at 1115, British Prime Minister Neville Chamberlain announced over the radio that because Germany had failed to withdraw troops from Poland by 1100 hours, a state of war existed between the United Kingdom and Germany.

The logbook of 609 Squadron pilot, David Crook declared in bold, red ink '1100 hrs, 3rd September, 1939. War declared on Germany' and in black ink below is written 'No flying'.

Britain was at war – and with it the part-timers of the Auxiliary Air Force and the RAF Volunteer Reserve were part-timers no more. When war broke out in 1939, the RAFVR ceased to recruit part-time members and instead served as the principal route for aircrew entry to the RAF. Recruitment to the Auxiliary Air Force ceased at the outbreak of war.[47] They would soon test the skills and training they had received in the preceding years. Would they be found wanting?

PHONEY WAR AND THE BATTLE OF FRANCE

The day before Chamberlain's announcement Jim Lacey was ordered to report to his RAFVR town centre in Hull. The next day he headed to Hedon Aero Club with other called-up reserve pilots. He heard the Prime Minister's broadcast that morning in the bar with a pint of bitter in his hand. But on the news that war had come he recalled soberly: 'The prospect of fighting in a war scared me stiff.'[1] He was soon sent to No. 501 (County of Gloucester) Squadron at Filton.

On the day that war broke out, Richard Hillary remembered 'all of us in the University Air Squadron reported that day to the Volunteer Reserve Centre at Oxford'.

He recalled, 'there was a definite prejudice in the Air Force against Volunteer Reserve Officers, and we had the added disadvantage of an Oxford attitude to life. We were expected to be superior; we were known as week-end pilots; we were known as the long-haired boys; we were to have the nonsense knocked out of us'.

He soon commissioned and was then reunited with university friends like Noel Agazarian and others from the University Air Squadron. Agazarian, he recalled distinctly.

> With an Armenian father and a French mother he was by nature cosmopolitan, intelligent, and a brilliant linguist, but an English education had discovered that he was an athlete, and his University triumphs had been of brawn

rather than brain. Of this he was very well aware and somewhat bewildered by it. These warring elements in his make-up made him a most amusing companion and a very good friend.

While Sergeant Lacey with his RAFVR pals supped their pints in contemplation, a glimpse of the world some in the AAF moved in was given by the predicament the wife of 605 Squadron's Adjutant, P/O Longsdon, found herself in at the outbreak of war. She was on holiday in Russia but was 'afforded invaluable assistance' by the Chief Counsellor, Gordon Verker, at the British Embassy in Moscow, who happened to be the brother-in-law of F/O Thomson (also of the squadron). Via this family connection, arrangements were made for her to fly to Stockholm and then to Shoreham via Amsterdam.[2]

Hugh Dundas and 616 Squadron marked the declaration of war occasion in boisterous style. 'That night we went off in a body to Margate's "Dreamland" and whirled around on everything which that notorious fairground had to offer. I had an anxious few moments on a particularly vicious device called an Octopus. There was an excess of beer and spirits inside me, and I thought that I was going to be airsick for the first time in my life'. Next morning, still queasy, they prepared to return to Doncaster.

Flying back in an Avro Tutor biplane, Dundas stopped at Duxford to refuel. There he saw Spitfires of 19 Squadron, lined up along the airfield boundary. 'It was my first view of a fighter squadron at readiness for action and I felt a strong sense of envy for those seemingly Godlike pilots with their beautiful machines, whose graceful lines I was then seeing for the first time'.[3]

Those early days of war heralded rapid re-equipment for some squadrons. No. 609 Squadron collected Spitfires from Eastleigh and Shawbury. No. 610 Squadron too began re-equipment with Hurricanes (although by 26 September they were ordered to transfer their Hurricanes to 605 Squadron and to re-equip with Spitfires).

PHONEY WAR AND THE BATTLE OF FRANCE

The Hurricane and the Spitfire would soon make up the majority of Fighter Command's strength.

Both were built around the liquid-cooled, Rolls-Royce Merlin engine and both carried eight 303-in Browning machine guns mounted in the wings.

But there were differences. Designed by Sydney Camm of Hawkers, the Hurricane first flew in 1935. The most numerous of RAF Fighter Command's aircraft during the Battle of Britain, it was of metal frame construction with a partly fabric-covered fuselage, making it a rugged, resilient design that could be repaired more easily than the Spitfire.

The Spitfire, meanwhile, came from the drawing board of Supermarine's Reginald Joseph Mitchell. He developed his designs of sleek, powerful seaplanes which won the Schneider Trophy in the early thirties to produce the fighter with an all-metal machine, a monocoque fuselage and graceful elliptical wings. Faster then the Hurricane, its top speed was 355 mph, compared to the Hurricane's 320 mph.

While both represented a step-change in capability for the RAF, for some the shock of the new wasn't quite to their liking. Earlier in the year, Jim Lacey was training on Hawker Fury biplanes with No. 1 Squadron when he first saw the Hurricane. With its nose 13ft 3in into the air, 3ft higher than the Fury, a wing span 10ft greater, a fuselage 5ft longer, and a weight of 6,000lb compared with its predecessor's 3,600lb – the Hurricane was a daunting sight.

Lacey walked round the new machine in silence, with a regular Flight Sergeant. When they had completed their inspection, the latter pushed his forage cap to the back of his head looking both disgusted and awed. 'Blimey. A single-seat troop carrier!' Lacey said that he did not feel that he would ever be able to fly one. Another Sergeant pilot, already qualified on them, gave some succinct advice. 'Don't touch that lever in the right-hand corner of the cockpit there while you're on the ground, or the aeroplane will fall down. Otherwise, she's exactly the same as a Fury'. Lacey climbed into the cockpit and took off. 'I didn't touch the lever in the right-hand corner while on the ground or in the air' he later admitted, 'nor did I touch it for the next two flights either. I had no confidence whatsoever in retractable undercarriages at that time and wasn't sure that the wheels would ever come down again.' But he would come to love the sturdy fighter which would work harmoniously with Lacey's innate flying talent to form a deadly combination.[4]

This robust assessment of the Hurricane from the Yorkshireman and Sergeant RAFVR pilot is in contrast to that of an officer pilot with an auxiliary squadron – one whose flying career began with the Oxford University Air Squadron – Richard Hillary. He was first introduced to the Spitfire with 603 Squadron.

The Spitfires stood in two lines outside 'A' Flight pilots' room. 'The dull grey-brown of the camouflage could not conceal the clear-cut beauty, the wicked simplicity of their lines'. Hillary hooked up his parachute and climbed into the low cockpit. The Flight Commander, John Kilmartin swung himself on to a wing and started to run through the instruments. 'I was conscious of his voice, but heard nothing of what he said. I was to fly a Spitfire. It was what I had most wanted through all the long dreary months of training. If I could fly a Spitfire, it would be worth it'. Like Lacey, his attention was drawn to the undercarriage handle. It was white enamel. 'Like a lavatory plug,' he thought. Kilmartin had said, 'See if you can make her talk.' That meant the whole bag of tricks, and I wanted ample room for mistakes and possible blacking-out. With one or two very sharp movements on the stick I blacked myself out for a few seconds, but the machine was sweeter to handle than any other that I had flown. I put it through every manoeuvre that I knew of and it responded beautifully. I ended with two flick rolls and turned back for home. I was filled with a sudden exhilarating confidence. I could fly a Spitfire; in any position I was its master. It remained to be seen whether I could fight in one'.[5]

No. 616 Squadron was re-equipping but it would not be in anything so modern or sleek just yet, Hugh Dundas recalled. 'Early in September, there came the magic moment when I was let loose for the first time in a [Gloster] Gauntlet. It is alarming, in retrospect, to consider that any fighter squadron should still at the beginning of the war have been equipped with such old-fashioned machines'. But to his eyes the Gauntlet epitomized everything a fighter plane should be. 'The stubby little radial-engined biplane, open cockpit set midway between nose and tail, seemed tailor-made for Biggles – or Errol Flynn'. That the Gauntlets were not well-suited to the needs of the time was soon brought home to him. 'There I was, climbing away from the airfield, goggles down, scarf neatly adjusted, when a twin-engined Hampden, belonging to a bomber squadron based at nearby Finningley, came alongside and passed me on the climb. The pilot made a rude and familiar sign as he soared contemptuously past me. I opened the throttle wide but could not keep up. I then understood why the older and wiser pilots in the squadron were so passionately anxious for our delightful little Gauntlets to be replaced by Spitfires or Hurricanes'.[6]

Meanwhile, pre-war RAFVR recruit Ray Holmes was doing some low flying training near his home on the River Dee. Flying over Hilbre Island, his instructor, a Sergeant Halton said he'd like to see where Ray lived so they circled his home on Grange Hill at 250 feet. 'Unfortunately', he recalled 'we had not allowed for the hill being 200 foot high' and when they landed back at Sealand, two military policemen met them as they climbed out of their cockpits and informed them they were under arrest for low-flying. They took them to the Chief Flying Instructor – 'a bumptious, bombastic, dyed-in-the-wool Squadron Leader' Ray remembered – who didn't have much time for reservists. With his blond handlebar moustache, he regarded 'VRs as an unavoidable wartime evil'. Despite the CFI's fury, he and his instructor were exonerated, but the mark it left on Ray's record would cost him a Commission he had been recommended for at that time.[7]

One squadron already flying Spitfires was 611 (West Lancashire). Based at Duxford with 19 and 66 Squadrons, they came under 12 Group. At Duxford, everywhere there were signs of preparation. Clearings had been made in trees on the boundary of the airfield for dispersal. Tents were pitched where groundcrews on the dawn shift would sleep. Two marquees had been pitched for use as an armoury store and a dining tent and hot meals were taken by truck to the dispersal areas for crews on duty. The men at the dispersal points had been busy constructing dug-outs and blast pens built of sandbags. Consisting of two walls of sandbags about 50 feet long and 5 feet high they were 4 feet wide at the base, tapered to 2 feet thick at the top. Their shape would become a familiar site in the coming months on airfields across southern England.[8]

No. 611's Commanding Officer, Squadron Leader James McComb – who was appointed on the day that war broke out – remembers those dramatic weeks. 'We had been at Duxford for a fortnight [for their summer camp] when war broke out. The message came through that with immediate effect 611 Squadron was to be embodied into the RAF for the duration. This was damned inconvenient for most of us because we had not given a thought to putting our civilian affairs in order before leaving for the camp.'

In those early days of wartime, the auxiliary squadron had to use its own initiative in fitting out their Spitfires. McComb recalled, 'At the beginning of the war our aircraft didn't have armoured windshields – the Air Ministry thought it was much too expensive – the pilots being cheaper than the glass and we didn't have mirrors either, so Barrie [Heath - fellow 611 pilot] and I went into Royston and bought some and had them screwed on to the Spitfires.'[9]

Since embodiment in late August, Hugh Dundas of 616 Squadron, like all members of the AAF and RAFVR now served full-time in the RAF. His day-job as solicitor was left behind as he trained to hone his skills as a pilot. 'All through that crisp, suspenseful September we flew and flew and flew. Every day, two or three times a day, I was sent up to cram into a few weeks an amount of training which normally stretched over several months.'[10]

What would the following weeks and months bring for those former part-timers of the AAF and RAFVR and the wider RAF of which they were now part?

PHONEY WAR AND THE BATTLE OF FRANCE

From the earliest months of the war, Scottish Auxiliary squadrons were at the forefront of the fight and both No. 602 (City of Glasgow) and No. 603 (City of Edinburgh) AAF fighter squadrons were tasked with guarding the east coast of Scotland and naval bases like Rosyth.

No. 603 based at Turnhouse and 602 at Drem, were quickly in action. The wonderfully titled history of No. 603 Squadron, 'The Greatest Squadron of them all' stated how on 16 October: 'The history of the great Glasgow Squadron [602] was inextricably linked with that of their sister auxiliary squadron in Edinburgh. But at no time were they more united as a fighting force than on this date'.[11]

Leading that action were pilots who had joined the Auxiliary squadrons many years before to fly in their spare time and many of them would become famous names in the annals of Auxiliary Air Force history.

Bright sun on 16 October made visibility to the east difficult, the 602 Squadron diary told, and out of that blinding sun would come their first taste of action. At 0943 Drem reported there were unidentified aircraft flying over the aerodrome above clouds. Three Spitfires of Blue Section took off at 0949 to investigate and patrol at 5,000 feet.

Leading Blue Section was Flt Lt George Pinkerton. A fruit farmer from Houston, Renfrewshire in Spitfire Mk1 L1019, he was born in Rutherglen and educated at Glasgow High School. He joined 602 Squadron in 1933.

His number two was F/O Archie McKellar in K9979. His family had moved to Glasgow in 1915 where his father started a plastering business. McKellar worked for the family firm. Nicknamed 'Shrimp' because of his short stature, a measure of his character came when he was learning his trade as a plasterer. The other apprentices took advantage of his small size and he promptly learned to box so that he could take care of himself.[12]

The young McKellar dreamed of learning to fly but his father wouldn't allow him to take lessons. The determined McKellar took them secretly at a flying club at Abbotsinch where he attained his 'A' licence. In 1936 he was invited to join 602 Squadron, was commissioned in November and awarded his wings on 11 July 1937.[13]

He was said to radiate cheerfulness, with the happy knack of making friends easily. Everyone called him Archie. He was kind too, as fellow 602 pilot Findlay Boyd recalled 'He would share his last ten shilling note with you.[14]

Also in Blue Section was F/O Paul Webb in K1079. Born in 1918 at Greenock and educated at Kelvinside Academy in Glasgow, in late 1937 he joined 602 Squadron while working at the National Bank of Scotland. In those early years he flew Hawker Hinds from Abbotsinch at weekends.[15]

At 1023 Blue Section sighted a He 111 flying east over clouds at 2,000 feet and Pinkerton led the section into line astern for an attack. Both Pinkerton and McKellar fired bursts at the Heinkel but it turned and escaped into cloud. They were the first shots to be fired in air-fighting over the British Isles during the Second World War and it was the first time the Spitfire had been in combat.[16] Further, fruitless patrols were staged through the morning, but at 1425, Blue Section was ordered into the air again. Five minutes later, No. 603 Squadron entered the fray and sent Red Section aloft, with Yellow Section following another five minutes later.

The leader of 603's Red Section was Flt Lt Patrick 'Patsy' Gifford in Spitfire Mk1 L1070. He joined 603 at Turnhouse while working in law and gained his wings in 1932. A qualified solicitor, he worked for the firm founded by his father Patrick Gifford. He worked there as a Procurator Fiscal, Deputy Clerk of Peace, Secretary to the local National Farmers Union and a member of the Town Council.[17]

Leading 603's Yellow Section was George Denholm in L1067, who we've already met. A comparatively early entrant, he commissioned on 27 June 1933. At 31, Denholm was considered to be rather old by his youthful pilots and they christened him 'Uncle George'.[18]

Also in Denholm's section was F/O James 'Black' Morton in L1049. Although born in Blackheath, London on 24 April 1916, he was educated at Loretto School, Musselburgh. At Pembroke College, Cambridge, he read Physics, Chemistry and Physiology and joined the University Air Squadron in February 1936. After leaving Cambridge he transferred to the RAFVR in July 1938 and worked for the Fife Coal Company at Cowdenbeath as a trainee manager. In May 1939 he joined 603 Squadron.[19]

The two sections from each Auxiliary squadron flew out across the Firth of Forth following reports that British warships at Rosyth had come under attack from 12 Ju 88s.

Their intended target was HMS *Hood* which was thought to be in the area, but the actual ships in the Forth were HMS *Edinburgh* and HMS *Southampton* at anchor, and HMS *Mohawk* which was underway east of the Forth Bridge. There was very little warning of the raid since the radar at Cockburnspath was not working, and only late notice was given by the Observer Corps. Now faced with an imminent attack, the ships manoeuvred wildly in efforts to confuse the attackers.[20]

Passengers on a train crossing the Forth Bridge were surprised to see great waterspouts leaping up near the bridge The diary of 602 Squadron told that the raiders dropped 'some 40 bombs'.[21] The ships survived (although the Admiral's barge and a pinnace moored alongside the *Southampton* were sunk) but some 16 seamen were killed, including her Captain and over 40 wounded – mainly on the *Mohawk*.[22]

Yellow Section of 603 intercepted three aircraft east of Dalkeith and despite the fact that the enemy aircraft broke formation and took advantage of clouds, rounds were fired at each one of them.[23]

Morton later recorded in his diary 'Over Dalkeith got in a burst of about 8-10 seconds…I was shaken to see something black fall off E/A shied violently at it'. The Junkers 'failed to make the next cloud and started to lose height'.

Gifford was credited with the destruction of this Ju 88 which crashed into the sea off Port Seton.[24]

Sent to patrol over Tranent, Pinkerton, leading 602 Squadron's Blue Section spotted a Ju 88 through a gap in the clouds. Having lost Webb, he led McKellar to the attack, diving from above with superchargers at full boost. McKellar opened fire, riddling its port wing with bullets. Both he and Pinkerton fired busts into the bomber as it dodged in and out of clouds. Rounds from both Spitfires hit the port and starboard engines. With fuel streaming from damaged wing tanks, the Ju 88 plunged down towards the sea.[25] Both Pinkerton and MacKellar were credited with its destruction.

The fighting in the air was fast and intense. One of the dogfights took place low over the suburbs of Edinburgh with an enemy bomber being chased at roof-top heights. It desperately twisted to avoid the guns of the Spitfire and fired its own rear guns at its pursuer as residents gazed up open-mouthed.[26]

Word was quickly sent of the AAF squadron's success and the next day, telegrams of congratulation poured in. Air Vice Marshal R.E. Saul lauded the achievements of the pilots who until recently were mere part-timers: 'Please convey to 602 and 603 my heartfelt congratulations…Our friend the enemy will have an even healthier respect for the Auxiliary squadrons in future.' But the message from AOC Fighter Command, Air Chief Marshall Sir Hugh Dowding, although short, became a proud, oft-quoted line for the AAF: 'Well done. First blood to the Auxiliaries'.

There was still a strong feeling of respect between enemies and something of a chivalrous mood. One of the survivors of the Ju 88 shot down by Blue Section was pilot Hauptmann Helmuth Pohle. George Pinkerton visited him in hospital a few days later and there was a clear respect between the two men. In an excerpt from one of Pinkerton's letters to Pohle after visiting him in hospital on 22 October 1939, he wrote:

> I much appreciated the opportunity of visiting you on Monday last and I hope you are now feeling more

comfortable and on the way to a speedy recovery from your injuries. We are at war but that doesn't stop me from acknowledging the very gallant fight which you put up.[27]

Four days after the action, the chaplains of both squadrons and 603 Squadron's pipe band were among those who attended the funeral at Portobello Cemetery of two of the German airmen shot down on 16 October.[28] Many of those involved in the action were recognised for the part they played. Flt Lt Gifford was awarded the DFC and his citation makes clear his vital contribution on that historic day: 'During October, 1939, this officer, leading a section of his squadron, sighted an enemy bomber over the mainland heading towards the sea at high speed. Flt Lt Gifford led the attack with skill, daring and determination, and as the result of a final burst of firing from his own guns the enemy aircraft crashed into the sea.' George Pinkerton also received the Distinguished Flying Cross, while Morton received a Mention in Despatches.

Ironically, on the same day another Auxiliary unit – No. 607 (County of Durham) Squadron – had arrived at Drem with 16 of its Gloster Gladiator MkIIs – the last biplane fighter to serve in the RAF. They were brought to readiness and three sorties of the nimble biplanes were sent up that afternoon. They patrolled the Firth of Forth at 10,000 feet, but made no contacts with the enemy, despite the success found by Nos. 602 and 603 Squadrons.

The only action they had came from HMS *Mohawk*, whose understandably twitchy gun crews opened fire on the Gladiators. The squadron was then ordered to return to Acklington at dawn the next day and disappointment at missing the action would be quickly forgotten. As they returned, two Do 18 flying boats left their base at Sylt for reconnaissance of Royal Naval shipping around the Firth of Forth and to search for downed crews from the previous day's raids.

At 1240, Blue Section of 'B' Flight, led by Flt Lt J. Sample with F/Os G.D. Craig and W.H.R. Whitty took off from Acklington.

At 10,000 feet they spotted one of the flying boats and Sample ordered the section to follow him as he dived at the Dornier from 8,000 feet.

The pilot of the Do 18 dived steeply down to 50 feet above the sea, denying the Gladiators a shooting opportunity. Sample called his section into line astern and each of the Gladiators made three passes on the Do 18, all firing bursts into the flying boat, registering hits with pieces of the flying boat seen to fly off. Fuel streamed from the stricken Dornier and it almost dipped a wing tip in the water as it tried to evade the pursuing biplanes.

By now the fighters had no ammunition and with fuel running low, they headed for home, with the flying boat trailing smoke in the opposite direction. However, it eventually landed on the sea and the crew members were picked up by the destroyer HMS *Juno*.[29]

One of the crew was killed in the attack and the three survivors were interrogated. With impressive English and knowledge about the auxiliary squadron and its former part-timers. Joe Kayll recalled that the 'very articulate' Luftwaffe pilot of the Do 18 commented that 'to be shot down by a bloody barrister in a bloody biplane is more than I can bloody well bear!'[30]

The news that they had in fact downed one of the Dorniers was greeted with jubilation at 607. 'Thus' the squadron diary proudly recorded 'the squadron scored its first victory of the war simultaneously with its first actual engagement'. First blood was very nearly to this auxiliary squadron.[31]

October saw more victories for the Scottish fighter squadrons. On 22 October, 'Patsy' Gifford led Red Section of 603 Squadron to intercept enemy aircraft reported to be attacking a convoy off St Abb's Head. They contacted a He 111 4 miles from the shore and pursued it out to sea and shot it down 7 miles out after it had turned back towards the shore.[32]

Nos. 602 and 603 again were in pursuit of another raider, a He 111 on 28 October. They attacked it at 14,000 feet over the Firth of

Forth. Two of the crew were dead from bullet wounds, the pilot was wounded and the observer was uninjured. The aircraft was riddled with bullet holes[33] and came down in the Lammermuir Hills, at Humbie. It was the first to fall on British soil in the war, with Archie McKellar of 602 Squadron credited with the He 111's destruction.[34]

After the excitement of these first victories in October, the war in the air settled into a pattern of inconclusive skirmishes.

On 27 November 1939, six Blenheims of 601 Squadron flew from Bircham Newton in a daylight raid on the seaplane base at Borkum in Germany. Among the pilots of 601 who took part in the raid was Sir Archibald Hope, Max Aitken, Willie Rhodes-Moorhouse and Raymond Davis. This was the first combat operation for the 'Millionaires' but the low-level attack caused little damage and all the aircraft return safely.[35]

No. 610 (County of Chester) Squadron too were tasked with patrols over the east coast. For them the North Sea around Norfolk and the Lincolnshire coast was their beat but they saw little action.

While there were few contacts with the enemy, a patrol on 3 February was particularly lively. Flt Lt A. Smith was sent out over the Norfolk coast to intercept following a report of an enemy aircraft approaching Wells from Cromer. He was unable to find it due to very poor visibility but as he flew across Overstrand, people on the beach waved and pointed to him the direction the enemy had flown. Still unable to find the intruder he headed for home only for 'small boys' to throw stones at his aircraft (although 'without registering any hits').

Alongside the bringing to readiness of the RAF, an immediate commitment by the British after war broke out was the formation of the British Expeditionary Force (BEF).

This was the contingent of the British Army sent to France in 1939 after Britain and France declared war on Nazi Germany on 3 September. General Lord Gort was appointed its commander and it quickly moved to take up positions along the Belgian–French border.

Two AAF squadrons were part of the Air Component – the RAF support for the BEF. The recently mobilised part-timers of Nos. 607 (County of Durham) and 615 (County of Surrey) would soon fly to France to help defend the British forces there, both flying the Gloster Gladiator. One 607 Squadron pilot had his own ideas as to why the Gladiator was sent. 'A' Flight Commander with No. 607 Squadron was Sqn Ldr Joe Kayll.[36]

He observed drily that they were sent with Gladiators to France, 'because [the RAF] did not want to spare Spitfires and Hurricanes.'[37]

In early November, 607 flew south from Acklington to Croydon, where 615 Squadron was based. On 15 November, they left in what must have been a dramatic exit with the 32 Gladiators of both squadrons taking to the sky together.

They then flew to Merville, where officers were billeted in the town and aircrew in a large grain site on the bank of the canal near the railway station. Both squadrons quickly began operations but encounters with the enemy were fleeting. On 20 November, a He 111 was sighted near the aerodrome and a section of 'A' Flight from 607 Squadron was sent up but the enemy aircraft evaded them in cloud.

Fruitless patrols then continued but as the weather worsened through November, the airfield became unusable. Sorties were launched sometimes following sightings of enemy aircraft; standing patrols often over the Channel were undertaken 'so far as serviceability of aircraft permits'.[38]

On 13 December, the squadrons moved again with 607 going from Merville to Vitry. Personnel were billeted in the village in farmyard stables, barns and houses. Officers and senior NCOs being for the most part in private houses. An officers' mess was set up, appropriately, at the Café de Grande Bretagne.

That winter was hard with roads 'in a very treacherous condition' with 2-3 inches of snow becoming frozen. The new year brought an unexpected visitor when on 9 January, Winston Churchill, then First Lord of the Admiralty – also the Honorary Air Commodore of 615 Squadron – came to Vitry.[39]

PHONEY WAR AND THE BATTLE OF FRANCE

Severe weather curtailed flying throughout January and into February when all 607's aircraft were unserviceable at various times. Joe Kayll remembered how the Auxiliary spirit served 607 well in the face of these difficulties. 'Flying ceased for lack of spares and only by some ingenuity did the Auxiliaries contrive to get airborne, generally on the pretext of air testing'. He recalled it was the 'it was the sheer enthusiasm of the Auxiliaries that made the squadron what it was.' The skills they had from they brought as part-timers from their civilian jobs were hugely beneficial he recalled. 'These', he recalled 'were often skilled workers from the shipyards, the mines and the factories'.[40]

Kayll would not be with 607 for much longer, but he wouldn't be going far and took over as OC 615 Squadron on 14 March. That month, moves began to finally re-equip both squadrons with replacements for the obsolete Gladiator. Personnel from 615 went for training on the Hurricane and 607 had two Hurricanes delivered on 15 March to familiarise themselves.

Meanwhile, much further north the picture was changing for the worse. On 9 April, Germany invaded Norway and Denmark. This heralded a big increase in activity around Scapa Flow naval base in the Orkneys and for 605 (County of Warwick) Squadron, which was based at Wick.

The following day while on convoy patrol, P/O Muirhead sighted an enemy aircraft and carried out two attacks before losing them in cloud. An hour later, F/O Leeson, leading Red Section saw two enemy aircraft at 14,000 feet climbed and brought down one with two crew members seen to bale out. In another raid later that day, F/O Gerry Edge was to play a leading role. He was commissioned in 605 Squadron in July 1936 while working for the family metal business. That day he attacked three He 111s, shot down one of them, possibly another, and damaged the third. A month later he shared a Do 17 off Dumner Head.

For the next six hours there was intense activity, far greater than anything the squadron had seen before. There were more sightings but no more kills. At 1045, the air raid siren sounded in nearby Wick and four aircraft from 605 with 43 and 111 Squadrons took off. Around 40 enemy aircraft raided Scapa Flow, coming over in successive waves, dropping bombs. But within weeks there was to be more dire news from the Continent.[41]

The 10 May was recorded in the diaries of many of the AAF squadrons like a bell sounding; crisp and clear and there is generally a single line. For 602 'Germany invaded Holland and Belgium – all leave stopped'. For 609 'Following Germany's invasion of the Low Countries, all RAF leave is cancelled'.

At Digby in Lincolnshire, for No. 611, the quiet of the long patrols on the east coast was shattered. At 1730 a message was received forecasting a possible raid by parachute troops in an hour, later varied to 2115. Rifles with ammunition were quickly issued to airmen and the night guard at dispersal was increased in strength.[42]

Some based in southern England leapt quickly into the fray. That morning, Blenheims of No. 600 (City of London) Squadron were engaged in a fierce fight with He 111s over northern France.

On patrol at 0340 P/O Anderson was in Blenheim Mk1 'P' vectored towards France in pursuit of a 'Bogey'. He sighted a He 111 which opened fire on him and the rear-gunner of the Heinkel brought down heavy and accurate fire on the Blenheim. But Gunner LAC Baker fired until his ammunition was gone and put the Heinkel's gunner out of action. Anderson dived to sea-level and returned to Manston where he landed riddled with bullet holes and hydraulics out of action.

By 1200 they had received that news Germany had invaded the Low Countries. Six aircraft took off to attack Waalhaven airfield in Rotterdam which had been taken by German parachutists.[43]

One of the Blenheims 'O' was flown by P/O Norman Hayes with gunner Cpl John Holmes. Hayes recalled it was a beautiful day as they approached the target, but columns of smoke from burning Rotterdam and The Hague betrayed the desperate fight the Dutch were putting up against the invading Germans. Smoke too was rising from the airfield as they went in for the attack. 'I picked a Ju 52 and shot it up...As I climbed I saw a Bf 110 attacking one of our Blenheims. Then I saw about eight Bf 110s 600 feet above us just peeling off onto our tails.' The fight then got 'very confusing'. He was grateful for the direction given by Cpl Holmes and he dodged the marauding twin-engined fighters. 'I soon found the situation was hopeless', he recalled 'and that my only chance was to get out as soon as I could. My airplane had been very badly hit and what worried me was the petrol leaking into the fuselage as my starboard tank had been hit'. He dived to ground level to get home.[44]

Encountering three He 111s on the way home, they used their remaining ammunition to break up this formation and returned safely.[45]

Limping home to Manston, on landing he reported to Wg Cdr Grice, the CO. He told them that they were the first to return. 'I had to tell him that we would be the only ones to return'. It was a grievous blow for the squadron. Hayes would receive the DFC and Holmes the DFM for the great courage they displayed that day.[46]

Meanwhile other Blenheims of 600 Squadron were fighting elsewhere. At 1330, four were sent to patrol to Zeebrugge. A He 111 was spotted and 4,000 rounds were pumped into it with many hits observed. The Heinkel was last seen diving towards the sea with considerable smoke pouring from it, 'hotly engaged by Dutch anti-aircraft fire', with two of 600's Blenheims targeted by the Dutch too.[47]

'B' Flight of No. 604 (County of Middlesex) Squadron took off from Kenley to escort 12 Blenheim Mk IVs to attack roads to beaches north of The Hague where enemy aircraft were known to have landed. Four Ju 52s were destroyed and three more were damaged.[48]

For some it meant an immediate move. For No. 601 (County of London) Squadron, two flights were ordered to RAF Hawkinge for operations and No. 610 (County of Chester) Squadron were ordered to move at once to Biggin Hill.[49]

No. 501 (County of Gloucester) Squadron went straight to the fight, flying to France on the day of the invasion to deploy to Bétheniville.

Operations began immediately on arrival and F/O Pickup shot down a Do 17 north of Vouziers.[50]

The squadrons already in France felt the force of the German attack immediately. At Vitry-en-Artois, France, members of No. 607 (County of Durham) Squadron were awoken at 0412 when the civilian '*Alerte*' was sounded followed immediately by the firing of Bofors guns.

Later a formation of nine enemy bombers was seen approaching the aerodrome at 300 feet, dropping to 30ft and passed over them releasing bombs. As they flew over, they opened fire on aircraft in dispersal, tankers and fuel dumps burst into flames and exploded throughout the evening.

The following day, 501 Squadron's groundcrew and remaining pilots arrived in Handley Page Harrow transport aircraft, but tragedy struck before they had even faced the enemy. The last aircraft to arrive crashed on landing, killing three.[51]

On the same day there was tumult at home too. Following the evacuation of British and French forces from Norway, the allied strategy lay in tatters. Although there was no actual vote of confidence, it was clear that Chamberlain no longer had the support of Parliament and Churchill replaced him as Prime Minister.

Just days later in his first speech to the House of Commons as Prime Minister on 13 May, Churchill spoke of the challenge ahead: 'We are in the preliminary stage of one of the greatest battles in history…. I would say to the House, as I said to those who have joined this government: I have nothing to offer but blood, toil, tears and sweat'.[52]

In France, 501 quickly recovered from its losses and did so by adding to its score in the most emphatic manner. On 12 May, 501 claimed six enemy aircraft – Donald McKay shot down a He 111 – the first of four kills in France for him and he damaged a Do 17 into the bargain three days later. Born in Pontefract, in 1917, McKay was working as a bank clerk when he joined the RAFVR in April 1937 and began his elementary flying training at 5 E&RFTS at Hanworth. He was then offered a six-month attachment to the regular RAF for continuous

PHONEY WAR AND THE BATTLE OF FRANCE

training with 43 Squadron and 111 Squadrons. He was called up on 1 September 1939 and joined 501 Squadron at Filton five days later.[53]

Another reservist pilot quickly started his account at Bétheniville. Pilot Officer Robert Dafforn applied to join the RAFVR in 1936 but was turned down because the slender 6 feet 6 inches tall, ex-Harrow pupil was considered by doctors to be too thin.

While working in the Exchange Equalisation Department of the Bank of England, he underwent a course of physical training, applied again and was accepted. He began his flying training at 8 E&RFTS, Woodley in October 1937. In mid-September 1939 he joined 501 Squadron at Filton. He claimed a Do 17 destroyed on the 11th, a He 111 on the 14th, a probable Me 110 on the 19th, a probable He 111 on the 20th and on the 27th a He 111 destroyed and another shared.[54]

The next day saw even greater efforts. The slight, red-haired lad from Wetherby who had honed his skill as a civilian flying instructor saw those hours of practice pay off. Sgt James Lacey – or 'Ginger' as he was universally known, was to shoot down three enemy aircraft that day – an Me 109, a He 111 and an Me 110. For this action, Lacey was later awarded the Croix de Guerre.

On 14 May, No. 504 (County of Nottingham) Squadron – who had only arrived in France two days earlier, had their baptism of fire. That afternoon Red Section – consisting of Sqn Ldr Parnall, Flight Lieutenant Royce, P/O Rennison and Sgt Hamblett on patrol sighted six He 111s escorted by Me 110s. The Hurricanes attacked the bombers and the Me 110s attacked them. Royce's machine was shot down but he baled out and successfully and managed to regain his own lines and later rejoined the squadron having probably shot down a He 111.

Sqn Ldr Parnall did not return from their patrol and according to Royce, he probably shot a He 111 down. Sgt Hamblett did not return either.

From Mansfield in Nottinghamshire, William Royce joined his local squadron, No. 504 (County of Nottingham) in June 1932 – then a Special Reserve unit. Appointed 'B' Flight Commander in January

1940 with the rank of Acting Flight Lieutenant, on 2 April he had damaged a He 115 floatplane. On this chaotic day, he took temporary command of the squadron that day when the CO was lost.[55]

Awarded the DFC on 31 May, his citation told how. 'This officer assumed command of a squadron after its three previous commanders had been lost. One day in May his squadron had completed seven sorties, including two ground attacks, by 1300 hours and were eager to go out yet again. Flight Lieutenant Royce shot down four enemy aircraft. He led the squadron in a most efficient and determined manner.'

On 16 May an early hero of the Auxiliary Air Force met his end. After having been posted away from No. 603 (City of Edinburgh) Squadron to take command of No. 3 Squadron in November following the shooting down of enemy raiders over the Firth of Forth, the now Sqn Ldr 'Patsy' Gifford was reported to have been killed when his Hurricane was shot down over Hamme-Mille, Belgium.[56]

On the same day, a pilot with No. 607 (County of Durham) Squadron, Jim Bazin was missing, and as fellow-flyer Francis Blackadder recalled in his diary, he had an interesting escape. 'He force-landed near Sedan after having tried without success to bale-out from the left-hand side: He was shot at so escaped into a wood and through a field to come to an area where he found a French motor-cyclist. He was taken to their (French) General HQ and made welcome, but they were in retreat – So he [Bazin] went to set fire to his machine [Hurricane], but a hail of bullets from the Hun line made him decide it was better to leave things as they were. He accompanied the General, who was getting all his men back across a canal and then blew up the bridge. Bazin eventually got conveyance home. The whole show was like the film 'Dawn Patrol' but it was given better reality'. A few days earlier on the 11th, Bazin shot down a He 111 north of Douai and next day he destroyed another near Brussels. From the Newcastle suburb of Jesmond, Jim Bazin joined his local auxiliary squadron in May 1935 while working in engineering with Armstrong Whitworth in the city.[57]

PHONEY WAR AND THE BATTLE OF FRANCE

By 17 May, the 'Millionaires' of 601 came to France and arrived at Merville. They quickly learned of the febrile situation with the hazards and confusion of war. Three aircraft of 'B' Flight patrolling over Brussels came under fire 'probably Belgian'. The Hurricanes left the patrol line but the leader was uncertain of the route back and F/O Branch became separated in the dark and force-landed, damaging his aircraft and returned by car of another 'Millionaire'. Others landed safely by their headlights. 'B' Flight then operated over France from Manston.[58]

Meanwhile 'A' Flight also was deployed to Merville. It was led by Max Aitken, the elder son of William Aitken, the newspaper tycoon Baron Beaverbrook who would become Minister of Aircraft Production in Churchill's government. A noted member of the social set and a keen sportsman in the 1930s, he joined 601 Squadron in 1935. He would have a successful time in France, claiming a He 111 destroyed plus another probable over Brussels on 18 May, a He 111 and a Ju 87 on the 19th, a probable Ju 87 and Me 110 the same day and on the 23rd a Me 109 damaged. Aitken returned to England and in early June he was promoted to Acting Squadron Leader and given command of 601 Squadron. He destroyed a He 111 off Brighton during the night of 25/26 June. For this and those victories in France he was awarded the DFC on 9 July. His final victory with 601 came on 7 July 1940 when he shared a Do 17 over the Channel with four other pilots. He was posted from the squadron on 20 July.

The next day, 504 Squadron flew to escort Blenheims to Cambrai. They were jumped by six Me 109s which appeared 3,000 feet above them. P/O Frisby gave the alarm over the radio, P/O Parsons heard and turned steeply left but Flt Lt Owen and P/O Rennington did not hear it and P/O Owen was shot down in flames but baled out.

A graphic demonstration of this brutal new phase of the war came when Owen was machine-gunned as he descended in his parachute. P/O Van Ments saw this and attacked the Me 109 which fired on his desperate comrade.[59]

By this time, the German panzers were sweeping through northern France and Belgium. On the same day, 607 Squadron had an insight into the chaos that was descending across the region. All personnel were warned to prepare to move with minimum kit and stores. At nightfall, the convoy left for Norrent-Fontes. The journey was slow as roads were full with French and Belgian soldiers advancing and refugees fleeing.[60]

Arriving in the early hours of the 19th personnel were accommodated in a deserted mining village nearby. That day, as the crisis deepened, No. 609 Squadron was ordered to move to Tangmere from where they could support the beleaguered BEF.[61]

A raid the next day showed that, successful though the RAF had been, they were being overwhelmed by the vast numbers they were facing. No. 601 Squadron met a formation of '50 or 60 He 111s and Ju 87s accompanied by six Me 110s.'[62]

By 20 May the situation was becoming frantic. All personnel of 607 Squadron were instructed to abandon all kit and equipment, and board transport which was supposedly forming up beyond the aerodrome boundary. This transport, however never materialised and personnel made their way in small groups to Le Havre via Boulogne amid very bad congestion. Dodging raids through the night, they boarded a ferry which took them to Dover. Others remaining at Norrent-Fontes flew to Hendon. Two pilots were dead, two were missing, believed to be PoWs. Between 10–20 May the squadron destroyed 72 enemy aircraft with a further 56 probably damaged.[63]

No. 607's AAF colleagues in France, 615 stayed put and on 20 May they moved to Norrent-Fontes and the squadron began to take a toll on the enemy. At 1200, 615 with 504 and the remnants of 607 attacked a convoy on the Arras-Cambrai road leaving 'lorries in flames and confusion'. At 1500, six aircraft patrolling Arras-Douai-Lens accounted for two He 111s. These successes were to be a parting shot and on 21 May, the squadron left for Boulogne arrived at Dover by 1430.[64]

A day later, 22 May, all 504 Squadron personnel were successfully evacuated from France. As 504 left, another AAF squadron would move south to operate over France and Belgium. On 22 May, 605 went to Hawkinge and were quickly in action.[65] Called to readiness at 0430, they patrolled Calais, Boulogne and 20 miles inland. A second patrol took off at 1115 South-West of Arras and was attacked by six Me 109s, resulting in the loss of F/O Austin and Sgt Moffatt. Yellow Section attacked five He111s, but P/O 'Bunny' Currant's Hurricane suffered damage to its oil feed and he had to force-land. He set fire to his aircraft and returned to his unit 24 hours later with a broken nose. F/O Wright attacked two He111s and he saw glycol streaming from one. The squadron diary told that four He111s had been claimed 'three conclusive.'

As the BEF retreated ever closer to the coast around Dunkirk, sorties focussed that part of the northern French coast. On 25 May at 0554, they escorted Blenheims on a reconnaissance mission to Gravelines. The squadron stayed on patrol after the Blenheims left and Yellow 3, P/O Muirhead in Hurricane P3423 spotted two Henschel 126s at 10,000 feet. He attacked them and shot one down.

A further patrol at 1110 saw them covering bombers over Calais then to Courtrai–Hazebrook–Dunkirk for an hour. They met a formation of Ju 87s between east of Calais and Gravelines and set upon them. A dogfight ensued and they also met a further formation of Ju 87s as they were proceeding to dive-bomb shipping off Gravelines. Two Ju 87s were shot down in the first encounter by F/Os Edge and Muirhead in Hurricanes N2557 and P3423 respectively plus one 'inconclusive' by P/O Cooper-Slipper flying in L2098. In the fight with the second formation, there was one 'conclusive' for Muirhead and two 'inconclusive' for F/Os Danielson in L2059 and Edge.[66] That May over France with 605, Gerry Edge racked up an incredible tally with the Auxiliary squadron – albeit before the Battle of Britain began. He would destroy seven enemy aircraft, including three Ju 87s in total in this period.[67]

By 26 May Allied forces in northern France had been pushed back to the coast, particularly around Dunkirk. As retreating allied troops streamed towards the port, Operation *Dynamo* – the Dunkirk evacuation of the BEF and other Allied troops to England was ordered to commence.

Hitler famously at this time issued his 'stop order' to the Wehrmacht that it should halt before reaching Dunkirk and the surrounding area. Goering argued that the Luftwaffe could finish off the BEF and so as the evacuation began, they began to pound Dunkirk.

It would be the job of the RAF to prevent the Lutfwaffe from doing this and to protect the evacuation fleet. Squadrons of the AAF were quickly in action. On 26 May, 616 Squadron was ordered to Rochford to mount offensive patrols over Dunkirk. The next day at 1810, 610 Squadron received an order to patrol the port area. At 18,000 feet, their Spitfires were met with an intense anti-aircraft barrage. Spotting a He 111 at 15,000 feet, Red Section dived to attack from above. Red 1 (Sqn Ldr Franks) in Spitfire N3201 made sure it was an enemy and ordered his wingmates – Red 2, F/O E.B.B. Smith in L1010, and Red 3, Sgt Medway in N3284, to attack. Red 2 fired all his ammunition into the fuselage and starboard engine which belched flames and black smoke. Red 3 continued the attack and fired a five second burst. Yellow and Blue Sections then joined the attack but Blue leader Flt Lt J. Ellis in 'L1000' broke his section away before opening fire as he saw the Heinkel by this time was on fire and diving steeply. The stricken Heinkel fired signal flares which then brought 30-40 Me 110s into the battle. A dogfight ensued which resulted in three Me 110s confirmed shot down and three unconfirmed as well as the He 111.[68]

In those frantic, long days, 605 Squadron, which had been moved to Hawkinge would be very close to the enemy, sometimes too close it would seem. On 26 May, they received reports of enemy parachutists near Dover. Orders were given to secure the camp and the all-clear was not sounded until 0230 the next day.

As the evacuation from Dunkirk gathered pace, 605 would be in the thick of the fight – fighting to protect the troops waiting to be picked up and the ships taking them to safety. At 1310 that day they sent nine aircraft to patrol around Calais–Dunkirk. At Dunkirk the harbour was reported to be burning fiercely, with smoke rising up to 4,000 feet. A formation of '4 or 5 Ju 88s' encountered over Dunkirk was about to dive-bomb the harbour. One was shot down in the sea, five miles north-east of Dunkirk by Red 2 P/O Cooper-Slipper in Hurricane L2059.

The remainder of the squadron attacked more Ju 88s and Red 3 fired 290 rounds into one, being hit in the fuselage and emitting a large cloud of black smoke. Red 1 put two bursts of into the aircraft killing the rear gunner. Eight 605 aircraft returned to base at 1430 but P/O Muirhead in N2346 was missing. A Hurricane was seen to go into two turns of a spin at 6,000 feet, 4 miles north of Dunkirk over the sea. The diary told it is considered that Muirhead's machine was brought down by AA fire, possibly friendly as white and black puffs were noted.

In 'perfect' weather at 0827 on 27 May, 605 were patrolling and engaged six Do 17s 5 miles south-east of Dunkirk. Though four aircraft returned to base at 1015, one 605 pilot, F/O Forbes, was missing. He was last seen near Poperinge prior to engaging a Do 17.

At 1440, eight 605 aircraft encountered six Do 17s south-east of Dunkirk, heading towards the port. Yellow 1 (P/O Danielson) in Hurricane P3581 followed by Yellow 4 attacked 3 Dorniers and Red 1 (Sqn Ldr Perry) in P3423 followed by Red Section attacked others. After the fight, their ammunition was almost gone and on breaking off, 605 encountered further formations of Me 109s near Dunkirk which were evaded and six of 605 returned to base at 1555.

Sqn Ldr Perry and F/O Danielson were missing, and the surviving pilots considered the losses 'entirely due to small numbers of our formations as compared the enemy and in consequence loss of protection'.[69]

The fighting over Dunkirk was fast and chaotic. On 28 May, 616 Squadron was ordered to patrol with 65 and 19 Squadrons over the Dunkirk beaches. On reaching the patrol position, two unidentified aircraft were being attacked by Spitfires. They were identified as Fleet Air Arm Skuas. The squadron became separated from the main formation. Immediately afterwards, Red and Green Sections were attacked by 30 Me 109s. P/O Holden accounted for an Me 109 and returned undamaged. F/O Moberley accounted for another unconfirmed.

It was clear to the pilots flying over the area how desperate the situation was at Dunkirk. On 28 May, 611 Squadron, so long ploughing their lonely furrow over the North Sea in uneventful patrols, sent a detachment from Digby for Martlesham Heath to patrol Dunkirk. No enemy aircraft were sighted but the column of smoke they saw rising 15,000 feet high over Dunkirk would be an ominous portent of trials to come.

As squadrons like 611 entered the fray, they allowed others to have respite. On the same day, 28 May, 605 received a signal posting them north to Drem for the squadron to reform.

No 611's fellows from the north-west – 610 – had success but suffered grievous blows protecting the evacuation. At 1645, four Me 109s were shot down in patrol over Dunkirk, but four of their pilots were missing: F/Os M.T. Kerr, J. Kerr-Wilson and A.R.J. Medcalf, and Sgt W.T. Medway all failed to return. By 1955 in a further patrol over Dunkirk Sqn Ldr A.L. Franks did not return and Sgt P.D. Jenkins baled out of his burning Spitfire with the wings falling off. Flt Lt J. Ellis attempted to signal to destroyers to pick him up but came under fire from them.[70]

As the pressure increased on the Dunkirk perimeter, so too did the pressure on squadrons to patrol the skies above it.

On 29 May, 616 Squadron joined Nos. 222, 19 and 44 Squadrons patrolling a 10-mile radius of Dunkirk from 0415 to 0600. The following day, 609 Squadron was ordered to stand by for action on the French coast. Four sections of three aircraft patrolled. They knew the reason for this work and were proud to do it: 'It is felt an honour for the Squadron to be chosen for such an important task as this one of covering the evacuation from Dunkirk' the diary told.

John Dundas, who we first met during the Munich Crisis in September 1938, was now becoming an accomplished fighter pilot and he destroyed a He 111 and shared a Do 17 on 31 May and damaged a He 111 on 1 June, all over Dunkirk.[71]

High-level contacts between the British and French governments continued amid the worsening military situation. On 31 May, four aircraft of 601 Squadron went to Warmwell and escorted two

Flamingo aircraft carrying the PM and his staff to Villecoublay, while five other aircraft went to Hendon and provided escort to France.

We met Flt Lt William Pancoast Clyde in the previous chapter after making his way back to 601 Squadron on the outbreak of war. He was sent as a member of 'A' Flight to operate from Merville and was part of Churchill's fighter escort when he went to Paris for meetings on 15 May and 31 May with the French government prior to the French collapse. On the 27th Clyde had shared two Me 110s destroyed and was awarded the DFC on 31 May 1940.[72] The citation read: 'This officer was posted to France in early May 1940 and has led his flight on many occasions with great skill and has set a high standard of morale and leadership'. Other DFCs were awarded that day. The citation of Flt Lt Walter Churchill of 605 Squadron told how 'this officer assumed command of a squadron shortly after its arrival in France and led it with marked success, inspiring his pilots and maintenance crews magnificently. Squadron Leader Joe Kayll, now CO of 615 Squadron was similarly honoured. His citation read 'Owing to his inspiring training and leadership this officer's squadron has destroyed 32 enemy aircraft'.

With daylight coming very early, 1 June saw 10 aircraft of 616 Squadron airborne at 0419. They were ordered to patrol Dunkirk beaches from 0500 to 0615 to protect shipping and evacuating troops. The patrols continued through the day and the frantic pace of operations can be gleaned from 616 Squadron's activity the following day:

> 0448 Eight aircraft were airborne to patrol Dunkirk from 0500 until 0615. On landing the squadron was to be placed at 30 minutes availability.
>
> 0708 Eight aircraft landed.
>
> 1110 'B' Flight released until 1800, 'A' Flight released from 1500 until 2100; whole squadron available from 2100 until one hour after dusk.

1230 'A' Flight to immediate readiness.

1358 Squadron 'Scramble', all aircraft (five) airborne 1403.

1525 five aircraft landed.

1600 Squadron released until dawn except for one section which was to be at 30 minutes availability.

1840 'A' Flight brought to immediate readiness later put it 30 minutes availability

2025 Squadron was released until dawn.[73]

But perhaps the finest example of the fierce fighting over Dunkirk came from 611 Squadron. On 2 June, the whole squadron flew to Martlesham, refuelled and left at 0700 together with four other squadrons for an offensive patrol over Dunkirk. By 0745 they were over the port.

Their formation consisted of five layers. Topmost was 32 Squadron, below them 66 Squadron, below again, 266 Squadron, next at 17,000 feet, was 611 Squadron and lowest at 14,000 feet was 92 Squadron.

As they approached Dunkirk, the 611 pilots again saw a thick column of smoke rising over the port. They saw that the sea between Dunkirk and Folkestone was 'thick with shipping'.

The squadron was flying south-westerly above the coastline and above the edge of the clouds, in sections at about 0805. Then the enemy aircraft were seen – a formation of bombers flying on a similar course, just below the cloud level.

They were attacked by 92 Squadron, while 611 Squadron took on their escorting fighters. The diary told how 'Almost at once a dog fight became general, and the pilots' individual combat reports are not easy to piece together'. Sqn Ldr J.E. McComb (Red 1) in Spitfire N3058 was leading the squadron whose pilots were all examples of the Auxiliary roots of the squadron.

Born in 1909, James Ellis McComb trained as a solicitor and worked for the Legal Department of Lancashire County Council. In early 1934 he joined 600 Squadron but transferred to his local unit,

PHONEY WAR AND THE BATTLE OF FRANCE

611 Squadron on 25 September 1936. He was appointed OC 611 Squadron at the outbreak of war.[74]

McComb saw two Me 109s approaching on his starboard bow and firing cannon. Turning the squadron into the attack, he saw them turn away. He got on their tails and fired a five-second burst at the nearest, and saw petrol streaming from the left side of the fuselage behind the pilot. At 15,000 feet it then disappeared in a left-hand spiral dive.

Later, at 10,000 feet he saw five He 111s flying in close formation, apparently unescorted. He attacked the leader from the right with a short burst, but then found an Me 110 attacking him with cannon fire from behind, so broke off his attack and spun down to 2,000 feet. On looking up he then saw only four He 111s.

P/O Jones (Red 3) in N3050 saw an Me 109 on the tail of a Spitfire and immediately attacked, getting in two short bursts. The enemy aircraft broke and dived through thick cloud. P/O Jones followed, attacking again with a long burst, and closed to 50 yards. He saw the pilot apparently trying to abandon his aircraft but was attacked from behind himself and saw holes appear in his port plane, but evaded by a quarter roll and steep dive. Flt Lt Leather (Yellow 1) in N3054 saw another Me 109 at 15,000 feet attacking a Spitfire (which may have been P/O Little's). He saw the Spitfire descending in a gentle spin with white smoke streaming from its engine. He attacked the Me 109 with a five-second burst from 50 yards astern and saw it turn over slowly and go into a spin. He was unable to watch it further as he was attacked with cannon and machine gun fire by another Me 109.

F/O Douglas Watkins in N3051 was flying as Yellow 2. From Heswall in Cheshire, after leaving Denstone College in Staffordshire he joined 611 Squadron in 1938 while he was apprenticed as an architect to S.A. Kelly of Liverpool. Called to full-time service on 21 September 1939, he'd already damaged a He 115 floatplane east of Spurn Head on 21 October.

He saw two Me 109s trying to get on his tail, but evaded them by climbing away into the sun. He saw another two Me 109s crossing his path just below him in line astern and attacked the second with a long continuous burst at 200 yards. He saw parts of its port wing break off, corrected his aim and saw the enemy aircraft shudder violently, do a flat climbing turn, and dive vertically out of sight.

F/O Barrie Heath (Blue 3) in N3061 was patrolling the Dunkirk beaches at 13,000 feet when he sighted 12 Ju 87s.

Born in 1916, Heath was the son of the senior director of Rootes Motors and was educated at Wrekin College and Pembroke College, Cambridge, where he read Mechanical Sciences. After learning to fly with the University Air Squadron, he was commissioned in the Reserve of Air Force Officers (RAFO) in May 1937, but relinquished this on being commissioned in the RAFVR in May 1938. He transferred to 611 Squadron in June 1939.

Having seen the Stukas, he attacked – coming down on the tail of the starboard of the two leaders with a 10 second burst and broke away at 25 yards. As Heath blazed away, return fire from the Stuka ceased. It shuddered violently, turned on its back and fell straight for the sea. He then attacked a single Ju 87 which at 5,000 feet was diving at a ship. He gave it a continuous burst which was seen to enter the fuselage, until all his ammunition was gone.

Another former part-time reservist over Dunkirk that day was (Green 2) P/O Dennis Adams in N3066. Educated at Liscard High School, Wallasey, Adams passed the entrance examination for Cambridge University but decided to do an apprenticeship in the leather industry, taking a job with a tannery in Northampton. He joined the F2 Reserve of Pilots on 14 April 1936 at 7 E&RFTS Desford on a course which required nine weeks full-time training in the first six months on Tiger Moths and two weeks in the second six months on Hawker Harts. When the RAFVR was formed in that year, Adams enlisted as a Sergeant-Pilot and spent his RAFVR weekends at Meir in Staffordshire. In 1938 he applied to join 610 Squadron, but there were no vacancies so he applied to 611 Squadron at Speke that July and was accepted. He was commissioned and given a £60 uniform allowance to spend at Gieves in Liverpool.

At the start of the engagement Adams saw two Me 109s below and to the left. F/O Crompton (Green 1) in N3064 dived down on them, and Adams, following at a distance, saw him being attacked by one, and turning to his right and diving. Adams then lost sight of his leader, but sighted four Ju 87s in a box formation, 500 feet above him at 8,000 feet. He attacked one in the box with two short bursts and saw him go straight down with black smoke pouring out and flames appearing.

Green 3, P/O Colin Macfie in N3060 lost his section early on. Born in Cheltenham in 1920, he studied at the Liverpool School of Architecture and joined 611 Squadron in early 1939. Still under training when war broke out, after gaining his wings he rejoined 611 at Digby.

Green Section was the rearguard of the squadron and was varying their course and formation to keep a lookout behind. He didn't see Green 1 and 2 diving away, so continued to patrol Dunkirk. His attention was attracted by anti-aircraft fire to the seaward and he saw six Ju 87s with escorting Me 109s above them, approaching the land. He attacked the last Ju 87 which broke formation and followed him through the pillar of smoke over Dunkirk. Macfie found him again, attacking shipping off the port, and got him pulling out of its dive with a long burst astern and then a deflection shot when he did a climbing turn to the right. The stricken dive-bomber continued to turn, but its nose dropped, and it hit the water and broke up.

Shortly afterwards he saw a Spitfire with no tail spinning into the beach. It is possible that this was Crompton's aircraft. Two pilots were missing – Crompton and Little. The remainder returned safely, but with aircraft in 'various conditions'.

Meanwhile Flt Lt Stoddart (Blue 1) in N3058 was at 13,000 feet when he was shot about before opening fire, but he got home.[75]

Born in Cressington Park, Liverpool in 1914, Kenneth Stoddart finished his degree at Cambridge and worked for the family businesses – Cearns and Brown Ltd and the United Mersey Supply Company – ships' suppliers in Liverpool. While working for them he joined No. 611 Squadron at Speke on 18 December 1936. He learned to fly in Avro Tutors then graduated to Hawker Harts and later Hinds. He converted to the Spitfire in May 1939 and from August 1939 he was a Flt Lt and commanded 'B' Flight at Digby.[76]

Stoddart cut a dashing figure with a profile in the *Liverpool Echo* describing his 'insouciant manner and casual references to "prangs" and drinking Pimms, while waiting for comrades to return, masked his true heroism and steely resolve'.

He had a lucky escape. Landing at Martlesham, he found his aircraft had been bit by a cannon shell in the fuselage just behind him. The shell had torn a large hole in one side of the fuselage, blown the canopy off and left the other side like a sieve. 'The armour plating, recently fitted behind seats of all our aircraft, was spattered at the back with bullet marks. His control wires were shot about, so that they were held by two strands only' the squadron diary told.

It had all taken just 20 minutes. In that dogfight the diary described how the squadron 'so effectively engaged the escorting enemy fighters that No. 92 Squadron were uninterrupted in their attack on the enemy bombers and were able to shoot down 23 of them ("some Heinkel 111s, some Ju 87s") without loss to themselves. According to the best estimates yet available, 611 Squadron accounted for eight (three Ju 87s, four Me 109s and an Me 110)' the squadron diary explained.[77]

The next day was 'brilliantly fine and hot'. Dowding visited and saw all pilots of the squadron, discussing with them the events of the previous day.

An indication of the strain they would all soon feel is signalled by the 609 Squadron diarist that day. North Weald and Northolt were now linked as a 'Four Squadron Sector' which had to have one squadron at readiness, two at 15 mins and one at 30 mins. 'This means the squadron never gets a release day and is constantly on station from dawn to dusk' the diarist complained.[78]

PHONEY WAR AND THE BATTLE OF FRANCE

In the wake of this success and the end of the evacuation, there was a message from Dowding to his pilots. Sent on 4 June, his note praised their skill and courage but steeled them for the fight to come. It read:

> My Dear Fighter Boys,
> I don't send out many congratulatory letters or signals, but I feel that I must take this occasion, when the intensive fighting in Northern France is for the time being over, to tell you how proud I am of you and the way in which you have fought since the 'Blitzkrieg' started.
>
> I wish I could have spent my time visiting you and hearing your accounts of the fighting, but I have occupied myself in working for you in other ways.
>
> I want you to know that my thoughts are always with you and that it is you and your fighting spirit that will crack the morale of the German Air Force and preserve your country through the trials which yet lie ahead.
>
> Good luck to you.
> H.C.T. Dowding[79]

By 4 June, the pilots of 605 Squadron were bruised and battered and were licking their wounds in distant Scotland. Precious leave was granted – equivalent to that awarded to the BEF i.e. a clear 48 hours – but there was wariness in resting for too long and there were signs all around that the next phase of the conflict was near. 'It is hoped pilots will be posted soon so that work can recommence. Idleness is grand but not conducive to winning the war. We must reform as soon as possible and so be ready to fight again'.

In his speech to the House of Commons on 4 June, Churchill gave thanks for what he called 'A miracle of deliverance'. But he cautioned 'We must be very careful not to assign to this deliverance the attributes of a victory. Wars are not won by evacuations'. However, he recognised the RAF's central role in allowing the evacuation to happen with the protection they gave from the air and defended it against those who believed the RAF had abandoned the BEF:

> Many of our soldiers coming back have not seen the Air Force at work; they saw only the bombers which escaped its protective attack. They underrate its achievements. I have heard much talk of this; that is why I go out of my way to say this.
>
> This was a great trial of strength between the British and German Air Forces. Can you conceive a greater objective for the Germans in the air than to make evacuation from these beaches impossible, and to sink all these ships which were displayed, almost to the extent of thousands? Could there have been an objective of greater military importance and significance for the whole purpose of the war than this? They tried hard, and they were beaten back. We got the Army away; and they have paid fourfold for any losses which they have inflicted.

He praised again the young pilots of Fighter Command. 'May it not also be that the cause of civilisation itself will be defended by the skill and devotion of a few thousand airmen?' He lauded them, 'going forth every morn to guard their native land and all that we stand for, holding in their hands these instruments of colossal and shattering power'. He said these pilots 'deserve our gratitude [who are] ready to give life and all for their native land.'

He finished with a rhetorical flourish which is still known well today. 'We shall go on to the end, we shall fight in France, we shall fight on the seas and oceans, we shall fight with growing confidence and growing strength in the air, we shall defend our Island, whatever the cost may be, we shall fight on the beaches, we shall fight on the landing grounds, we shall fight in the fields and in the streets, we shall fight in the hills; we shall never surrender.'[80]

PHONEY WAR AND THE BATTLE OF FRANCE

As breath was drawn after the hellish month of retreat and evacuation, on 8 June squadrons received this signal from Sir Archibald Sinclair, Secretary of State for Air. 'The War Cabinet have expressed their high appreciation of the fine work of the Royal Air Force in covering the evacuation of the British and French Forces from Dunkirk. All ranks have done magnificently'.[81]

On 9 June, the French government fled Paris as the Germans swept onwards through France. The next day Italy declared war against France and Britain and on 11 June three sections from 609 Squadron escorted the aircraft to Orléans.

P/O Michael Appleby was one of 609's pilots chosen to escort Churchill and his War Cabinet to France. They rendezvoused with the PM's Flamingo aircraft at Warmwell, and flew with some difficulty – owing to the large difference in speeds of the slow transport.

While Churchill and the British delegation met their French counterpart, Appleby recalled they looked for something to eat. Finding on the airfield only 'a wooden hut festooned with nude pin-ups and lots of champagne bottles, all empty', they found a wayside bistro, at which 'much wine was consumed' before they turned in for the night aboard a train. The following morning, their return trip nearly ended in disaster, owing to a shortage of fuel and starter batteries. But for the timely assistance of an RAF unit still based nearby, Churchill and the War Cabinet would have been compelled to take-off without their escort.[82] They were again selected to escort the Prime Minister to another urgent meeting at Tours a few days later – one of the last Churchill would make to France before the armistice.

By 12 June, in Scotland, the 602 Squadron diarist recorded with horror: 'News from France very grave. Jerry tanks within 15 miles of Paris'. The next day General Weygand declared Paris an open city and, on the 14th, the Germans entered Paris unopposed.[83]

On the same day, Operation *Aerial* began – the evacuation of the remaining Allied military forces and civilians from ports in western France, such as Saint Nazaire.

The end for France was rapidly approaching it seemed. On 18 June, 501 Squadron had orders to evacuate the squadron from France. Some went to Jersey to cover the evacuation of the BEF from Cherbourg. Jim Lacey returned to England when the squadron was withdrawn on 19 June and went to Croydon after a brief stay on the Channel Islands. Having probably destroyed a Do 17 on the 21st, Donald McKay destroyed two He 111s and probably a Do 17 on the 27th.[84]

On 20 June, 605 Squadron welcomed someone who had already found their mark early on in the war and would find it many times yet. Due to the prolonged illness of a Flight Commander, the CO requested that F/O Archie McKellar of 602 Squadron be re-posted to 605 Squadron – and would now arrive as Flt Lt McKellar.[85]

The way he transferred to 605 Squadron was another indication of his agile brain and how swiftly he saw and seized a chance - just as he did in combat. The CO of 605 Squadron, Wing Commander Walter Churchill went to Drem to reform 605 Squadron, and gloomily preoccupied by the task, he strolled into the mess where he was approached by a sprightly pilot with a twinkle in his eye and his hair immaculately brushed into place. 'I'm sorry to hear that my services will not be required as your squadron leader,' the smiling Scot said in a friendly manner. 'I understand you are waiting for another member of your old squadron. It was just the job I wanted.' A telephone call later to the Air Officer Commanding and Archie McKellar had got the job.[86]

Two days later, on 22 June, the French signed an armistice with Germany and two days later with Italy.

Amid the dire news from the Continent, following the completion of the Dunkirk evacuation, there was good news for Sqn Ldr Joe Kayll of 615 Squadron. On 22 June he got a probable He 111 and another damaged. Having been gazetted on 31 May that he was to receive a double award of the DSO and DFC, he was decorated by the King on 27 June at Kenley. He marked his achievement with an Me 109 destroyed and another damaged on the 30th.[87]

PHONEY WAR AND THE BATTLE OF FRANCE

On 18 June, Churchill spoke to the House of Commons but his words quickly travelled across the country and beyond, stiffening sinew and bracing all for the coming storm:

> What General Weygand called the Battle of France is over. I expect that the Battle of Britain is about to begin. Upon this battle depends the survival of Christian civilization. Upon it depends our own British life, and the long continuity of our institutions and our Empire. The whole fury and might of the enemy must very soon be turned on us. Hitler knows that he will have to break us in this Island or lose the war. If we can stand up to him, all Europe may be free and the life of the world may move forward into broad, sunlit uplands. But if we fail, then the whole world, including the United States, including all that we have known and cared for, will sink into the abyss of a new Dark Age made more sinister, and perhaps more protracted, by the lights of perverted science. Let us therefore brace ourselves to our duties, and so bear ourselves that, if the British Empire and its Commonwealth last for a thousand years, men will still say, '*This* was their finest hour.'[88]

Already blooded in battle, those members of the Auxiliary Air Force and its proud squadrons together with their fellow part-timers of the RAFVR, would soon show the stuff of which they were made and the skill they brought from their many and varied backgrounds. They would do so in a battle – the first to be fought entirely in the air – which would be for the country's very survival as a free nation.

PRELUDE AND FIRST ATTACKS, 26 JUNE – 16 JULY

3

Scattered and limited day and night attacks and mine-laying sorties, directed mainly against ports and shipping and towns with aircraft factories.

The Battle of France and the air battles over Dunkirk had depleted Fighter Command but following the French armistice in June 1940 there was a pause for a few weeks which allowed Dowding the chance to rest those squadrons most battered by the fighting over France, train new pilots and hone the command and control system which would be essential in the battle to come.

Looking back, Dowding admitted that 'it is difficult to fix the exact date when the Battle of Britain can be said to have begun. Operations of various kinds merged into one another almost insensibly.' There were grounds for choosing 10 August 1940 when the Luftwaffe began full-scale attacks on objectives on land. Instead, he chose, 'somewhat arbitrarily', 10 July, when German formations began hitting convoys in the Channel. His reasoning was that 'the weight and scale of the attack indicates that the primary object was rather to bring our Fighters to battle than to destroy the hulls and cargoes of the small ships engaged in the coastal trade.'[1]

As Dowding admitted, the phases and stages of the battle were indistinct. Although the Battle of Britain is generally accepted to have begun on 10 July, some (including the RAF Museum) see the first phase of the battle as beginning on 26 June.

PRELUDE AND FIRST ATTACKS, 26 JUNE – 16 JULY

Those scattered small scale probing attacks, what the Germans called *Störangriffe* (nuisance raids), both day and night, armed reconnaissance and mine-laying sorties featured strongly. From 4 July, the daylight *Kanalkampf* (Channel Battles) began against shipping. This became a stern test for Fighter Command and some AAF squadrons in particular.

At this point, as the battle was on the verge of joining, it would be helpful to describe the structures that the squadrons and pilots of the RAF fought under and the peculiar language they used.

Radar, developed from the mid-thirties, led by the research of Robert Watson Watt, was vital to the air defence of the UK. By the summer of 1940 there would be 22 so-called 'Chain Home' stations (the codename for the ring of coastal early warning radar posts) supplemented by 30 'Chain Home Low' stations. Each was sited to ensure that every aircraft approaching from the east or south would be detected by at least two stations.

This technology, then known as RDF (Range and Direction Finding) equipment, was at the heart of what became known as the Dowding System. This was a highly efficient network devised to make maximum use of the enormous amount of information coming from radar and Observer Corps sites. That information had to be quickly analysed and made into something usable by Fighter Command.

The information on approaching aircraft - their direction, altitude, approximate speed and size of formation was sifted by 'Filterers' who collated the radar information and displayed it on a gridded map and this picture was then passed on to the main Operations room and the appropriate Groups and sectors.

Plotting tables were used to display information on the developing picture built up from radar and Observer Corps information processed by the Filterers. It took just four minutes between an RDF operator identifying a plot to this information appearing in the Operations rooms.

Fighter Command, by the time the Battle of Britain began, was divided into Groups 10-14 and they were; No 10, covering South-West

England and South Wales; No 11, covering South-East England; No 12, covering East England; No 13, covering North-East England, South Scotland and Northern Ireland and No 14, covering North Scotland. No 9, covering North-West England and North Wales; was added on 9 August. Of these, No 11 Group based at Uxbridge under the command of Air Vice-Marshal Keith Park, bore the brunt of the Luftwaffe's assaults with No 10 Group also seeing intensive attacks.

The Groups in turn were subdivided into Sectors and each had its own control room, linked by secure telephone landlines to the Group operations room which was in turn connected with the main control centre at Fighter Command Headquarters at RAF Bentley Priory, where Dowding was based.

Fighter airfields formed the centre of each sector which in turn would have several satellites. For example, in 11 Group, Hornchurch had its satellite airfields at Gravesend, Rochford, Manston and Hawkinge.

When enemy aircraft were reported in a Group's area, the duty controller in the group operations room, in consultation with the group commander, decided which sector would deal with it and which aircraft would be 'scrambled'. A 'scramble' would start with a telephone ringing in the dispersal hut to be answered by an airman who would then shout 'scramble!' and the code for area to be patrolled. Pilots would dash to their aircraft which had already been started by ground crew. As soon as the flight reported ready, the Leader cleared them for take-off. The sector controller then was given control of the fighters and his job was to put his aircraft into the best position to intercept the raiders.

His instructions might say something like: 'Vector zero-eight-zero. Thirty bandits approaching Thames estuary.' 'Vector', plus a number giving degrees, gave the pilot a course to steer.

Squadrons which were given call signs, such as 'Turkey' for 605 and 'Villa' for 602, would send fighters up in Sections referenced by colour. So 'Red Section' might consist of three aircraft, with its commander called 'Red Leader'. Orders and information were passed

PRELUDE AND FIRST ATTACKS, 26 JUNE – 16 JULY

down the command chain using a code. They might be cruising at an economical speed, called 'Liner'.

Red Leader might then call 'Buster' to throttle up to maximum cruising speed. 'Bandits at Angels four,' the Controller might say to them. 'Angels' meant altitude, so 'Angels four' meant 4,000 feet and enemy aircraft were 'bandits'.

He might also call 'bandits at ten o'clock' – meaning the enemy was in the direction of the minute hand pointing to ten – gave an accurate fix on where their opponents were.

The signal – 'Tally Ho!' – from the squadron or flight commander, meant that the enemy had been sighted and battle was about to be joined.[2]

Following the bruising campaign over Dunkirk, 609 had a new boss. After joining the regular RAF in 1932, Horace Stanley 'George' Darley joined another Auxiliary Air Force unit when he was appointed Adjutant and Flying Instructor at 602 Squadron at Abbotsinch on 6 June 1938, moving on 2 December 1938 to 611 Squadron AAF at Speke, on the same duties. After time as a Controller at Debden from September and then from May 1940 he was posted to Merville in France, as Controller with 63 Wing of the Air Component of the BEF. On 26 June he joined 609 Squadron at Northolt and took command on the 28th.[3]

The squadron had taken a battering over Dunkirk and the new boss found them in a somewhat demoralised state. P/O John Bisdee, who we met earlier, remembered Darley's impact. 'He really pulled the Squadron together after the beating we had taken at Dunkirk. Darley insisted on an enormous amount of squadron and individual training. He used to act as a target. He'd fly along and everybody practised attacks on him – quarter attacks, head-on attacks and every other kind of attack.'

Darley himself recalled how urgent it was to inspire them. 'I realized when I took command of the squadron that I had to do something with these people'. The pilots ranged in age from 30 down to 19. 'The older chaps were depressed from having lost close friends over Dunkirk. There was a danger the morale of the younger ones, who'd just joined the squadron as replacements, might be affected'. Time was not on his side so he got them all together – the airmen as well, because, he reasoned 'lack of morale at the top doesn't take long to filter down and I gave them all a good talking to. I didn't hold back. I told them exactly what was wrong with them. I told them I knew about their personal and flying problems. But we had a job to do and they would have to change their ways'. The reaction was muted. 'There was a bit of a deadly hush and some of the men sucked their teeth. They didn't like it at all. But things did improve. I tried to analyse for them what had been responsible for their high rate of casualties at Dunkirk. I asked them what they had done, and what they had done next, and what they should have done. The remarkable thing was, they'd never sat down and analysed what had happened'. They then trained hard. 'I had the new boys go up with their flight commanders, and sometimes with myself. I'd see if the chap could stay in formation. We'd practice dog-fights to see who could handle his aircraft and look after himself. We did rolls and turns to see if [he] could stay on your tail and shoot you down.'[4]

As Darley had recognised, the fighting over Dunkirk had shown that the RAF's fighter tactics had been found wanting and were quickly changing.

Many pilots were caught out because they were still using formations and tactics taught before the war and because the lessons learnt at Dunkirk had not been fully digested. Before the war RAF squadrons flew compact formations of three aircraft and tactics were standardised in 'Fighting Arca Attacks'. There were five different forms of attack and it was recognised that in terms of flying discipline and spectacle they were excellent, but tactically they were worthless. In the speed and fury of these encounters there was rarely enough time to get sights on the target because keeping station was seen as important. Following the command "Attack No. 1 – Go", the fighters would swing into line astern behind the leader, follow him in an orderly queue up to the bomber, fire a quick shot when their turn came and then swing away after the leader again, presenting their vulnerable undersides to the enemy. Compared to the tactics the Germans had learned over the years in the Spanish Civil War, Poland and France, Fighting Area Attacks were disastrous. Soon the British would be imitating the Germans.

By flying loose formations, the Germans found they could hold position more easily, and keep a better look-out. By flying at different heights, they could cover each other and scan the sky more effectively. The Germans devised a highly effective formation, based on two aircraft called the 'Rotte'. The pair were separated by some 200 yards and the wingman, or number two, was responsible for covering the leader from attack via the quarter or behind. The 'Schwarme' was two pairs, and the RAF adopted it, called it a finger-four because each plane flew in a position corresponding to the finger-tips. Here, the leader is the longest finger, the number two is the index finger, and three and four are the third and little finger-tips. Number two would always fly on the sun side of the leader, slightly below so that the other pilots could see him well below the sun's glare. Two pairs of eyes remained stepped-up down-sun of the leader scanning the danger area. These lessons were still being learned by Fighter Command in the opening phase of the Battle of Britain at this time.[5]

It was not just a question of formations. How the fighters' guns were set up was crucial – and controversial.

The RAF stipulated that the eight guns of a Spitfire or Hurricane had to be aligned so their fire converged at 650 yards. It was said by a pilot that this merely guaranteed the indifferent shot a few hits, but the good shot was penalised. Pilots had already found that a German bomber could take heavy fire from their .303 machine-guns and would still fly. To shoot an enemy aircraft from the sky, it was essential to get close. More and more pilots unofficially aligned their guns to converge at 200 or 300 yards. Aces like Sailor Malan and Al Deere believed that 250 yards 'harmonization' and the incendiary bullets normally loaded into at least two guns (two carrying armour-piercing rounds and the remaining four normal ammunition) made the difference between damaging and destroying an enemy aircraft. It was the men who flew very close and who had the superb judgement to be able to make a killing deflection shot (aiming at where the enemy will be when your bullets get there) against a target moving at 300–400mph in three dimensions, who would be the aces of the Battle of Britain.[6]

Despite the outdated tactics used over France, in early June, in recognition of 607 Squadron's operations in France, three of its pilots were decorated, with Flt Lt W.F. Blackadder receiving a DSO and there were DFCs for Sqn Ldr J. Sample and F/O W.E. Gore. All three had signed up with 607 Squadron as reservists some years before war broke out. William Gore was working as an electrical engineer with the Reyrolles Hebburn Company when he joined in 1934.

John Sample joined the same year and commenced training at RAF Usworth, some thirty miles from his home. He was the fifth man to apply for pilot training there and he gained his 'A' licence flying an Avro 504. A gifted musician, he was accomplished on a number of different instruments including the flute, concertina and Northumbrian pipes.

William Blackadder would join two years later and was Captain of the Northern Rugby Club and played for Scotland against England in the Calcutta Cup of 1938. His citation stated that he had shot down three enemy aircraft and carried out several very important reconnaissances of bridges and roads.[7]

In Scotland, 602 and 603 continued to have success with raids on the east coast. One of those to find their mark was Flt Lt Alexander 'Sandy' Johnstone. Born in Glasgow in 1916 and educated at Kelvinside Academy, Glasgow, he was working for a footwear firm in Edinburgh when he joined 602 Squadron in late 1934. By 1938, he had clearly become accomplished in his part-time role with the AAF and he went to work for Scottish Aviation as a navigation instructor at 12 E&RFTS and No. 1 Civil Air Navigation School at Prestwick. Still with 602 Squadron he went to RAF Manston in August 1938 for a service navigation course. On 16 October he shared in damaging two He 111s over the Firth of Forth, that first engagement of the war with enemy aircraft over the British Isles.

On 25 June, he shot down a He 111 at night. The following day, there was what the 603 diary recorded as the 'first air-raid over Turnhouse'. Two enemy aircraft were brought down with George Denholm claiming a probable He 111. On 30 June RAFVR man P/O Ronald Berry damaged a Ju 88.[8]

Born in Hull in 1917 Ronald Berry was educated at Riley High School and Hull Technical College. After leaving he was employed in the Hull Corporation's Treasurer Department and while working there he joined the RAFVR in April 1937. He recalled, 'It was not easy to get into the RAFVR and I got myself really fit by running round my local park'. As well as doing his weekend flying training at nearby 4 E&RFTS at Brough, he also joined Hull Aero Club for additional training. In February 1939 he spent three weeks with the RAF and was attached to 66 Squadron at Duxford where he was able to fly the Spitfire. 'Ras' Berry went on to become a noted fighter ace.[9]

On 1 July, Blue Section of 602 Squadron was sent up and intercepted a Ju 88. It jettisoned its bombs which dropped in the sea half a mile from Dunbar and the section attacked at about 1,000 feet as it was entering clouds. On reappearing, the Junkers was attacked by F/O Webb from the beam. When last seen the aircraft was emitting a long trail of smoke.[10]

On 3 July, Johnstone appeared to have success again. Blue Section intercepted a Do 17 at 14,000 feet and he gave it a seven second burst as it dived at about 1,000 yards, which he claimed that it had been damaged.[11]

No. 603 Squadron had success on 2 July too. At 1346, Green Section, led by P/O Carbury, with P/Os Berry and Stapleton was ordered to investigate an aircraft flying over Montrose. Discovering it was a Ju 88, they attacked and it was shot down into the sea. There were three survivors.

Although not a part-time auxiliary, a pilot who brought honour to 603 was New Zealander Brian Carbury, leader of Green Section that day. He went to England in 1937 and successfully applied for an RAF short service commission. Just before the outbreak of war Carbury was attached to 603 Squadron to assist with Spitfire training. His temporary posting became permanent in late September 1939. He played an important part in 603's coastal patrols early in the war, damaging a He 111 on 7 December and on 7 March 1940 he shared in the destruction of another He 111 east of Aberdeen. His tally grew on 3 July with this share in a Ju 88 and his record would grow throughout the battle.[12]

At 1543, a Section, led by Sqn Ldr George Denholm, with P/O D. Stewart-Clark and Sgt Archer, attacked a He 111 25 miles north-east of Peterhead which came down in the sea. All the section was reported to have received hits in their machines. Red Section, meanwhile, led by P/O Ritchie with P/O Gilroy and Sgt Caister, attacked a Ju 88 off Stonehaven. It was seen by coastguards to crash into the sea.

Further south, but still operating over the North Sea, 616 Squadron also were enjoying success that day. Green Section scrambled at 0900 with F/Os Moberley, and H. Dundas. They encountered and shot down a Do 17 at 4,500 feet, all making two attacks and the Dornier crashed into the sea. F/O Dundas received three rounds in the wing which broke his aileron cable. Later another Do 17 was encountered and F/O Dundas and F/S Berryhard gave short bursts but the enemy aircraft escaped with the engine thought to be out of action as was the rear gunner.[13]

The Scottish squadrons continued their pursuit of sometimes lone raiders over the North Sea. On 6 July, Red Section of 603 led by P/O Gilroy with P/O Stewart-Clark and Sgt Caister attacked a Do 215 100 miles east-north-east of Aberdeen. The enemy aircraft was seen to crash in flames into the sea.[14]

Another 602 pilot whose tally would continue to grow scored his first success on 7 July. Born in 1916 in East Kilbride, Robert

PRELUDE AND FIRST ATTACKS, 26 JUNE – 16 JULY

Findlay Boyd worked as a mining engineer before the war and joined No. 602 Squadron in 1935 and was commissioned as a pilot officer later that year. He was promoted to Flying Officer two years later.

He was involved in the early successes of the two Scottish Auxiliary squadrons in October 1939 but had to wait until 7 July to claim his first success when he shared in the destruction of a Ju 88 off St. Abb's Head. These early successes presaged many more in the months to come as the battle intensified.[15]

Around this time a new front in this phase of the battle was developing.

The *Kanalkampf* (Channel Battle) was the German term for air operations by the Luftwaffe against the RAF over the English Channel in July 1940.

Why was shipping continuing to be put in harm's way? The answer was energy – or more precisely, coal. Coal fuelled practically all Britain's need for generating electricity, rail transport and heating homes. British power stations ran on coal as did the railways, manufacturing industry and shipbuilding.

Without it, industry and indeed the wider country would have ground to a halt. The bulk of the coal reserves in Britain were found in Scotland, north-east England and Wales and the greatest areas of demand were in the south and south-east of England.

Writing in *The Road to Wigan Pier*, published in 1937, George Orwell told how vital coal was to the functioning of British economy and society.

'Our civilization ... is founded on coal, more completely than one realizes until one stops to think about it. The machines that keep us alive, and the machines that make machines, are all directly or indirectly dependent upon coal.'

Coal convoys were slow and in easy range of enemy aircraft flying from France but the land transport capacity was insufficient to meet demand.[16]

Soon, the main elements of this phase were in full swing. The *Störangriffe* ('nuisance raids'), scattered small scale probing attacks both day and night, armed reconnaissance and mine-laying sorties and from 4 July, and the daylight *Kanalkampf* against shipping.

As the pressure from the Luftwaffe increased, one Auxiliary squadron returned to the fight. On 2 July 1940, 'The Chesters' went back to Biggin Hill, where they had been stationed prior to the Dunkirk evacuation. No. 610 shared the airfield with 32 Squadron's Hawker Hurricanes – and they built a formidable partnership until the end of August 1940, flying repeated daily patrols from Biggin Hill and the forward airfield at RAF Hawkinge, Kent.[17]

A few days later 609 Squadron entered the fray. Moving to Middle Wallop on 6 July, they would also operate from Warmwell. By the next day, one flight of 609 would be at readiness at Warmwell during the hours of daylight. Its proximity to Portland and Weymouth meant protecting convoys in this stretch of the Channel – in the firing line of the *Kanalkampf* – was to be their lot over the coming weeks. It would prove to be a difficult time which saw them suffer many grievous blows.

On 9 July one of 609's former part-timers announced his arrival. David Crook, the Huddersfield native who joined 609 Squadron after leaving Cambridge University, was mobilised the day after getting married. On 10 May, at the news of the opening of the German offensive in Europe, he damaged his knee leaping from bed and had to go into hospital for an operation, missing the Dunkirk action in consequence.[18]

Crook was ordered aloft at 1835 alongside P/O Appleby in N3023 that evening with Green Section in Spitfire P9322 led by F/O Drummond-Hay in R6637. In his account of his time as a fighter pilot: *Spitfire Pilot: A Personal Account of the Battle of Britain*. 'Peter' is F/O Drummond-Hay, 'Michael' is P/O Appleby.

Crook recalled:

PRELUDE AND FIRST ATTACKS, 26 JUNE – 16 JULY

At about 6.30 pm we were ordered to patrol Weymouth… we [took off] circled round for about three-quarters of an hour and saw nothing at all. Peter was getting very fed up with this apparently unnecessary flying, and we circled round the aerodrome and asked permission to land. We were told, however, to continue our patrol and turned out again over Weymouth at about 7,000 feet. A moment later, looking out towards the left, I saw an aircraft dive into a layer of cloud about two miles away and then reappear. I immediately called up Peter on the R/T, and he swung us into line astern, and turned left towards the enemy. A moment later I saw one or two more Huns appear and recognized them as Junkers 87 dive bombers. I immediately turned on my reflector sights, put my gun button on to 'fire' and settled down to enjoy a little slaughter of a few Ju 87s, as they are rather helpless machines.

But as they sped towards the hapless Stukas, they were in for a rude awakening.

'We were now travelling at high speed and rapidly approaching the enemy, when I happened to look round behind. To my intense surprise and dismay, I saw at least nine Messerschmitt 110s about 2,000 feet above us. They were just starting to dive on us when I saw them, and as they were diving, they were overtaking us rapidly. This completely altered the situation. We were now hopelessly outnumbered, and in a very dangerous position, and altogether I began to see that if we were not jolly quick, we should all be dead in a few seconds'. Calling Peter and Michael he shouted desperately, 'Look out behind, Messerschmitts behind' – all the time looking over his shoulder at the leading enemy fighter, who was now almost in range. 'But though I kept shouting, both Peter and Michael continued straight on at the bombers ahead, and they were now almost in range and about to open fire. I have never felt so desperate or so helpless in my life, as when, despite my warnings, these two flew steadily on, apparently quite oblivious of the fact that they were going to be struck down from the rear in a few seconds'. At that moment the leading Me 110 opened fire at him and he saw the German's shells and tracer bullets going past just above his head. 'They were jolly close too. I immediately did a very violent turn to the left and dived through a layer of cloud just below. I emerged from the cloud going at very high speed – probably over 400 mph, and saw a Ju 87 just ahead of me. I opened fire (my first real shot of the war), and he seemed to fly right through my tracer bullets, but when I turned round to follow him, he had disappeared'. Crook climbed up into the cloud again to try to rejoin the others. 'I saw an Me 110 some distance above me, and I pulled up into a steep climb and fired at him but without result. He turned away immediately, and I lost him. At that moment I saw dimly a machine moving in the cloud on my left and flying parallel to me. I stalked him through the cloud, and when he emerged into a patch of clear sky I saw that it was a Ju 87'. Now he had the upper hand once more and he used his position to devastating effect.

> I was in an ideal position to attack and opened fire and put the remainder of my ammunition – about 2,000 rounds – into him at very close range. Even in the heat of the moment I well remember my amazement at the shattering effect of my fire. Pieces flew off his fuselage and cockpit covering, a stream of smoke appeared from the engine, and a moment later a great sheet of flame licked out from the engine cowling and he dived down vertically. The flames enveloped the whole machine and he went straight down, apparently quite slowly, for about five thousand feet, till he was just a shapeless burning mass of wreckage.

Crook followed him down 'absolutely fascinated by the sight', seeing him hit the sea with 'a great burst of white foam'. The Stuka disappeared immediately, and apart from a green patch in the water 'there was no sign that anything had happened', he recalled. 'The crew made no attempt to get out, and they were obviously killed by my first burst of fire. I had often wondered what would be my feelings when killing somebody like this, and especially when seeing them go down in flames. I was rather surprised to reflect afterwards that my only feeling had been one of considerable elation – and a sort of bewildered surprise because it had all been so easy. I turned back for the coast, and started to call up "Peter" and "Michael" on the R/T. But there was no response.'

Unsettled by the action, he made a dreadful landing, overshooting so badly that he nearly turned the Spitfire on its nose as he tried to pull up before hitting a hedge on the perimeter. 'I got out to talk to Michael and found to my surprise that my hand was quite shaky and even my voice was unsteady' he recalled, adding, 'I had just been in action. I had just been in action for the first time and shot somebody down, and the full significance of that rather startling fact was beginning to dawn on me now that I had time to think.'[19]

F/O Drummond-Hay failed to return and notwithstanding Crook's success, his loss and the odds they were fighting against were beginning to tell. Rumours of further moves were having an 'unsettling effect' on the squadron. The squadron diary described the events of the day:

> At 0800, five aircraft of 'B' Flt intercepted a number of Ju 87s attacking a convoy off Portland. Flight Lieutenant Barran was shot down and his body was recovered from the sea. P/O Mitchell is reported as missing.

It pulled no punches in describing their situation:

> The utter futility of sending very small sections of fighters to cope with the intense enemy activity on the Portland area is bitterly resented by the pilots. The fact that they have been sent off to make an interception – as a section

or possible a flight – only to find themselves heavily outnumbered by enemy fighters acting as guard to the bombers is discouraging because the British fighter then finds himself unable to do his job of destroying the bombers and is compelled to fight a defensive action. The situation is keenly felt by this squadron whose 'score' of enemy aircraft is in too close a ratio of its own losses. It is felt that we happen to have been very unlucky in that both Dunkirk and at Portland our contacts with the enemy have taken place where the numerical odds were rather too unreasonable.[20]

Despite his success, Crook felt despondent.

It is difficult to describe my feelings during the next few days. We had lost three pilots in 36 hours, all of them in fights in which we had been hopelessly outnumbered, and I felt that there was now nothing left to care about, because obviously from the law of probability, one could not expect to survive many more encounters of a similar nature.[21]

Crook felt Barran's loss personally too. In his logbook, he wrote 'Pip Barran was one of the original Auxiliaries of 609. He was a grand person, with a terrific personality and very tough'.

Other squadrons, like 501 were sent to fight off the Dorset coast. After becoming operational again on 3 July, the next day they received orders to move from Croydon to Middle Wallop. However, they suffered blows too. On 10 July, Green Section was engaged by enemy aircraft while on convoy patrol off Portland Bill. Sgt Dixon descended by parachute and was lost. Two days later the squadron operated from the satellite airfield at Warmwell for the first time. Numerous patrols were carried out, one of which took off at 1515. In an engagement over the English Channel off Portland, P/O D.A. Hewitt crashed into the sea while attacking a Dornier and was lost.

PRELUDE AND FIRST ATTACKS, 26 JUNE – 16 JULY

On 13 July, 609 Squadron had success over the Channel. Yellow Section was sent up, consisting of F/Os J. Dundas, Overton and P/O Miller in Spitfires R6643, L1082 and L1065 respectively, to patrol over a convoy at 4,000 feet west of Swanage. They couldn't find the convoy as it was not in the position given, but P/O. Miller saw many enemy aircraft 15,000 feet above, south of Portland. Dundas and Miller climbed above them and attacked from the sun. Firing 800 rounds, P/O Dundas shot down one Me 110 but then was attacked by Me 110s himself. He broke off the engagement and landed at Warmwell. P/O Miller carried out a short inconclusive attack on Me 110s and then fired all his rounds into a Do 17, which was seen by members of 238 Squadron who were also engaged, flying out to sea with his port engine on fire and losing height rapidly. Overton could not gain height quickly enough, so broke away and did not engage.

The previous day, 615 (County of Surrey) Squadron had a visit from their Honorary Air Commodore – Prime Minister Winston Churchill. He visited the station at 1830, and spoke to several officers, before watching the whole squadron take off 'in dirty weather for Hawkinge', where they were obliged to spend the night. He left in a DH Flamingo for Northolt. The PM was accompanied by AOC 11 Group AVM Keith Park who also talked to pilots in the crew room and flew his own Hurricane to Northolt.[22]

The following day saw a graphic account being given of a dogfight over Dover. It has become famous as capturing the intensity of the conflict taking place in the skies above Britain.

BBC commentator Charles Gardner visited Dover on the afternoon of Sunday, 14 July hoping to witness one of the air battles which had been raging over the Channel. At around 1500 he watched as the ships came under attack and he began to record his broadcast, which while capturing the frantic air battle, was questioned by some as presenting this life-or-death struggle as something closer to a game of cricket.

In the air at the time were three Hurricanes from No. 615 Squadron's Red Section. At 1600, they were patrolling convoy near Dover, when they were attacked by 40 Ju 87s which were escorted by Me 109s. This was the battle witnessed by Gardner, who breathlessly told: 'The Germans are dive-bombing a convoy out to sea! There are one, two, three, four, five, six, seven German dive-bombers! – Junkers Eighty-Sevens! There's one going down on its target now – Bomb! No! He missed the ships – it hasn't hit a single ship. There are about ten ships in the convoy, but he hasn't hit a single one and – There! You can hear our anti-aircraft going at them now. There are one, two, three, four, five, six – there are about ten German machines dive-bombing the British convoy, which is just out to sea in the Channel.'

Tragically, Gardner seemed to think he was witnessing a great victory for the RAF when in fact he saw three Hurricanes heavily outnumbered. Watching as the spectacle unfolded, Gardner exclaimed breathlessly:

> There's one going down in flames! Somebody's hit a German and he's coming down with a long streak – coming down completely out of control – a long streak of smoke. And now a man's baled out by parachute! The pilot's baled out by parachute! He's a Junkers eighty-seven and he's going slap into the sea. And there he goes – SMASH! A terrific column of water and there was a Junkers eight-seven. Only one man got out by parachute, so presumably there was only a crew of one in it!

This was in fact, P/O Michael Mudie (Red 3) of 615 Squadron who was shot down but baled out. Red 1 and 2 put several bursts into Ju 87s but were unable to observe the result as they were being attacked. Later the squadron's remaining nine aircraft took off from Hawkinge to assist Red Section. F/Os Gayner and F/O Collard each shot down one Ju 87, as did P/O Hugo who saw it catch fire and fall into the sea.

Mudie, badly wounded, was rescued from the sea by the Navy and admitted to Dover Hospital. On arrival at the hospital his wounds were recorded as burns and a gunshot wound to the face. He died the next day, aged 24.[23]

The same day, just days after visiting 'his' Auxiliary squadron, Churchill defiantly appraised the situation in a speech broadcast by the BBC:

> And now it has come to us to stand alone in the breach, and face the worst that the tyrant's might and enmity can do. Bearing ourselves humbly before God, but conscious that we serve an unfolding purpose, we are ready to defend our native land against the invasion by which it is threatened. We are fighting by ourselves alone; but we are not fighting for ourselves alone. Here in this strong City of Refuge which enshrines the title-deeds of human progress and is of deep consequence to Christian civilisation; here, girt about by the seas and oceans where the Navy reigns; shielded from above by the prowess and devotion of our airmen – we await undismayed the impending assault. Perhaps it will come tonight. Perhaps it will come next week. Perhaps it will never come. We must show ourselves equally capable of meeting a sudden violent shock, or what is perhaps a harder test, a prolonged vigil. But be the ordeal sharp or long, or both, we shall seek no terms, we shall tolerate no parley; we may show mercy – we shall ask for none.[24]

By the 16 July the RAF had been sorely tested. The experience of squadrons like 609 showed both tactics and strategy needed to be refined still. By drawing the RAF into a battle of attrition over the Channel they were losing precious fighters.

On 16 July, Adolf Hitler issued Directive 16 to the Wehrmacht (German armed forces), ordering preparations for an invasion of Britain, under the codename *Unternehmen Seelöwe* (Operation *Sealion*).[25]

The directive from the Führer read:

> 'Since England, in spite of her hopeless military situation, shows no signs of being ready to come to an understanding, I have decided to prepare a landing operation against England, and, if necessary, to carry it out. The aim of this operation will be to eliminate the English homeland as a base for the prosecution of the war against Germany and, if necessary, to occupy it completely. I therefore order as follows: The landing will be in the form of a surprise crossing on a wide front from about Ramsgate to the area west of the Isle of Wight. Units of the Air Force will act as artillery, and units of the Navy as engineers. The possible advantages of limited operations before the general crossing (e.g. the occupation of the Isle of Wight or of the county of Cornwall) are to be considered from the points of view of each branch of the Armed Forces and the results reported to me. I reserve the decision to myself.
>
> Preparations for the entire operation must be completed by the middle of August. These preparations must also create such conditions as will make a landing in England possible, the English Air Force must be so reduced morally and physically that it is unable to deliver any significant attack against the German crossing. The invasion will bear the cover name *Seelöwe*.
>
> ADOLF HITLER, DIRECTIVE No. 16,
16 JULY 1940

The task given to the Luftwaffe came sharply into focus – it must destroy the RAF and make way for an invasion. The scene was set for the Battle of Britain to reach a new, more intensive stage.

CHANNEL BATTLES, 17 JULY – 12 AUGUST   4

Increasing and larger daylight attacks against shipping in the English Channel, ports along the South and East coasts and some coastal airfields, with increased night attacks against the West, Midlands, and East Coast, RAF facilities and the aircraft industry.

For 603 Squadron, July saw them continue their patrols over the North Sea, catching raiders. Taking off at 1524, Red Section sighted a He 111 off Fraserburgh and attacked it causing the bomber to crash into the sea. They saw two survivors enter a rubber boat. Red 2 was hit by return fire from the Heinkel's gunner in the starboard main plane. Returning to Turnhouse later that afternoon, the kill was confirmed and shared between Morton, Ritchie and Stewart-Clark.

On 19 July Fighter Command reinforced its forward coastal airfields as the weather improved, and nine convoys were at sea off the coast. Around 0800 4 Do 17s slipped undetected over Glasgow and carried out a destructive attack on the Rolls-Royce works before escaping. In the day, Fighter Command lost ten fighters, five pilots killed and five wounded, against four Luftwaffe aircraft shot down (although thirteen were claimed).[1]

Meanwhile that day there was to be a pivotal message from Berlin. Hitler addressed the Reichstag at the Kroll Opera House, Berlin, giving his account of the war to date and extending a peace offer to Britain:

> I have summoned you to this meeting in the midst of our tremendous struggle for the freedom and the future

of the German nation. I have done so, firstly, because I considered it imperative to give our people an insight into the events, unique in history, that lie behind us, secondly, because I wished to express my gratitude to our magnificent soldiers, and thirdly, with the intention of appealing, once more and for the last time, to common sense in general. In this hour I feel it to be my duty before my own conscience to appeal once more to reason and common sense in Great Britain as much as elsewhere. I consider myself in position to make this appeal since I am not the vanquished begging favours, but the victor speaking in the name of reason. Possibly Mr Churchill will again brush aside this statement of mine by saying that it is merely born of fear and doubt in final victory. In that case I shall have relieved my conscience in regard to the things to come.[2]

Churchill's answer, was brief and spiky. 'I do not propose to say anything in reply to Hitler's speech, not being on speaking terms with him.'

Another of 501 Squadron's pilots who, like 'Ginger' Lacey, was a former RAFVR part-timer was Kenneth 'Hawkeye' Lee. Born in Birmingham in 1915, he joined the RAFVR in January 1937, while working as a trainee technician in a paint factory. In January 1939, like many RAFVR pilots, he joined a regular RAF unit for six-months of training, in his case 111 Squadron. He was posted to 501 Squadron on the outbreak of war and went with them to France in May 1940. He claimed two victories during the initial period and then a further two over Dunkirk during the evacuation of the BEF. On 10 June he had just attacked a formation of He 111s without apparent result, and had run out of ammunition when his Hurricane blew up. He baled out, but hit the tailplane, coming down at Le Mans. During the panic of evacuation that night, his right hand was accidentally crushed, and it was some weeks before he was fit for flying again.[3]

Lee recalled that 501's pilots slept in their new base at Gravesend and then every morning flew their Hurricanes down to Hawkinge near the coast. There they would disperse around the perimeter of the large grass airfield. There were four small tents where the pilots sat waiting for the scramble, writing letters, reading the papers, playing cards.

Often they were on stand-by until dusk and three or four times a day the 'scramble' call would come.

One of the others was teaching Lee and his friend Johnny Gibson how to play bridge. They'd put their cards down carefully with the intention of finishing the rubber later, and dash for their Hurricanes.

Jim Lacey recalled on the afternoon of the 20 July the pilots of 501 were sunning themselves at dispersal, when a panic call came from the Ops Room. Once airborne the controller told them a convoy was being attacked near Jersey. By the time they came upon it, it was halfway between Portland Bill and the Channel Islands.

Lee recalled that their tactics had not changed – they still flew the standard 'number one' attack and the old Vic formations. It was the only thing that the new pilots were capable of. But by now most of them had their guns set to converge closer than the recommended 300 yards.

The fighter controller would come on the R/T: 'Blue Leader, Blue Leader, Vector 120, Angels 15.' You'd see black in the distance and you'd be climbing and climbing and climbing all the time pressing on.[4]

At first they saw the swarm of Ju 87s, diving steeply and then the escorting Me 109s were upon them. The leader's R/T crackled 'Tally Ho!'

As Lacey broke he quickly looked for his first target. An Me 109 was turning towards him, 200 yards dead ahead. Lacey banked hard over, watching the German pilot try to bring his guns to bear. As the 109 flashed by, 50 yards ahead, Lacey opened fire. The German twisted down away and Lacey followed. Once more the Me 109 attempted to turn inward and again Lacey turned with him, holding the inside position.

Sharply, the German pulled up and stall-turned in the opposite direction. Lacey fired a long burst into the Me 109's fuselage, behind the cockpit. The enemy dived sharply, trying to escape. Lacey followed and held him in his sights at 150 yards, pouring another four-second burst; hitting the engine.

Lacey recalled: 'I can clearly remember watching him slanting down the sky at a hell of a steep angle. A beautiful little blue and grey mottled aircraft with white and black crosses standing out startlingly clear, getting smaller and smaller; and thinking what a terribly small splash he made when he went straight into the Channel.'

As his gaze lifted from the downed fighter, he quickly saw another Me 109 some three-quarters of a mile away, flying due north. He cooly appraised the tactics of his foe:

> I thought, 'Well, he's making a fool of himself. He's going due north. He'll have to turn any moment now and then I've got him.' He pulled up in a climbing turn to starboard and remembered thinking he looked exactly like the other one a beautiful blue and grey mottled effect with the sun shining on him from the south.

As he pulled up in a climbing turn, Lacey pulled up inside him as he came into his sights.

> Then as his turn continued, and I was reducing the deflection, I could see him coming back towards me; I thought for one awful moment that he was going to attempt to crash into me. Then I suddenly saw the aeroplane almost stagger as my bullets were hitting it. It didn't catch fire or break up or anything like that. Its propeller just started

> to slow down until I could almost see it turning over. We flashed past each other, a few feet apart, going in opposite directions; and by the time I had whipped round, my new Flight Commander, 'Pan' Cox, latched on to this 109; he didn't fire until he was in to about 20 yards: and once again the dive of that 109 got steeper and steeper and it went in almost right beside the oily patch marking the place where my first one had gone in.

The Yorkshireman was modest in victory. 'I put no claim in the for the half-share in that because it was Pan Cox's first success. I was getting a bit blasé by that time'.[5]

Lee recalled seeing a 'great cloud of them' [Ju 87s] dive-bombing Dover harbour and some ships out to sea. 'There the buggers are. Tally Ho!' Lee dived down and straight through the Dover flak, which should have stopped once the Hurricanes came into view but as usual didn't. Called 'Flaming onions' the exploding shells gave bright flashes and the acrid smell of cordite which seeped into Lee's cockpit.

> You'd try to judge the curve; you're climbing to come round behind them. You go in and squirt off your guns and hope bits will fall off and when you've used all your ammunition you just pull out and go back and get some more.

And now there were Stukas everywhere. Large and ungainly with distinctive cranked shaped wings, they looked defenceless. But the rear gunner fired away. 'Soon sort him out' Lee recalled. Pouring fire with all eight Brownings into the pilot and the engine, he manoeuvred closer 'to finish the bastard off for good'. His thumb pressed the fire button. There was a roar in his ears and then the Stuka began to fall apart and plunge down into the sea.

As well as his skill and judgement, Lee relied on good luck charms and superstitions to keep him safe. A girlfriend had given him a little 'Jiminy Cricket' doll as a charm and he always made sure he had it in the cockpit, just as he always liked to take a leak against the tailwheel before he took off. A superstition that many pilots had. And, he recalled, you always needed a pee before going into combat.

Another 501 pilot flying with Lacey and Lee was P/O Edmund Sylvester. As Lee remembered he was one of 501's best.[6]

Born at Trowbridge, Wiltshire in 1914, he attended Harrow School from 1928 to 1930, then, while working as a solicitor, he was commissioned in 501 Squadron in January 1939. He quickly found his mark when the squadron went to France in May 1940. He shared a He 111 on 12 May and later shared a Do 17. On 25 May, Sylvester failed to return from a patrol, and was last seen diving down with his engine smoking near Abbeville. He turned up the next day, having made a forced-landing after his aircraft was damaged by return fire from a Do 17 which he badly damaged. He was forced down on another occasion at Limésy.[7]

A reason for his many scrapes, Lee recalled, was that Sylvester liked to get in close, with the result that he took more than his fair share of punishment. He'd been shot down so many times in France that, under his seat, he carried an escape kit including a razor and a clean shirt. 'Back then he always seemed to land in the grounds of some chateau, and he would come back a couple of days later with a huge grin on his face, having been wined and dined by some beautiful aristocrat, or so he always said'.[8]

Being in possession of two Caterpillar Club badges for parachute descents, Sylvester was clearly something of a survivor.

On this day Lee had lent Sylvester his Hurricane, but left his Jiminy Cricket doll inside. But it didn't bring Sylvester luck and his Hurricane was shot down in the Channel in Lyme Bay.

The squadron diary simply recorded: 'Numerous patrols carried out over the English Channel while the squadron was operating from the Forward Base [Warmwell]. P/O EJH Sylvester was reported missing'.⁹

'This time,' Lee recalled 'there were no pretty ladies, no nice meals and no need for a clean shirt. Silly bugger – he should have pissed on the tailwheel'.¹⁰

The 24 July was to be an eventful day for 610 Squadron, in particular for two ex-part-timers. Edward Smith was born in 1915 in Formby, Lancashire. While working for Shell Refineries at Stanlow in Cheshire he joined 610 Squadron in 1936. He saw action over Dunkirk ad the Channel, destroying a He 111 on 27 May and sharing and damaging a Do 17 on 3 and 9 July respectively. He became a Flight Commander in July.¹¹

Another was Sgt Horatio Chandler. We met him earlier as one of the AAF's NCO pilots. On qualifying as a Sergeant Pilot in March 1940, he served briefly with 501 Squadron, before returning to 610. On 24 July he destroyed an Me 109 and on 12 August he damaged an Me 109.¹²

On 24 July, Smith led Red Section aloft at 1112. They were ordered to patrol Dover in Spitfire R6976 at 12,000 feet alongside Blue and Green Sections. Flying at 14,000 feet south of Dover, Smith sighted 9 to 12 Me 109s below, approaching head-on in open formation, line abreast. He attacked one of them, firing several short bursts, causing it to smoke heavily and dive vertically out of control. Sgt Chandler in P9503, who confirmed this, met three unidentified aircraft below. He wheeled round and attacked and saw pieces falling away from the enemy aircraft after closing to 30 yards. It gave no return fire and Red 2 was convinced that it was out of control. Red 5 (Sgt Parsons), in R6530 confirmed this and said the enemy aircraft was destroyed. Two Me 109s were confirmed and one 'Chance Vought' (French Air Force machine, believed to be used by Luftwaffe) was also confirmed. They returned to Biggin Hill at 1210.¹³

It was later confirmed that this 'Chance Vought' was in fact a Royal Navy Blackburn Skua which was shot down in error.¹⁴

Coincidentally, Parsons was also a part-timer who had joined the RAFVR while actually making Spitfires.

Sgt Claude Parsons, of Halterworth, Romsey, Hampshire was born in1914 and worked in the Vickers-Armstrong Supermarine factory at Eastleigh on the Spitfire production line. Parsons joined the RAFVR in April 1939 and after completing his training, he requested to fly Spitfires but was sent to a Hurricane OTU. He eventually was reunited with his beloved fighter when he was posted to 610 Squadron – which flew the Spitfire – at Gravesend on 15 June.

Parsons also damaged a Do 17 on this day and destroyed an Me 109 on the following day.[15]

If there was no let-up that day for the convoys, there was certainly none for 610 and for Chandler. He was one of seven 610 Squadron pilots, who took off with in their Spitfires at 1827. Ordered to patrol a convoy west of Folkestone, they saw about 18 enemy aircraft bombing destroyers in mid-Channel. Suddenly Me 109s appeared – they counted 24 – and a battle was joined at 10,000 feet. P/O Morris in Spitfire N3284 shot down an Me 109 in flames and saw it hit the sea. Sgt Chandler in R6630 chased an Me 109 for five minutes and eventually shot it down, seeing it go down burning. Sgt Else in P9496 gave chase to an Me 109 which desperately trying to shake him off, flew over Hawkinge at 500 feet. He managed to engage the enemy aircraft and it was observed to go down in the sea off Folkestone by soldiers.

Former Spitfire worker, Sgt Parsons, placed himself on the tail of an Me 109 and at about 300 yards opened fire for two seconds. The German fighter went down vertically, apparently out of control. Parsons then attacked another Me 109 from below which gave out clouds of smoke and fell 'burning furiously'. Sgt Else confirmed both these victories. Meanwhile Flt Lt Smith in L1000 attacked an Me 109 which broke away emitting black smoke. The estimate for the encounter was five Me 109s confirmed and three unconfirmed.

CHANNEL BATTLES, 17 JULY – 12 AUGUST

One 602 Squadron pilot who opened his account on 24 July was Sgt Andrew McDowall. Born in 1913 Kirkinner, Wigtownshire, he joined the squadron while working as an engineer on Clydeside before the war. He was originally an Aircrafthand and later re-mustered as an Airman u/t Pilot as part of the programme to train non-commissioned pilots in the AAF which began in early 1939. McDowall completed his training and rejoined 602 Squadron around May 1940.

Flying from Drem, during a night patrol over East Kinton, McDowall was informed by control that there was a bandit approaching from the east at 4,000 feet. At around 0400, McDowall saw the He 111 in searchlights flying towards him and he opened fired from head-on. After giving a five second burst at 400 yards, he saw tracer going into the bomber and broke away upwards. Before the attack could be renewed he lost sight of the Heinkel. He saw parachutes break away from the aircraft which dived apparently out of control. The squadron diary told how it was later found that these had mines attached the Heinkel dived towards the sea and was later confirmed shot down. It would be the first of many for the auxiliary sergeant pilot from Galloway.[16]

Some squadrons moved back towards the east. No. 501, who went from Croydon to Middle Wallop at the beginning of the month, now were sent to Gravesend on 25 July.

Once a civilian airfield on the south bank of the Thames Gravesend sat within the Biggin Hill Sector alongside Nos. 32, 600 and 610 Squadrons. Accommodation was rudimentary – for Lacey and fellow sergeants at least. They slept on camp beds in an empty house just inside the barbed wire fence that skirted the airfield and ate their meals in a hut behind one of the hangars. The officers lived in the control tower.

In an echo of the adventurous pre-war days, a hangar on the airfield housed the de Havilland Comet in which Scott and Black had won the Mildenhall to Melbourne air race in 1934.

They were quickly in action. On 26 July, Lacey recalled: 'Things were getting hectic'. In his logbook, there are four patrols recorded on 27 July, and two flights from Gravesend to Hawkinge and back, amounting to almost four hours' flying in one day with six take-offs and six landings four calls from the Tannoy to 'scramble, scramble, scramble'. Flight Commander 'Pan' Cox was shot down – apparently by anti-aircraft batteries at Dover.

This almost constant action meant the pilots were constantly fatigued. While there was physical effort in flying a fighter, this was dwarfed by the mental effort.

Lacey's biographer Richard Townshend-Bickers summed up the strain the pilots were under: 'At all times the fighter pilot had to keep his reactions razor sharp. When he was simultaneously holding his position accurately in a formation and scanning the sky for the enemy, his whole nervous system protested under the burden. Already the fighter pilots of the RAF were doing more work in one week than mind and body could reasonably support'.

Despite the physical strain, these young men – who were at most in their early twenties – retained a sense of mischief and indeed fun amidst the unending fight. Photographs of Lacey taken at this time show a smooth-faced boy who looks 18 and not the 23 that he was. With his forage cap at a daringly rakish angle, spikes of straw-coloured hair poking through, gave him the look of an unruly schoolboy. For him and his comrades, despite facing incessant danger, almost constant states of alert and the death of friends, the war was still very much a game to the 'fighter boys' as Dowding always called them.

On the airfield was a small factory making fuel tanks for Spitfires The factory workers were subjected to gentle leg-pulling by the young pilots. When the pilots returned after a sortie and the workers were emerging from their air-raid shelters, the sergeant pilots delighted in loudly asking each other how they got on and replying modestly 'Oh, not too badly. I got a 109 and a Do 17'. 'What about you?' they'd retort 'Not as well as you. I only got a He 111.'

CHANNEL BATTLES, 17 JULY – 12 AUGUST

The workers would listen agog and would rush to buy the pilots beer in the local pubs that evening.[17]

Still the scrambles continued. On 29 July, 501 took part in a 'major engagement' over Dover. An enemy formation of Ju 87s and Me 109s was encountered with six of them destroyed (confirmed or probably destroyed) and six damaged. McKay claimed one of the Stukas, unconfirmed.[18]

On 29 July, operating from their forward base at Hawkinge, on the Kent coast, 501 were in action over Dover once more. Of a large formation of Ju 87s and Me 109s, they shot down six and damaged four.

Amid the threat of impending invasion and the continual strain on the young pilots and groundcrew, there were diversions. The RAF played cricket against the Fire Service at Lords, and the rush to see an evening paper was as much concerned with seeing how the teams had done as with learning about the war situation.[19]

One former part-timer recalled how there were moves to ease the strain on the pilots. Michael Appleby was born in Edmonton, Middlesex in 1913 and was educated at the Leys School, Cambridge. Interested in aviation from an early age, he joined No. 609 (West Riding) Squadron in December 1938.

The now Pilot Officer recalled that towards the end of July, Dowding ruled that pilots should have at least eight hours stand down time in 24 and at least 24 hours continuous time off once a week.

> To enable us to do this we had a further intake of newly qualified pilots, including the pre-war RAFVR pilot, John Bisdee. Being Orderly Officer one evening I took a phone call from a newly-posted pilot, who wanted to know if it would be possible for him to postpone his arrival until the next day, as he wanted to see his parents in London on the way down from training school. To

this I agreed. Next day arrived Noel Agazarian, of French and Armenian ancestry, who had been sent down from Oxford having intended to read for the Bar. He was by nature a cosmopolitan and brilliant linguist, and his flying was typical of his slapdash but brilliant improvisation.[20]

Agazarian was to have great success in the battle. His first victory came on 11 August 1940 when he destroyed an Me 110 and the day later he shot down two Me 109s and damaged an Me 110. In September he shared a He 111 on the 25th, destroyed a Me 109 and damaged two Do 17s on the 26th, shot down an Me 110 on the 27th and damaged a He 111 on the 30th. His final victory of the battle was on 15 October when he destroyed an Me 109.

There were other changes for 609 and during August the composition of the squadron altered rapidly. On 5 August two Polish Officers – P/O Nowierski and P/O Ostazsewski reported for duty with the Squadron and were drafted to 'B' Flight. The diary told how: 'Neither could speak much English at the time but both rapidly acquired efficiency on Spitfires'.

They took the places of P/O Blayney and F/O Little who were posted away due to medical reasons. F/O Edge was also posted away. All were pre-war part-timers and the diary explained: 'Thus three of the seven auxiliary Pilots remaining in the squadron were posted in one month, leaving P/O J. Dundas, P/O Goodwin. P/O Appleby and P/O Crook as sole champions of the auxiliary attitude in the squadron'. Nevertheless, those bearers of the auxiliary spirit continued to play a leading and successful role in the squadron.[21]

On 9 August, 609 Squadron faced a series of intensive attacks on a convoy which was attempting to sail that day from the Needles to Weymouth Bay. Pilot Office Appleby shot down a balloon-strafing Me 110 but his machine was 'slightly peppered'. Those remaining auxiliaries would continue to contribute hugely to 609's tally as the battle raged on.

CHANNEL BATTLES, 17 JULY – 12 AUGUST

The squadron dispersed frequently to Warmwell from Middle Wallop, which possessed, according to John Dundas in the squadron diary, 'the two chief characteristics of a forward operating station – action and discomfort'. The pilots had arrived with cockpits 'optimistically bulging' with sponge bags, pyjamas and other articles of toilet which they got very little opportunity to use'. Sleeping accommodation was provided for visiting squadrons in the sergeants' quarters but after some experience of this, pilots preferred to live in in tents at the dispersal areas. These were furnished with 'beds, dirty blankets and an assortment of unreliable telephones'. As it had not rained for a very long time the surrounding terrain came to consist of dust and stones which blew into the tents whenever an aeroplane was 'run-up' in the vicinity.[22]

In late July it had sometimes been quiet, as Michael Appleby recalled:

> On 18 July I did five sorties, on one of which, a patrol of Lyme Regis, Swanage and Weymouth, I acted as Section Leader, that is the leading aircraft of a section of three, but nothing of any event occurred so as the weather closed in we returned and patrolled base for half an hour before landing.[23]

But by early August things had changed.

> On 8 August, I flew four times, on one of those sorties as number two to Squadron Leader Darley when he put me in such a position over some Me 109s attacking a convoy off the Isle of Wight that I had nothing to do but press the firing button.

Appleby remembered that he 'gave him all there was and both engine cowlings and the upper part of the cockpit cover came off and he dived into the sea', much to the delight, they subsequently heard, of the Royal Navy.

He recalled too the accuracy of the enemy rear gunner's return fire, which scored three hits, 'one through the prop near the root, another in the wing just below the cockpit, and one in the wing tip'. Nonetheless, pilot and 'peppered' Spitfire returned to base.

'I will never forget', he said 'The strain of waiting at dispersal'. This was greatly emphasised by the field telephone:

> Every time it rang everyone would just stop until the operator answering would call out, perhaps, 'Sergeant so-and-so required in Sick Quarters', at which point we all promptly relaxed. On the other hand, when it was a scramble, we all rushed to our aircraft, preceded by the fitter and rigger, popped into the cockpit, set our parachute and safety harnesses, quite tight too, and having got the throttle mixture control and airscrew pitch controls set, the fitter operated the starter battery and the engine started. Then off we would go, taking off in formation, and after that who knew what would happen?[24]

From Middle Wallop 609 Squadron patrolled the Dorset coast.

On Sunday, 11 August the weather was glorious and by 0945 it was clear that a major raid was building up over Cherbourg with the Royal Navy's installations at Portland a possible target. No. 11 Group scrambled the Hurricanes of 1 Squadron and 10 Group sent up the Spitfires of 609 Squadron, while six more squadrons were placed at readiness. Soon the largest raid so far dispatched against England – 165 bombers and escorts – approached Portland.[25]

David Crook of 609 Squadron remembered this day as having their 'first really big action of the war.' At about 1130 they were ordered to patrol over Weymouth Bay and were joined by several other squadrons. They soon saw a big enemy fighter formation out to sea, and went out to attack it, climbing the whole time, as they were flying at about 24,000 feet. 'The Messerschmitts [Me 110s] had formed their usual defensive circle, going round and round on each other's tails. This makes an attack rather difficult, as if you attack one Hun, there is always another one behind you. We were now about a thousand feet above the Mes at 25,000 feet, and the CO turned round and the whole of 609 went down to attack'.

They came down on top of the enemy formation, 'going at terrific speed,' He selected an Me 110 ahead of him going across in front. He fired at him but his bullets passed behind him. 'I then closed in on him from behind and fired a good burst at practically point-blank range. Some black smoke poured from his port engine and he turned up to the right and stalled. I could not see what happened after this as I narrowly missed hitting his port wing. It flashed past so close that instinctively I ducked my head'. There were many more enemy fighters above him and 'a terrific fight was going on'. Unable see another target in a good position and realising it was 'rather an unhealthy spot in which to linger', he turned and dived back to the coast to refuel and rearm.

To his surprise, 'after such a fierce scrap' all returned safely. 'We had shot down about five Me 110s and several more (like mine) were probably destroyed, but it is almost impossible to stay and see definite results in the middle of such a mix-up'. He had learned much that day about the bare necessities of dogfighting: 'All that you can do is to fire a good burst at some enemy and then, hit or miss, get away quickly'.

Some bombers had got through to Weymouth and Portland, and they'd seen an enormous column of smoke rising from a blazing oil tank. The Germans, in spite of their great numerical superiority, had suffered considerable losses.[26]

For 601, operating from Tangmere successes were mounting. On 8 August a true 'Legionnaire' of the 'Millionaires' Squadron', John Keswick Ulick Blake McGrath had destroyed two Me 109s. Born in Tonbridge, Kent in 1919 he attended Harrow School from 1933 to 1937. He joined 601 Squadron at Hendon on 1 January 1939 and began his flying training. McGrath was called to full-time service on 25 August when the AAF was embodied and he was commissioned. He was then posted to 6 FTS Little Rissington on 7 September 1939 for further training.[27]

There, he remained true to the ways of the 'Millionaires' Squadron'. As the first 'Auxiliaries' to attend a war course, at Little Rissington, he and his comrades came under regular RAF discipline. One rule forbade the use of private cars, a rule swiftly abandoned when McGrath turned up in an Alvis Speed-Twenty, while his squadron-mate Peter Dunning-White came in a Rolls Royce – complete with valet. As well as these 'Legionnaires', another attending was Michael Appleby of 609, who turned up in a 'drop-head Hillman'.[28]

McGrath rejoined the squadron at Hendon on 5 May in the days before the German invasion of the Low Countries and notched up an impressive tally over Dunkirk.

On 22 May, he was with 'B' Flight of 601, detached from Tangmere to operate from Manston when he destroyed an Me 109 over Arras. Over Dunkirk on 27 May he destroyed an Me 109 and probably a second, and on the 30th he destroyed an Me 110 and probably another.

On the day after the Battle of Britain started – 11 July, he dispatched a He 111 which crashed into the sea off Portsmouth. That August, there were further victories for McGrath, with two more Me 109s destroyed, on the 8th.[29]

Another pre-war part-timer and archetypal 'Millionaire' enjoying success was (Sir) Archibald Philip Hope. Hope was born in 1912 and succeeded his father as the 17th Baronet of Craighall in 1924. He was educated at Eton and Balliol College, Oxford where he read Modern History. He learned to fly with the University Air Squadron and joined 601 Squadron at Hendon in late 1934. He flew one of the six Blenheims of 601 which attacked the seaplane base at Borkum on 28 November.

When operating over France he had a run of bad luck. As 'A' Flight Commander Hope led his flight to Merville on 16 May. He crash-landed in his Hurricane near Bapaume and the next day was shot down by return fire from Dorniers he was attacking. On the 27th, flying from Tangmere again, Hope was attacked by Me 110s and was shot down between Calais and Dunkirk.

Heading for land he flew as far away from the advancing Germans as possible and crash-landed on a beach. He set fire to his Hurricane and was then taken by a French farmer to Bergues, where there was a British Brigade HQ, before being taken to Dunkirk, where he spent a night on the dunes. The next day he boarded a British destroyer which took him to Dover, Hope phoned 601 and a Magister aircraft picked him up at Hawkinge, still carrying his parachute.

On 11 August he reprised these misfortunes with a claim of two probable Ju 87s.[30]

Another 'Legionnaire' with impeccable 'Millionaire' credentials was William Rhodes-Moorhouse. He was born in Brompton Square, Kensington, West London in 1914. The son of 2nd Lt William Barnard Rhodes-Moorhouse, a First World War RFC pilot who won the Victoria Cross, and was indeed the first airman to receive the VC.

Educated at Eton, he spent part of the winter holidays skiing in Switzerland with his mother and friends. One of this group was Gordon 'Mouse' Cleaver – who would later serve alongside him in 601 Squadron. Cleaver's mother, Adelaide, owned a Percival Gull aircraft and encouraged William's interest in flying. While at Eton, he learned to fly and received his license at the age of 17.

After leaving Eton, William travelled in the USA and Africa and then, in 1936, married Amalia Demetriadi, daughter of Sir Stephen Demetriadi. The noted beauty was reputedly offered the role of Scarlet O'Hara in the film *Gone With the Wind* but turned it down.

A proficient skier, William was selected as a member of the 1936 British Olympic ski team but broke his shoulder while practicing for the ski-jump and wasn't able to compete.

The year later William joined 601 (County of London) Squadron, eventually flying the Blenheim Mk1. It was in this aircraft type that he took part in one of the early operations of the war, the attack on the German seaplane base at Borkum.[31]

Doubtless inspired by William's experience, the brother of Amalia, Richard 'Dick' Demetriadi, joined 601 Squadron in 1938 to serve alongside his brother-in-law and was commissioned in that July.[32]

On 16 May 1940, William went with 'A' Flight to France and destroyed a He 111 on 18 May and an Me 109 on 22 May. Through July he had also shared in the destruction of two Do 17s and on 16 July shared a Ju 88 and destroyed another. In recognition of this success in the air, he was awarded the DFC on 30 July. The 11 August, however, was to be a momentous day for him – and for Dick.[33]

Sometime between 0930 and 0940, what looked like a raid assembling over the Cherbourg Peninsula was spotted by the Isle of Wight radar station at Ventnor Park and AOC 10 Group, AVM Brand, decided this was most likely the enemy's main effort of the day and organised a response.[34]

No. 601 was part of that response with two waves being scrambled. The first took off at 0945 when a section of five Hurricanes took off, flown by Flt Lt Rhodes-Moorhouse, F/Os Gillan and Dickie, P/O Fiske and Sgt Hawkings. At 1000 a further section of four Hurricanes took off, flown by F/Os Davis, Demetriadi, Smithers and Cleaver.

The Hurricanes attacked the heavily escorted formation off the Dorset coast, but were themselves attacked from all sides. They claimed 12 enemy aircraft, including two probable Me 109s shot down by Rhodes-Moorhouse, but paid a high price.

Out of those who took off that morning Gillan, Dickie, Smithers and Demetriadi were reported as 'missing believed killed'.

CHANNEL BATTLES, 17 JULY – 12 AUGUST

The abrupt loss of four pilots, hopelessly outnumbered in the kind of fighter-to-fighter melee that Dowding had sought to avoid, meant 601 Squadron lost a quarter of its fighting force in one day. It was a brutal foretaste of combat against superior numbers.[35]

Of those lost that day, three were pre-war part-timers. The only regular pilot was F/O James Gillan. Born in Aberdeen he joined the RAF in January 1936 on a short service commission. He was posted to 601 Squadron at Tangmere on 3 August 1940.

Julian Smithers was born in Knockholt, Kent in 1915 and was educated at Eton. He then entered the city and joined 601 Squadron in 1938 while working for his father's stockbroking firm. After completing his training Smithers arrived at 5 OTU Aston Down on 6 May 1940 and converted to Hurricanes to rejoin 601 in late May. His body was washed up in France and he is buried in Sainte Marie Cemetery, Le Havre, France.[36]

From an altogether different social sphere was William Dickie. The Dundee man joined the RAFVR in January 1939 and was called up at the outbreak of war. After completing his flying training as a Sergeant, he was commissioned and arrived at 6 OTU on 27 May 1940. He joined 601 Squadron at Middle Wallop on 8 June. On 7 July Dickie had shared in the destruction of a Do 17. He was 24.[37]

The last of the four was William Rhodes-Moorhouse's brother-in-law, Richard Demetriadi. The 21-year-old's body was washed ashore in France and he is buried in Cayeux-sur-Mer Communal Cemetery.[38]

Among those in the second wave was John McGrath. Taking off on a later sortie at 1000, he was No2 Yellow Section. After patrolling between Portland and St Catherine's Point for 15 minutes they sighted a dogfight to the south of them and flew towards it. He recalled, 'I saw an Me 110 crossing from left to right of me at approx 150 yards. E/A coincidentally didn't see me and began a left hand turn, baring the underneath of his aircraft to me. I fired just too soon and let him fly through my bullets. I saw a lot of bullets hit him. E/A rolled onto his back and dived vertically into the sea. I banked an circled left to see E/A crash into the sea. Nobody escaped by parachute'.

After this he climbed again to approx 22,000 feet and saw another Me 110 on his right. It proved impossible for either to get in position. 'We both turned simultaneously towards eachother but neither could get a shot. I stall-turned to the right and E/A stall-turned to the left. Being able to turn quicker, I got my sights on him far sooner and opened fire at close quarters (150 yards) and continued firing [for 3-4 seconds]. E/A continued firing. E/A flew right through my fire. The attack was practically head-on. The Me 110 broke up and dived out of control. I followed him down and gave one more short burst at him (this was unnecessary I consider). Nobody jumped and E/A sank almost directly on contact with the sea (nobody seen on surface).'

He gave chase to an Me 109 heading for France and belching smoke but low on fuel broke off the pursuit. He returned to base alone and landed at 1110.[39]

On 12 August the Luftwaffe began a systematic assault on Fighter Command's forward airfields and radar stations, striking at Manston, Lympne and Hawkinge in the south-east and radar installations in Kent, Sussex and on the Isle of Wight. No. 600 (City of London) Squadron – which was operating Blenheims in the night-fighter role – was based at Manston and was caught in this offensive.

The squadron diary recorded the first heavy bombing attack on the aerodrome and the impact it had. There was 'damage to the aerodrome surface, 150 bombs or so being dropped. Hangars on the far side of the drome were damaged. One of our aircraft was seriously damaged. As the aerodrome was impossible for night-flying a section was sent to operate from Hornchurch for the night phase'.[40]

The attacks continued as recalled by the famous New Zealand fighter ace, Al Deere, who was full of praise for the bravery of 600 Squadron. He recalled the attack on the base which his unit, No. 54 Squadron, shared with the Auxiliary squadron and told of the aerodrome 'half hidden in mushrooms of smoke which drifted across its now bomb cratered surface'. The first of the many attacks that were to be made on Manston had been launched. 'All that day the German formations continued their onslaught. First Manston, then Hawkinge, then Lympne and further along the coast the radar stations'.

He remembered the airfield as 'a shambles of gutted hangars and smouldering dispersal buildings.' As the bombs exploded in the chalky ground – the distinctive Kent geology which gives the iconic white cliffs – all was immersed in 'a thin film of white chalk dust which drifted across the airfield and settled on men, buildings and parked aircraft in the manner, and with the appearance. of a light snow storm. The rows of yellow flags, marking the safety lane for landing, and the chalk-coated men and materials were to become symbolic of Manston in the days that followed, and remain as a lasting impression with all those who worked and operated from there in August 1940'.[41]

Fellow Blenheim unit, No.604 (County of Middlesex) Squadron had the previous day, sent two aircraft from Middle Wallop to investigate an enemy seaplane. They found a He59 in the sea with its engines running, 30 miles from the French coast. They attacked it and set it on fire. They were set upon themselves by six Me 109s but their escort of Spitfires from 152 Squadron damaged two of them and the Blenheims and Spitfires returned unscathed. The Luftwaffe claimed that the He59 seaplanes were used for air sea rescue work and painted many white with red crosses. The British, however, claimed they were being used as reconnaissance aircraft and therefore were legitimate targets.[42]

No. 501 Squadron and Jim Lacey in particular had a busy day. The squadron diary reported that in the morning, the weather 'was fine and clear'. Its Hurricanes left for Hawkinge at 0624 and patrolled from 0938 to 1015. No interceptions were made. Later they were ordered to patrol east of North Foreland and over the Thames Estuary off Westgate. They encountered between 30 and 40 Ju 87s flying around 4,000 feet over the Thames and attacked.

Lacey recalled a frantic encounter. At 1130 when airborne on their way to Hawkinge from Gravesend, the Controller at Biggin Hill called them sharply. 'Vector zero-eight-zero. Thirty bandits approaching Thames estuary.'

Occasionally the R/T crackled as a section leader chided one of his wingmen for keeping bad formation; once or twice someone called out that he had spotted what looked like a formation dead ahead … and then they all saw them.

'Nasty, wicked-looking little Ju 87s diving absolutely vertically, trying to bomb a destroyer. The destroyer was putting up a magnificent show; doing everything except slow rolls.' There was an escort of Me 109s, but the Hurricanes went straight for the Stukas. Lacey picked out one which was streaking eastward at sea level. The dryness in his mouth he'd had before was gone, now that nervous anticipation had given way to the excitement of the chase. With his right flying boot hooked into the toe-strap of the rudder bar and his left tapping on the floor of the cockpit, he overtook his quarry and lined it up for a deflection shot from above and to the left. A three-second burst, and he broke to the right to come in again from that side. Another three-second burst, a spurt of smoke and flame appeared. The dive-bomber plunged down into the sea and a pillar of water foamed up, engulfing the downed Stuka.

Pulling the stick hard back Lacey climbed furiously to 4,000 feet again and fastened his eyes on another Ju 87. It dropped its bombs into the estuary as soon as it saw him coming, and turned east. Throttling back, Lacey opened fire from 250 yards dead astern, while tracer from the rear guns hurtled past his wings and over his cockpit canopy.

But now Lacey's mouth was dry once more. Each streak of tracer looked like it was going to slice through him. He kept his thumb on the firing button, feeling the shuddering of his Hurricane as its eight Brownings hammered at the rear position. Suddenly, the tracer in the air ahead cleared. The gunner was no more, slumped over his mounting.

Two Hurricanes of No. 501 (County of Gloucester) Squadron taking off from Hawkinge on 15 August 1940. Both aircraft were lost three days later on 18 August. (Crown copyright/MoD)

Sgt James 'Ginger' Lacey of No. 501 (County of Gloucester) Squadron was one of the highest scoring aces of the Battle of Britain. He is credited with destroying 18 enemy aircraft during the Battle of Britain. (Crown copyright/MoD)

A formation of three Westland Wallaces of No. 501 (County of Gloucester) Squadron based at Filton in September 1933. (Crown copyright/MoD)

Above: The main section of the Do 17 rammed by Sergeant Ray Holmes of No. 504 (County of Nottingham) Squadron plummets to the ground in central London. (Courtesy of Battle of Britain Monument)

Left: Sergeant Ray Holmes.

A group of pilots from No. 504 (County of Nottingham) Squadron enjoy a pint at the White Hart in Brasted, Kent during the Battle of Britain. (Crown copyright/MoD)

Avro 504N training aircraft of No. 601 (County of London) Squadron at Hendon in 1929. Many AAF pilots learned to fly in these venerable training aircraft – like future CO of No. 504 (County of Nottingham) Squadron John Sample while he was with No. 607 (County of Durham) Squadron. (Crown copyright/MoD)

A Hurricane of No. 601 (County of London) Squadron is serviced by groundcrew at Tangmere in July 1940. (Crown copyright/MoD)

Flying Officer Raymond Davis of No. 601 (County of London) Squadron, in front of one of the Blenheim Mk Is he flew, pictured in 1939. Raymond is is credited with destroying nine enemy aircraft during the Battle of Britain. (Courtesy of Carolyn Horton)

Pilots of No. 601 (County of London) Squadron scramble at Northolt. (Crown copyright/MoD)

A crowd of onlookers gather to view the wreckage of a He 111 – the first enemy aircraft to be brought down on British soil at Humbie, near Edinburgh after being pursued by No. 602 (City of Glasgow) and No. 603 (City of Edinburgh) Squadrons. (Crown copyright/MoD)

Right: Findlay Boyd of No. 602 (City of Glasgow) Squadron is credited with destroying nine enemy aircraft during the Battle of Britain, including perhaps the fastest victory of the battle, shooting down a Ju 87 just seconds after taking off.

Below: A Westland Wallace of No. 602 (City of Glasgow) Squadron flies over Mount Everest in April 1933. (Courtesy of Dougal McIntire)

HM King George VI with No. 602 (City of Glasgow) Squadron at Drem during a visit to the station on 26 February 1940. (Crown copyright/MoD)

Aircrew living quarters of No. 602 (City of Glasgow) Squadron at Westhampnett, summer 1940. (Courtesy of 602 (City of Glasgow) Squadron Museum Association)

A Spitfire of No. 602 (City of Glasgow) Squadron at Westhampnett, summer 1940. (Courtesy of 602 (City of Glasgow) Squadron Museum Association)

Richard Hillary of No. 603 (City of Edinburgh) Squadron. (Courtesy of and copyright the David Ross Collection)

No. 603 (City of Edinburgh) Squadron had their own piper and are pictured here arriving in style at Hornchurch in August 1940. (Courtesy of 603 Squadron Association)

'A' Flight 603 Squadron in October 1939. From left to right; Bill Caister, Ken Macdonald, George Gilroy, Jim Morton, Pat Gifford, George Denholm and Ian Ritchie. (Courtesy of 603 Squadron Association)

Right: Sqn Ldr Archie McKellar originally of No. 602 (City of Glasgow) Squadron and later with No. 605 (County of Warwick) Squadron is credited with destroying 17 enemy aircraft during the Battle of Britain, including shooting down five within 24 hours, making him an 'ace in a day'.

Below: Pilot Officer Cecil Reginald Young, a pilot with No. 607 (County of Durham) Squadron, pictured with one of the squadron's pet dogs at Tangmere in September 1940. (Crown copyright/MoD)

Pilots of No. 609 (West Riding) Squadron – Flying Officer David Crook, left, with Pilot Officer Geoffrey Gaunt. (Courtesy of Battle of Britain Monument)

Spitfires of No. 610 (County of Chester) Squadron, based at Biggin Hill, in July 1940. (Crown copyright/MoD)

Barrie Heath of No. 611 (West Lancashire) Squadron gives a mock German salute with piece of crashed German aircraft. (Courtesy of Aldon Ferguson)

Barrie Heath of No. 611 (West Lancashire) Squadron on the Spitfire named after his brother, Grahame Heath, who lost his life in the First World War. The aircraft was presented to the RAF by Barrie and Grahame's father, George Heath. (Courtesy of Aldon Ferguson)

Winston Churchill wearing his uniform as Honorary Air Commodore of No. 615 (County of Surrey) Squadron with the unit's Officer Commanding, Sqn Ldr Joe Kayll during a visit to the squadron. (Courtesy of Battle of Britain Monument)

Gloster Gladiators and pilots of No. 615 (County of Surrey) Squadron at Vitry-en-Artois in early January 1940. (Crown copyright/MoD)

A pair of Hurricanes from No. 615 (County of Surrey) Squadron return to Northolt after a sortie. (Crown copyright/MoD)

John Dundas (below) and brother Hugh (Left) both flew in the Battle of Britain – John with No. 609 (West Riding) Squadron and Hugh with No. 616 (South Yorkshire) Squadron. (Both pictures courtesy of Battle of Britain Monument)

CHANNEL BATTLES, 17 JULY – 12 AUGUST

Jim was within 100 yards now and getting closer. At 50 yards the enemy edged a bank of cloud and Lacey opened fire once more. The Ju 87 rolled to the left, out of control, a dense plume of black smoke belching from its engine. Then he lost sight of it and having not seen it hit the ground he could only claim it as a probable.[43]

In the afternoon, the squadron met another formation, this time west of Ramsgate. They broke it up and attacked individually.

At 1240 they scrambled from Gravesend towards Manston and Ramsgate where they found 30 Me 110s and 20 Me 109s at 5,000 feet. Lacey dived down onto an Me 110, began shooting at 250 yards and continued till he was out of ammunition. White smoke belched from the engines and he saw the pilot bale out. Two Me 109s were on his tail, he had no ammunition left, so he opened the throttle and escaped into a big cloud away from their attentions.

One Me 110 was destroyed and two Me 110s were damaged. The squadron (18 aircraft) took off from Hawkinge at 1725 and landed at Gravesend at 1840. They were unable to operate from Hawkinge thanks to the damage from bombing in the savage attacks that day. Several aircraft were destroyed confirmed and unconfirmed. P/O Lukasewicz, however, was reported missing believed killed.[44]

After landing, Lacey wolfed down a lunch of bully beef sandwiches and tea at dispersal. He was falling asleep in a canvas chair when someone shook his shoulder to tell him there was a visiting Air Marshal at the airfield. 'I'll stand up when he gets around here – if I'm awake.' The Yorkshireman gruffly replied.

Then, just as a formation of He 111s and Ju 88s swept over the airfield, the air raid sirens sounded. As the bombs burst around the aerodrome, Lacey, the pilots and the Air Marshal dived into the trenches for cover.

Amid the carnage in the air and on the ground, the day finished with a party at Gravesend to celebrate Lacey's award of the Distinguished Flying Medal. Although he and his pals were now becoming more and more skilled in aerial combat, they were exhausted by the strain of the endless scrambles and dogfights. By now, Lacey recalled that every time the loudspeaker hummed before blaring out a call to scramble, he had to rush from his bed in the dispersal hut or from the grass under his Hurricane's wing where he was lying and vomit.[45]

There was also success and recognition for 615 Squadron. At 0945 the whole squadron took off and remained in the air for one hour and forty-five minutes. Although there was plenty of enemy activity, no enemy aircraft were sighted. After landing and refuelling, the squadron were sent off again at 1220 towards Southampton. On the way there they were vectored to intercept a raid near Beachy Head and ran into Me 109s. Red Section attacked and Flt Lt Gaunce in Hurricane P2966 was confirmed to have shot one down. One burst into flames and the other blew up and dived into the sea. Gaunce's engine was covered in oil from the enemy aircraft when he returned. P/O Hugo in P3160 shot down one which fell into the sea and he saw the pilot was waving. Hugo landed to report this at Hawkinge, and a boat was despatched to rescue the pilot. P/O McClintock in N2328 in his first combat attacked one Me 109 and damaged it for certain.

In total the squadron diary claimed the following from the day's encounters: two Me 109s confirmed, one unconfirmed and one damaged. The success was capped by the announcement that Gaunce, Hugo and F/O Collard had been awarded the DFC.[46]

It would prove to be another big day for the former part-timers of 610 Squadron.

Horatio Chandler added to his toll when he damaged an Me 109. Meanwhile Sgt Bernard Gardner had only joined 610 Squadron in late July but on 12 August he would announce his arrival in emphatic style.

Having joined the RAFVR in September 1937 while working as a draughtsman at the Ordnance Survey Office, the former Tauntons School pupil from Bassett in Hampshire, was called up on 1 September 1939. He completed his training at 11 FTS and joined 610 Squadron

CHANNEL BATTLES, 17 JULY – 12 AUGUST

at Biggin Hill on 27 July. On this day he destroyed an Me 109 and took on a whole formation of bombers on his own.

The CO, Sqn Ldr Ellis recorded 'Sergeant Gardner was engaged with enemy bombers and fighters over Dover, and after shooting down a 'He 113' [Me 109] he attacked, single handed, ten Dornier 215s. During this attack his aircraft was hit several times and Sergeant Gardner received an incendiary bullet in the left arm. Despite fainting twice in the air, he successfully force-landed at Wye with his undercarriage retracted and was taken to Ashford Hospital.'

Another member of 610 was not to be so fortunate. Edward Smith, the former oil refinery worker who we met earlier, was the only member of his section to return from a scramble on 11 August, while next day he was shot down by Me 109s, baling out of his Spitfire into the Channel with burns to his face and neck.[47]

No. 609 Squadron was to come face-to-face again with the sheer, shocking scale of the Luftwaffe attacks being mounted against the south coast that day. Of the Auxiliary pilots John Dundas and David Crook were to be sorely tested.

They flew two of the 12 Spitfires were sent aloft at 1200 heading for the coast off Portsmouth and the Isle of Wight.

David Crook was due for 24-hours' leave and was having a bath when he was called to readiness. Quickly wiping the soap from his face, he made it to his Spitfire to find the radio was dead. Later taking off, he couldn't find his squadron-mates but headed for the anti-aircraft barrage he could clearly see over Portsmouth. He was astonished at the sheer number of enemy aircraft he faced.

> A powerful force of German aircraft was circling over the east end of the Isle of Wight, and I went out towards them, climbing all the time. As I got nearer, I was staggered by the number of Huns in the sky. I think we had always imagined that raids might be carried out by three or four

squadrons at the most – some forty or fifty aircraft. And here, circling and sweeping all over the sky, were at least 200 Huns! 'My God,' I muttered to myself, 'what a party.' I was not the only person to be impressed. Several other people (not only in 609) who were also in this fight told me afterwards that their main impression had been one of blank astonishment at the numbers of aircraft involved. As somebody remarked – 'There was the whole German air force, bar Goering.' Later in the summer we got used to seeing these enormous formations, but this first occasion certainly made us think a bit.

'A' Flight led the attack against the Me 110s, flying straight into their circle, taking full beam shots and breaking away downwards. There were estimated to be at least 80 Me 110s in this one formation.[48]

Crook recalled: 'I climbed out towards the Huns and saw three formations of Messerschmitts circling round, one above the other, between about 20,000 and 28,000 feet. Each layer had formed into the usual German defensive circle, going round and round on each other's tails.'

He got into position about 2,000 feet above the Me 110s and then dived straight down into the middle of the circle. As he descended, he selected a target and 'blazed away madly at him...getting in a few seconds' effective fire at very close range'.

After giving him a good burst 'at practically point-blank range' the Me 110 turned to the right, appeared to stall, and started to turn over on to his back.

Unable to see any results as he flashed right through the enemy formation at high speed, he narrowly missed a collision with one fighter and continuing to dive before he could pull out. He pushed his Spitfire to the limit. 'I think I was doing well over 500 mph and the strain of pulling out was considerable'. Looking round he saw an Me 110, enveloped in a sheet of flame, which fell past him within

200 yards. 'I don't know if this was my victim or not, but I definitely think it was, as I had seen no other British fighters in the vicinity when I attacked'.

'There were a lot of Huns all round and above me, and I decided it might be a good idea if I moved on elsewhere'.

Surrounded by enemy aircraft and with very little ammunition left, he turned on his back and dived away to the English coast, and shortly afterwards landed safely at the aerodrome. All from 609 returned safely, and all had a fruitful time with 'six or seven Huns and several more probables, including mine' destroyed. Crook recalled 'my dive through the Hun circle had been so fast and the pull out so violent (probably in the heat of the moment I pulled out far more quickly than I realized), that as a result both wings of my Spitfire were damaged and she had to go back to the factory for repairs'.

He recalled it was a boiling summer's day and they all were soaked in sweat when they got back. Charles 'Teeny' Overton and John Dundas both headed straight to the mess and 'drank a pint of iced Pimms apiece, after which they felt much better and swapped experiences'.[49]

The day's fighting, the squadron diary told, yielded 'a very satisfactory score' for no losses with many confirmed victories. One Me 110 falling to each of F/Os Dundas and Goodwin, P/Os Staples and Overton and Sgt Feary. P/O Crook is recorded as shooting down two Me 109s, however, he recalls them as Me 110s.[50] As night fell on this opening day of the Luftwaffe's offensive to destroy the RAF, the West Riding squadron looked at itself and liked what it saw.[51]

As the 12 August drew to a close, Fighter Command and its AAF and RAFVR pilots were holding their own against the Luftwaffe. But as Crook observed on seeing this last raid over Portsmouth, the scale of the attacks was growing. The rest of August and into September would see them and their airfields battered by continual attacks, some of enormous scale. It would be a most dangerous time when they would be close to being overwhelmed.

THE HARDEST DAYS, 13 AUGUST – 6 SEPTEMBER

Large-scale daylight attacks against RAF airfields in South-East England, with the object of exhausting the RAF's ability to provide a defence. Night attacks continued.

Adler Tag (Eagle Day), was the name given to the day of the launch of the main Luftwaffe assault *Adlerangriff* (Eagle Attack) against the RAF, but was postponed from the 10th to the 13th August because of poor weather.

The aim was to force Fighter Command out of the south-east corner of England within four days, and destroy the RAF completely within four weeks.

During the next three weeks, the Luftwaffe attempted to exhaust Fighter Command by forcing it to battle against continued attacks on its ground installations, which were moved further inland. Airfields in southern England were subject to intensive daylight raids, while night attacks continued against ports, shipping and the aircraft industry.

But the day began inauspiciously for the Luftwaffe. On the morning of 13 August, Goering personally issued an order again postponing *Adler Tag* due to poor weather.[1]

As the weather improved in mid-afternoon new orders were suddenly passed to the Luftwaffe's Air Fleets. *Adlerangriff* was 'on' after all. There were to be massive attacks on Fighter Command's airfields throughout southern England, spearheaded by the Stuka squadrons.

THE HARDEST DAYS, 13 AUGUST – 6 SEPTEMBER

Other engagements were being fought out all over southern England. Six of nine Stukas on their way to attack Middle Wallop were shot down by Spitfires of 609 Squadron after their Me 109 escort had turned back, short of fuel.

For 601 Squadron, the day was to be both eventful and fruitful. Perhaps they took advantage of operating in what an optimist might term a 'target-rich environment'.

William Clyde, known throughout his life as Billy, had won the World University Skiing Championship in 1935, the same year he joined 601 Squadron with his friend Max Aitken. Quickness of thought and co-ordination of hand, eye and mind, which gave him his prowess at keeping control while hurtling down a ski slope, presaged his talents as a fighter pilot. Alongside McGrath and Hope he was to make 13 August one of 601's most successful days.

Leading Blue Section in Hurricane P2920, he took off on his first sortie that day at 0630 and the Section was vectored to the Arundel-Petworth area. In his combat report, he told how they sighted Ju 88s flying south over 10/10 cloud near Arundel at 10,000 feet and Red, Blue and Green Sections climbed above the enemy. It was now around 0645, and he led his section against the formation of 21 Ju 88s. He attacked one Ju 88 and saw it back away from the formation. Blue 2 later attacked this aircraft with a definite result, 'although he jettisoned his bombs and one engine was smoking' as the squadron diary told.

He then turned and attacked another Ju 88 on the outside of the formation from quarter and it slowed down and dived straight into cloud with both engines smoking. 'I think this was a good probable' Clyde recalled. But he hadn't escaped unscathed. 'I was unable to follow it down as my aircraft had been hit in both mainplanes and in the oil pump. I had been hit by splinters in the leg' – later it had been found that a bullet had come through the front armour plating and pierced the air pipe making the guns unserviceable and some of his flying controls had been shot away, meaning he could only control one elevator. He landed at 0710. It had been a lively start to the day, but there was much more to come. Later in the day he claimed three Me 110s destroyed, a probable Ju 88 and a damaged Me 110.[2]

John McGrath too was involved in this sortie and recalled the patrol in his combat report. Flying as No. 2 in Yellow Section, they took off at 0630 and were told to climb to 10,000 feet as quickly as possible. They sighted '30–40 Ju 88s – many of escort fighters Me 109 and 110s; flying north over Haslemere at 12,000 feet'. After getting the enemy to the left, their attack was about to be delivered when the Germans aircraft turned left and passed under them. 'We could not keep formation. I chased the first formation of bombers and found two stragglers very exposed going just out to sea. I did three beam attacks on it and after the second he went into a shallow dive with smoke coming from the fuselage.

'I placed myself in front and beneath him. Again, did a beam attack from his right. After this his starboard engine caught fire and he spiralled through cloud in to the sea. There was an explosion and bits of wreckage could be seen floating.'

He climbed again and found another straggler who was travelling very fast and could not manoeuvre into position. 'I fired three or four bursts from astern at 200 yards closing to 100 yards. Both engines were burning fiercely and I saw an explosion in the centre of the fuselage after which smoke poured out of the enemy aircraft and it went into a shallow dive. All guns pointing to the rear had ceased firing. I watched him go down to the clouds but due to no ammunition I had to return to base as there was a danger of meeting the escort fighters and needed to refuel and rearm'. He landed back at 0700.[3]

At 1150 they were scrambled again with Clyde leading Blue Section of 'B' Flight. They saw 20–30 Me 110s at 20,000 feet above cloud west of Swanage. Clyde recalled: 'The Me 110s were in a defensive circle and a big dog fight was going on. Around 1215, I attacked one Me 110 and had one long burst and he went over on his back with one engine smoking and went straight down in a vertical dive. I then had

THE HARDEST DAYS, 13 AUGUST – 6 SEPTEMBER

a long burst at another machine and saw my bullets hitting the seat over on his back and dived but could not follow as another machine was on my tail. I had one more burst and finished ammunition to no effect. I then dived to the sea and assisted the motorboat picking up survivors – I saw four British and one German picked up.' In this action he had one Me 110 confirmed and one probable/damaged.

The noon battle was, in terms of numbers of aircraft to fall out of the sky in a short time, the fiercest 601 had ever known. The experience of Clive Mayers, described by him and Archie Hope in their official reports within minutes of returning to Tangmere, are powerful.

While this and other actions were large, sometimes vast, they all reduced to desperate struggles between individuals. Hope's report gives an incredible insight into the very personal duels which took place among the swarms of aircraft which criss-crossed the skies over southern England that summer.

At around 1215 Hope led 'A' Flight towards Portland. 'I saw about 20–30 aircraft going round in circles. We were at 20,000 feet and their highest aircraft was just below us. The squadron went into line astern, and I turned left towards the enemy aircraft who were still circling left-handed in a sort of spiral about 3,000 feet deep. I went for the top Me 110 and fired. It continued to turn, and I followed on its tail firing until it appeared to go down and I thought I had gone down far enough'. He continued to shadow his prey. 'It had continued to turn left, and I was by now circling with the enemy aircraft, so I turned to go against their circle. I fired a short burst at the enemy head-on and as I passed'. The slender twin-engined fighter desperately tried to evade Hope in his pursuing Hurricane. 'He tightened his turn and pulled straight up across me so that I could see all his pale blue underneath and I finished my bullets to his bottom in a full deflection shot'. It seemed this was enough. 'I then spiralled steeply down and watched the sea. I saw one parachute go in and circled it for a minute or two until I saw a boat going straight for it'. The chivalrous nature of the fight revealed itself as Hope desperately tried to ensure his erstwhile foe was rescued.

> I marked the place by the oil where an aircraft had gone in and went south-west to where I found two more pilots in the water, one British and the other doubtful. By this time, I had been joined by Blue 1 and 2 and I left them to circle the last two while I went back to the others. In the end all were picked up although we had considerable difficulty in showing the boat where the German was. The boat that had picked up the first pilot went straight back to shore and I couldn't make it come towards the others. I took one look around Weymouth Bay without seeing any more and set off for home as I was getting short of petrol. I am convinced that unless we had circled these three pilots in the water at least three of them would not have been picked up.

To continue their frantic signalling for the downed pilots to be rescued, showed equal concern for the British and German pilots – in spite of the desperate fight they were in. It is remarkable how they retained their humanity and the knowledge that they were fighting humans as well as machines.[4]

One of those shot down was P/O Howard Clive Mayers. Born in Sydney, Australia he joined the University Air Squadron in 1929 while reading Engineering at Jesus College, Cambridge. He was later commissioned in the Reserve of Air Force Officers (RAFO) in 1930. He had damaged an Me 110 and was watching it enter cloud at 7,000 feet when:

> My Hurricane was hit by what seemed a tornado. I felt pain in my right buttock and leg, felt the engine stop, heard hissing noises and smelt fumes. My first reaction was to

pull back the stick and there was no response. The next thing I remember was falling through the air at high speed and feeling my helmet, flying boots and socks torn off. Lack of oxygen must have dulled my senses as the combat ended at 19,000 feet and my parachute opened just above the clouds at 7,000 feet. At about 5,000 feet between two layers of cloud an Me 110 fired at me while being chased closely by a Hurricane. This Hurricane was Hope's, and as that fight subsided, he called over the R/T for others with sufficient fuel to help him direct the rescue launches to the numerous pilots, both British and German, in the water.

Mayers was among the first to be rescued:

> I landed in the water about three miles from Portland. Just before landing I saw an MTB [motor torpedo boat] about a mile away but the CO [of the MTB] told me later they didn't see me coming down although they saw a German parachutist not two hundred yards from me. He saw Hope's Hurricane searching the bay, waved at me and spent some considerable time in attracting the attention of the rescue launch ... I am quite sure that if it hadn't been for Flight Lieutenant Hope the MTB wouldn't have found me.

After Mayers was rescued, Hope had directed the launch to the German pilot, lying face downward and apparently lifeless, who proved when fished from the sea to be very much alive. Mayers was towelling himself and sipping hot cocoa when there was a commotion on the deck. A seaman, with good intentions and a sharp knife, was about to cut the life jacket off the Luftwaffe pilot, but the German, thinking he was about to be murdered, put up an obstinate fight. He was allowed to keep his wet clothes on.[5]

That day 601 Squadron carried out 43 hours 25 mins flying by day and 9 hours by night – consisting of seven interception flights during the day and one at night. The squadron accounted for 14 enemy aircraft destroyed, 15 probably destroyed and 16 damaged. Incredibly of those 14 destroyed, three Me 110s fell to the guns of Raymond Davis. This would bring the tally of the former mining engineer to four.'[6]

The spare detail of his combat report describes this extraordinary success. 'Squadron took off at 1100. I was Yellow 1. We climbed west to 20,000 feet over Portland. We had been told to go for fighters and saw them to the south dog-fighting. We joined in. I attacked defensive circle on right rotation in position to do head-on attacks. After one or two bursts saw Me[110] I fired at break away. I followed and put in burst from 200 yards astern. He stall-turned and dived into sea. I was then at 15,000 feet so climbed to south and attacked from south with sun at my back, again doing head-on attacks against the defensive circle. My second burst set a machine on fire between starboard engine and fuselage. He disappeared into cloud belching flames. I then saw an enemy aircraft by itself. As I turned towards him he did the same and I gave him a burst head-on. We both stall-turned and I attacked head-on again. He went into a gentle right-hand turn and dived. As I was out of ammunition I followed him down to the sea. My camera was switched on in this combat and I took a picture of the splash. An RAF launch nearby over which I flew should confirm this last machine. I landed at 1225.[7]

John McGrath, took off with Yellow Section at 1535 and told in his Combat Report how they intercepted a formation of Me 110s and He 111s north of Southampton. 'I attacked an Me 110 and gave some short bursts after which he dived to the clouds towards France. I followed him with his two engines smoking violently. I chased him out towards the sea where I caught him long enough to give him one long burst to finish him off. The pilot jumped but his parachute did not open. I was by now approx 30 miles south of Selsey Bill. I turned and climbed above a low layer of cloud and noticed a 'He 113' [probably

THE HARDEST DAYS, 13 AUGUST – 6 SEPTEMBER

an Me 109] who tried to stop me returning. I twisted about in the cloud with 2 chasing and circling above. I called base for assistance but realised it could not arrive in time so again dived through cloud and a He 113 [*sic*] overshot me. I gave him a full deflection shot and finished my ammunition. Smoke came from the enemy aircraft but I didn't watch it. He had fired at me but was a long way in front of me.' He landed back safely at 1700.[8]

In spite of the fierce fight they waged that day, not one pilot was lost, and 601 shared with No. 609 Squadron the great honours of the day when each claimed 14 of the enemy.[9]

David Crook recalled 13 August was 'a very lucky thirteenth for us'. At midday the squadron flew down to Warmwell and at about 1600 they were ordered to patrol Weymouth at 15,000 feet. 'We took off, thirteen machines in all, with the CO leading, and climbed up over Weymouth'. Soon he heard something which would give them a decisive edge. 'After a few minutes I began to hear a German voice talking on the R/T, faintly at first and then growing in volume. By a curious chance this German raid had a wavelength almost identical with our own and the voice we heard was that of the German commander talking to his formation as they approached us across the Channel. About a quarter of an hour later we saw a large German formation approaching below us'. There were around 60 enemy aircraft – Ju 87s escorted by Me 109s above with some Me 110s about 2 miles behind.

> A Hurricane squadron [possibly 601] attacked the Me 110s as soon as they crossed the coast and they never got through to where we were. Meanwhile the bombers with their fighter escort still circling above them, passed beneath us. We were up at almost 20,000 feet in the sun and I don't think they ever saw us till the very last moment. The CO gave a terrific 'Tally ho' and led us round in a big semi-circle so that we were now behind them, and we prepared to attack.[10]

F/O John Dundas was a spare pilot and joined Red Section as Red 4 in Spitfire R6690. Above cloud at 10,000 feet he sighted fighters above him. Given the lead by Red 1 he climbed into the sun at 18,000 feet with the flight in line astern behind him. They turned in towards three Vic formations of Ju 87s (18 in each formation) silhouetted against cloud below them, heading north. It was the beginning of a massacre.

He recalled 'Red 1 then took the lead and I fell into line astern as Red 4.' The first three aircraft of Red Section dived on rear section of three Ju 87s out of the sun. E/A (Enemy Aircraft) took no avoiding action. After three attacks carried out singly from line astern by Red 1 and 2, the 3 Ju 87s were all destroyed.

> I attacked the starboard Ju 87 of the next section to port, opening fire at 250 yds. Though well-throttled back I had rather too much overtaking speed and had closed to point blank range within 4-secs. I saw E/A burst into flames and dive into cloud. I broke away and then attacked a second Ju 87 which was already being attacked by a Spitfire as I closed in. For this reason, I had to hold my fire till I was too close and could only get in a two second burst, all but colliding with E/A as I broke away. During this attack I ran into some rear-gun fire and a bullet punctured my oil system. I came down through cloud with no oil pressure and forced landed on Warmwell aerodrome with a dead prop.

Another former part-timer who enjoyed success that day was Michael Staples. Born in 1917 in India, he was educated at Ampleforth College. A player for Bedford Rugby Club, he joined the RAFVR in November 1938 while employed as a technician working on accounting and tabulating machines. After completing his training and converting to Spitfires he joined 609 Squadron at Middle Wallop on 8 July.[11]

THE HARDEST DAYS, 13 AUGUST – 6 SEPTEMBER

Flying as Yellow 3 in L1008 his combat report gives a flavour of the aerial carnage 609 inflicted on the marauding Germans that day.

> Yellow Section was flying astern of Red section. Red and Yellow Leaders put their Sections in line astern and then gave the orders to put off and pick a target among a large number of Ju 87s which we saw to the left and 2,000 feet below us. I was the last to attack end saw many 87s diving towards the ground out of control and all emitting a great deal of black smoke as a result of the attack of the other members of the flight. I had a short burst at a Ju 87 but seeing a better target, another 87, I attacked from dead astern, opening fire at about 150 yds and giving six-second burst, I closed to within 20 or 30 yds and saw the enemy aircraft wobble severely, I then broke away to avoid a collision and did not see the enemy formation again. The engagement took place at 14,000 feet.

David Crook had shot down an Me 109 in a frantic encounter. When he returned, the groundcrews 'were in a great state of excitement'. They could hear a terrific fight going on above the clouds but saw nothing except several German machines falling in flames. 'All the machines were now coming into land and everybody's eyes were fixed on the wings. Yes – they were all covered with black streaks from the smoke of the guns – everybody had fired. There was the usual anxious counting – only ten back – where are the others – they should be back by now – I hope to God everybody's OK – good enough, here they come. Thank God, everybody's OK'. They all stood round in small groups talking excitedly and exchanging experiences. 'It is very amusing to observe the exhilaration and excitement which everybody betrays after a successful action like this; It soon became obvious that this had been our best effort yet. Thirteen enemy machines had been destroyed in about four minutes. Six more were probably destroyed or damaged, while our only damage sustained was one bullet through somebody's wing. I think this was the record bag for one squadron in one fight during the whole of the Battle of Britain. Just after I broke away to attack my Messerschmitt, the whole squadron had dived right into the centre of the German formation and the massacre started. One pilot looked round in the middle of the action and in one small patch of sky he saw five German dive bombers going down in flames, still more or less in formation. We all heard the German commander saying desperately, time after time, "*Achtung, Achtung, Spit und Hurri*" – meaning presumably, "Look out, look out, Spitfires and Hurricanes".[12]

P/O Michael Appleby in N3223, who was credited with an Me 109 and a Ju 87 damaged, recalled it was a pivotal moment for the squadron and for its boss. 'This was both a turning point for our Squadron, and a great success for our CO, George Darley, because of the tactics he had adopted in getting us in the right position at the right time, providing the information received from our radar people was reliable'.

John Dundas writing in the squadron diary struck an understandably jubilant note:

> Thirteen Spitfires left Warmwell for a memorable Tea-time Party over Lyme Bay, and an unlucky day for the species Ju 87, of which no less than 14 suffered destruction or damage in a record Squadron 'Bag', which also included five or the escorting Messerschmitts. The enemy formations, consisting of about 40 dive-bombers in four Vic formations, with about as many Me 110s and 109s stepped up above then, heading northwards from the Channel and was surprised by 609 Squadron's down-sun attack. All thirteen of our pilots fired their guns.[13]

Little did 609 Squadron know, but from the cliffs above Portland, Winston Churchill, and a gathering of 'Top Brass' – Lieutenant

Generals Alan Brooke, C-in-C, Home Forces; Claude Auchinleck, G.O.C-in-C., Southern Command; and the 5th Corps' Major General Bernard Montgomery, had paused from a survey of coastal defences to marvel at the spectacle.[14]

Meanwhile, 602 arrived in Sussex that day at 1715. The airfield at Westhampnett was basic with grass runways. The officers' mess was in a farm on the edge of the airfield and the airmen were billeted in the old kennels on the Goodwood estate. There were a couple of huts for dispersal.

They were relieving 145 Squadron and 602 Squadron's first arrivals at Westhampnett were astounded to see a Hurricane on its back in the middle of the field. The CO of 145 Squadron, Sqn Ldr John Peel, greeted 602's CO, his arm in a sling after being injured and explained they could do with a rest.

The boss of 602, Sqn Ldr Sandy Johnstone, later recalled: 'Johnny Peel was waiting to greet us. He said his outfit had been taking a bit of stick from Jerry and was now reduced to four aircraft and four pilots. That was his Hurricane in the middle of the airfield, he told me. He had brought it down without any aileron control. However, he was glad to say that the smoke rising from behind the hedge was coming from a burning Me 109.' Johnstone thought that Westhampnett 'was beginning to sound more like Calamity Corner'.[15]

That day, Dowding's controllers were getting the measure of the German Me 109 'free sweeps', and were refusing to be drawn. Dowding's men had destroyed 34 German aircraft and lost 12 in the air. Of the 47 destroyed on the ground, only one was a fighter. By any measure the day had been an impressive victory for the defenders.[16]

Air Chief Marshal Sir Hugh Dowding was indeed relieved. 'Pacing his office at 1000, on Tuesday, 14 August, thumbs, as always, hooked in his tunic belt, Dowding's normally pallid cheeks were flushed with excitement'. The normally taciturn Dowding was unusually animated, more than Lieutenant General Sir Frederick Pile, Chief of Anti-Aircraft Command had ever known him. Dowding exclaimed,

'Pile, it's a miracle.' And for the RAF, Eagle Day had indeed proved a miracle. And while the Luftwaffe had flown an impressive 1,485 sorties, successfully strafing 9 airfields, too many strikes had been launched at bases outside Fighter Command. Detling and Eastchurch had paid a heavy price – both Coastal Command bases. So too did Odiham and Andover – army co-operation airfields.[17]

After their success on Eagle Day, the next day saw 609 Squadron on the receiving end. Middle Wallop was raided by three twin-engined enemy bombers who scored direct hits on their hangar, and 'made a shambles of the offices'. While attempting to close the hangar doors, Cpl R.W. Smith, LAC H. Thorley and LAC L. Wilson, were all killed, and Cpl P.H. Appleby admitted to hospital, injured. But again 609 hit back. David Crook damaged a He 111 which John Dundas subsequently destroyed and added a 'Probable' Do 17 on his own, while Sgt Feary destroyed the Ju 88 that had been attacking the aerodrome.[18] 604 Squadron were also based at Middle Wallop and also bore the brunt of this raid – losing three of their Blenheims and having a fourth damaged.

The tally of John Dundas was increasing all the time. He destroyed a Ju 87 and damaged a second in the previous day's rout by 609 over Portland.

His days covering international affairs for the *Yorkshire Post* must have seemed a distant memory when he reported from the Munich conference as Chamberlain desperately sought to avert war. Dundas had continued his day-job at the paper and flying with 609 at the weekends and on summer camp. War, of course did come in spite of Chamberlain's efforts and nearly a year had gone by since he had declared war on Germany and the foe which had seemed distant then was now the enemy at the gate.

The next day saw him stalking his prey at no small risk. Flying as Yellow 1, Dundas recalled that his Section was ordered to patrol Boscombe Down at 18,000 feet. 'I climbed through 10/10 cloud to cloud ceiling which was 15,000 feet, when in position I saw a twin engine aircraft approaching from the south'. It flew above him. Dundas wheeled round and with the enemy 600–300 yards away 'put a burst of one second and one of four seconds into the enemy aircraft'. But it was not enough and it slipped away. 'Enemy went straight into thick cloud and I lost him', Dundas wrote.

However, there was more quarry for him. He heard on the radio at least two enemy aircraft approaching Salisbury at 15,000 feet. Climbing to 17,000 feet he found four Do 17s in box formation flying south. 'Saw another Spitfire making stern attack over Salisbury. Got within 800 yards of starboard beam of formation and 500 feet. Above in front and from this position made two beam and quarter attacks at leader and saw my shots pass in front of his nose.' On the third attack he broke away too steeply into cloud and blacked out. 'When I came round, I had difficulty in locating the enemy but found them still on course.' He then selected a fourth member of the box formation and 'did a good quarter attack on him firing a six-second burst.' He left formation but 'I lost him in clouds.' As he was returning, he met a Ju 88 three miles west of their base flying south. Dundas saw that the bomber was already damaged and as he attacked it he saw its under-carriage coming down. 'I gave him the rest of my ammunition at close range from dead astern, saw a black puff of smoke come from the engine and crash on the ammunition store, five miles south-west of the aerodrome.' He was credited with destroying a Do 17 and sharing in the destruction of the Ju 88.[19]

Meanwhile, in Kent, Al Deere remembered the severity of the attacks on the airfield and again was impressed with 600 Squadron. 'All next day the German assault on our coastal airfields continued with Manston once again the pivot of the attacks. At the end of the second day the airfield was in a sorry state. The power supply was cut; the telephone cable, over which came our orders, was severely damaged, the hangar area was a shambles; and there was extensive damage to administrative buildings'. However, 600 Squadron pilots enacted some sort of revenge when they brought down an Me 110 one of nine which attacked the airfield that day. A second one was brought down by Bofors fire from the station defence; 600 Squadron's victim being picked off with a Lewis gun mounted on the top of their dugout. Deere wondered: 'How those 600 pilots stick it. I don't know.'[20]

An improvised 'Armadillo' armoured car designed for airfield defence was fitted with a machine gun to help boost the airfield's defences, as did the officers who took pot shots at low-flying attackers with their .303 rifles.[21]

Their good humour and resolve had its roots in the camaraderie of the pre-war part-time days. The squadron used to hold its annual camp at Tangmere.

High jinks were also apparent at the camp, particularly at the end of a day's work when the officers would head down to Bognor.

The famous Mr Butlin had even then a fun fair at Bognor, and an undeclared state of war existed between his attendants and 600 Squadron. Butlin's was subjected to a series of sporadic but highly co-ordinated raids for the express purpose of capturing the current collector arms of the dodgems, in effect, the enemy's colours. Surprise was the order of the day, one moment of relative peace, the next thing a grand melee with protagonists locked in battle on individual dodgems.[22]

The 15 August saw some of the heaviest fighting of the battle so far. Banking on tactical surprise, Luftflotte 5 based in Norway launched two simultaneous thrusts in the north and north-east. At 1208, radar plotted a formation of enemy aircraft opposite the Firth of Forth over 90 miles away, estimated to be of around 30 aircraft in their sections flying towards Tynemouth. Among the squadrons sent aloft by the 13 Group Controller was 605 Squadron over Tyneside.

This momentous day would be among the most successful for many former reservist pilots. One of them was Archie McKellar. After shooting down his first back in October 1939, McKellar had to wait until this day to taste success once more, but the former plasterer's victories would herald further success for 605 Squadron.

'B' Flight was ordered off at 1215, from 'available' and was in the air within 10 minutes. They were vectored to what was described as a 'big air battle off Newcastle', involving 150 enemy aircraft. The flight, led by Flt Lt McKellar made contact.[23]

In his combat report, McKellar described the action: 'I was Blue 1 Commander of 'B' Flight which left Drem at 1205 and patrolled Acklington, Tyneside area at 10,000–20,000 feet. Owing to lack of orders from control I kept my Flight patrolling around Newcastle as I considered it to be the most vulnerable and important target for the enemy.' At 1310 Blue and Green sections observed large formations of enemy aircraft approaching Tyneside from the south-east at 12,000–14,000 feet and he ordered Blue Section and Green Section into line astern, follow him into the sun and to do a diving attack on the large formation. 'I also called the Controller and informed them about the enemy aircraft and that "Cockle" "B" Flt was going to engage the large formation and did a dive attack in formation on the last enemy aircraft of the first formation which was stepped up in box formation'. He gave a three-second burst from 250 yards and the enemy aircraft dropped off in a spiral dive. While carrying out this attack he was hit in the wings by the rear enemy aircraft formation from behind. By then they were over Newcastle so he ordered 'B' Flight to make individual attacks as the best way of breaking up the formation and defeating the object of the enemy which would appear to be the bombing of Tyneside.

'I climbed up again into the sun and engaged the leader of the second formation with full beam attack following No. 2 of the formation with a quarter attack giving an eight second burst from 400 feet on No. 1 25 yards on No. 2 and breaking through the formation'. As a result, he saw grey-white smoke coming from the enemy aircraft's engines. 'The enemy aircraft probably crashed in to the sea,' he added, 'but I had no time to follow their downward course as I was breaking through the formation'. After breaking and climbing he saw that the second formation now appeared to be three straggling aircraft which were trying to join up with the main formation. At the same time he counted seven enemy aircraft all spinning down into cloud and into the sea. Climbing again into the sun he engaged the first straggler in a beam to quarter attack from 100–200 yards with a three second burst, probably killing the top gunner and saw grey smoke coming from the starboard engine of the enemy aircraft.[24]

The action resulted in seven confirmed and one unconfirmed, the diary told. 'Flight Lieutenant McKellar himself bagged three, P/O Passy one, P/O Currant one, and P/O Muirhead and P/O Currant shared'. The official figure at that moment were four confirmed, four probable and one damaged. It was what the squadron diary described as 'a red-letter day' for the squadron and 'a brilliant performance by the Flt'.[25]

Having re-opened his combat tally in spectacular fashion, as later described his action in a letter to his mother.

> On Thursday, at 12 o'clock, I was sent off with my Flight to patrol Newcastle at 20,000 feet. We all arrived safely and remained there until 1.30, when I saw 70 to 80 Nasties in one big formation, followed by a second formation of 20 to 30. They were approaching Newcastle from the south. I whipped into them with my Flight. I got three down, with one more possible, and the rest of the boys got five down and seven possible – possible being when the Hun breaks away from the formation with engines out or flames coming but is not seen to crash. By this time there was a lot more of our fighters, so everyone gave the Nasties the fright of their lives. I was very proud. The Air Vice-Marshal came along and congratulated the Flight on their good show. It really was, as the majority were all new and inexperienced. Two of the boys were shot

down, but without damage to one, and only scalp and head wounds to the other, so I reckon it was pretty good going.[26]

A connoisseur of good food and good wine who smoked a pipe and enjoyed a good cigar. 'You can tell Uncle Archie that I shall be looking for that box of cigars', he added in his letter to his mother. As well as enjoying the good things in life, McKellar took fierce pride in his appearance. Always he was immaculate. No matter what happened, he shaved and groomed himself every morning during the Battle of Britain, even when many fighter pilots went unshaved for two or three days. He insisted on those he led following his example. 'If I have to die, I want to die clean,' he remarked to his colleague, Squadron Leader 'Bunny' Currant.

McKellar's success here showed how he had established himself as a Flight Commander at 605. His CO, Wing Commander Churchill paid tribute to how well the Scotsman worked with his fellow Flight Commander Gerry Edge, telling of 'the most charming triangular friendship I have ever known,' adding 'I used to think that I was a good Flight Commander, but those two boys were marvellous. They used to conspire together to think up new ideas for the squadron and to make things easy for me.'[27]

Also in action over Tyneside was 607 (County of Durham) Squadron. It would also be a fruitful day for them. Five Sections took off from Usworth at 1315. In command that day was Flt Lt Francis Blackadder, as James Vick was on leave.

They faced around 40-60 He 111s and Do 17s in two Vic formations between 10-12,000 feet at sea eight miles east of the Tyne.

Also leading Red Section, Blackadder gave the shout 'Tally Ho' as the enemy was spotted 5,000ft below over Whitley Bay.

P/O Harry Welford was to single out a He 111. 'I chased a Heinkel and filled the poor devil with lead until first one and then the other engine stopped and I had the sadistic satisfaction of seeing the plane go into the sea.'[28]

This was to be his first victory and he celebrated by flying his Hurricane at rooftop height down Newcastle's Northumberland Street on his way back to Usworth.

As 607 Squadron pursued the He 111s down the Durham coastline, Blackadder was to make a claim for a He 111 destroyed off Seaham Harbour. P/O Dudley Craig claimed two He 111s, pursuing one for some sixty miles out to sea before problems with oil pressure forced him to turn back. Sgt Burnell-Phillips claimed a further two He 111s destroyed.

The Squadron diary stated that the tally for the squadron was: six He 111s and two Do 17s destroyed; five He 111s and one Do 17 as probable's; four He 111s and one Do 17 with no losses.[29]

For John McGrath of 601 Squadron it was to be a spectacular day – but would be a climax to his part in the battle.

After destroying a Do 17 and an Me 109 and damaging a Ju 88 on the 14th, he was scrambled in the late afternoon on 15 August, and destroyed a Ju 88 and damaged another. Immediately after attacking this aircraft, he himself was shot down over Selsey Bill by an Me 109 (which he incorrectly claimed to be a 'He 113'). He suffered severe head injuries from which he nearly died. In consequence he spent most of the next six months in hospital. The same day he was awarded the DFC, for victories over Dunkirk. His citation read: 'In May, 1940, during a patrol over Arras, P/O McGrath destroyed a Messerschmitt 109. A few days later, near Dunkirk, he shot down a Messerschmitt 110. Since then, he has destroyed a further three enemy aircraft and possibly another seven. He has displayed great courage and determination.'[30] John McGrath's total tally since the beginning of the Battle of Britain would come to 15 victories.[31]

That day F/O Gordon 'Mouse' Cleaver also succumbed to enemy fire. After education at Harrow School, Cleaver worked for the family firms. His father was a partner in Robinson and Cleaver's, a large store in Belfast and another business in the Province was the Royal Irish Linen Warehouse which manufactured aviation and nursing clothing. He had a love of skiing – which he shared with many other 601 'Legionnaires' such as Billy Fiske, Roger Bushell and Max Aitken. He joined 601 Squadron, in 1937 alongside these friends from the ski slopes and was commissioned that April.

He'd had many victories since then. On the 27 May, he claimed two Me 110s destroyed over the Dunkirk area. A Ju 87 destroyed and a probable He 111 on 11 July, and an Me 109 destroyed on the 26th. On 11 August an Me 109 and an Me 110 probably destroyed and an Me 110 probably destroyed on the 13th.[32]

Two days later he was shot down in combat over Winchester. When his hood was shattered by enemy fire, Cleaver's eyes were filled with perspex splinters. Almost sightless, he managed to bale out and landed outside Southampton and was taken to hospital in Salisbury. He would not fly again, being now blind in the right eye and with seriously reduced vision in the left eye. Cleaver was awarded the DFC on 13 September and his citation recognised the courage he showed. 'Flying Officer Cleaver has now destroyed seven enemy aircraft and possibly another two. In August, 1940, whilst his base was being subjected to intense bombing, he led his- section with great determination and courage and after destroying one of the attacking aircraft he was severely wounded in both eyes. Despite this, he refused to abandon his aircraft and effected a successful landing. He has displayed great determination and devotion to duty.'

Following the war, Cleaver had further operations on his eyes and it was noticed that the perspex fragments which remained from his shattered cockpit hood lay dormant in them without ill-effect. This discovery led to the use of similar material to replace natural lenses affected by cataracts with the first operation taking place in 1949.[33]

On this day, the 601 Squadron diary recorded that they had destroyed eight enemy aircraft, three probably destroyed and three more damaged.

Meanwhile, at Leconfield, 616 Squadron were finally seeing some combat. Hugh Dundas recalled they were impatient with the lack of action and yearned to join the fight that was happening further south. The convoy patrols continued day in, day out, with little sign of enemy activity. 'For a month we had been reading and hearing of the fierce actions fought daily over the Channel by the squadrons of 11 and 10 Groups.' His brother John had been involved in several fights from Middle Wallop, 'I heard that his personal score was mounting and I was desperately anxious to emulate his success'. Their wait came to an end on 15 August.

The day looked like being a particularly quiet and at noon they were stood down from 'readiness' and the whole squadron was put on thirty minutes' standby. They were all having lunch together in the officers' mess, 'no doubt' he recalled 'grumbling about the inactive role we were playing compared with squadrons in the south, when the tannoy crackled into life: "616 Squadron scramble – 616 Squadron scramble all aircraft."' His immediate reaction was 'That was ridiculous! The controller must have taken leave of his senses. It was quite unheard of to be ordered to scramble while having lunch at thirty minutes' notice'. The voice over the tannoy continued to repeat the order 'in tones of urgency and excitement'. All was suddenly frantic. 'A telephone rang and someone rushed into the dining-room shouting at us to get down to our dispersal point immediately. We downed tools, ran from the mess and jumped into the first available cars'. As they tore round the perimeter track they saw the groundcrew running to the waiting Spitfires. 'Outside the dispersal hut Corporal Durham, the usually phlegmatic operations clerk from South Yorkshire, was jumping up and down, waving his arms'. He shouted in his broad Yorkshire accent with 'the usual epithets thrown in' instructing them to take off at once. Action was coming to Leconfield at last.

They sprinted to their Spitfires and took off in twos and threes. They were ordered to fly out to sea at top speed and intercept many bandits approaching the coast south of Flamborough Head.

He set a course and rammed the throttle 'through the gate', to get the maximum power output, 'permissible for only a very limited time'. Some of the others were ahead of him, some behind. 'We did not bother to wait for each other or try to form up into flights and sections. We raced individually across the coast and out to sea. About 15 miles east of Bridlington I saw them, to the left front, and slightly below – the thin, pencil shapes of German twin-engined bombers, flying in a loose, straggling, scattered formation towards the coast'.

Switching on his reflector sight, he set the range for 25 yards and turned the gun button to the 'fire' position. 'Wheeling down in a diving turn, I curved towards the nearest bomber, judging my rate of turn and dive to bring me in astern'. What he described as 'a light' flashed from the rear of the aircraft. It was the rear-gunner firing and tracer bullets 'nosed lazily past'. He opened up with his eight Brownings and the firing stopped. The bomber turned and lost height. 'First a gush of black smoke, then a steady stream poured back from its engine cowlings and it fell steeply towards the calm summer sea'.

Turning to look for a second target he saw other Spitfires fastening on to the German planes on all sides. 'Beneath me a damaged bomber turned back out to sea and I decided to go in and finish it off. It was a foolish decision made in the heat of the moment, for I should have looked for an undamaged plane still making for the coast'. By the time he'd caught up with it and knocked it down he was several miles further out to sea. 'The sky was empty and I judged that my ammunition was nearly exhausted. Hot and elated I set course back to base' He touched down only twenty-five minutes after taking off and the rest of the squadron aircraft were straggling in, singly or in pairs. 'Everyone seemed to have fired his guns', he said.

The squadron claimed eight enemy aircraft destroyed – four probably destroyed and two damaged of which he claimed one and a half. None of their aircraft were damaged and only a small number of the enemy penetrated inland.[34]

On 16 August, the Luftwaffe mounted another big push with attacks over Kent and the Thames Estuary, Sussex and Hampshire, and between Harwich and the Isle of Wight. The strongest German activity was directed against Fighter Command.

That day, Tangmere came under heavy attack. Taking off from there at 1225, Raymond Davis of 601 Squadron led Yellow Section on patrol and climbed to 20,000 feet. Detling told them there were bandits coming in from the south. They saw the Ju 87s at about 10,000 feet but could see no escort so dived to attack. Just then the first Stuka dived for Tangmere. By the time they reached them four had delivered their attack on the airfield and were heading south. He recalled 'I chased with one Ju 87 and gave several bursts'. He had crippled the dive-bomber but its end would not seem so violent as others were. 'He went down under control and landed near Bognor, crashing through some trees and hedges'. He observed though, 'No one got out'. He himself came under heavy, 'fairly accurate' fire from the Ju 87 and his aircraft was hit in the radiator so he returned to Tangmere and landed at 1305.[35]

He would have landed just as another wave of dive-bombers attacked the airfield, because before 1300, the CO of 602 Squadron led them off at the sight of Ju 87s bombing the beleaguered base. From nearby Westhampnett they could hear the din of diving Stukas, explosions and gunfire. Among those who took off was 'B' Flight commander, Flt Lt Findlay Boyd. Like Davis, Boyd flying Spitfire N3227 would see another unusual victory, but his was more bizarre. He just about to retract his undercarriage when he saw a Ju 87 streak in front of him. It was pulling out of its dive after dropping its load. Boyd pressed the trigger and fired a short burst and saw the enemy aircraft crash into the ground. He banked sharply, made a half-circuit of the airfield and landed to rearm at 1309. It had been a lively few minutes containing with what must have been the swiftest victory of the Battle of Britain.[36]

It was a sobering moment for Boyd. The 602 boss, 'Sandy' Johnstone recalled the rapid victory and Boyd's reaction. 'He'd just taken off…when a Stuka dived right in front of him. He just turned his firing button and blew this aircraft into the ground. It just exploded in front of him. That was his first big action. He was so shaken, he just continued to circuit and landed back at Westhampnett'. He remembered too the frantic battle they joined to defend Tangmere that day. 'The rest of us had meantime got together as best we could. We were in a tremendous melee of aircraft. We just fired blindly at everything that was nearby. We got a fair bag this day, and amazingly no casualties'.[37]

The Germans had christened the 15 August 'Black Thursday', but although their losses had been heavy that day, Goering persisted with trying to put RAF stations out of action.[38]

A Staffel of Ju 87s rose from its base in Normandy and set course directly for southern England. Archibald Hope led the waiting patrol of Hurricanes, having taken off at 1645. The Hurricanes were at the north end of the airfield at 20,000 feet, turning to port and ideally positioned to attack the Stukas, below them and to the south, presenting irresistible targets. As Hope dipped his wing he had a fleeting glimpse of a bomb exploding within 50 yards of his parked car near dispersal and felt all the more justified. Almost every Hurricane scored a kill or a 'damaged', and the surviving Stukas were chased out to sea.[39]

On Sunday 18 August 1940 the Luftwaffe launched three major air assaults against targets in southern England. Taking place between lunchtime and teatime, three big Luftwaffe raids were attempted. The targets were the airfields at Kenley, Biggin Hill, Gosport, Ford, Thorney Island, Hornchurch and North Weald, and the radar station at Poling. That day, 602 had been released from operations and it was the first chance for the pilots to rest after five days almost continuously at readiness for 16 hours per day; it was a chance too, for the groundcrews to carry out much-needed maintenance work on the aircraft.

Among those pilots was John Dunlop Urie. Born on 12 October 1915, he came from Glasgow and attended the Kelvinside Academy there, studying science subjects. He was working for his father's company, City Bakeries, when he joined 602 Squadron in June 1935.

He had already shared in the destruction of a He 111 which was laying mines 15 miles east of May Island on 22 December. After being appointed a Flight Commander in April 1940, Urie damaged a Ju 88 on 9 July, 10 miles east of Fifeness.

The day would bring a new intensity in the attacks from the Luftwaffe as it tried its utmost to destroy Fighter Command's airfields flying hundreds of sorties to pound targets across the South-East and South of England. The radar station at Poling would also face this onslaught. The RAF would resist with vigour, but it would be a costly day for both sides.

As 602 rested a raid of Ju 87s and Me 109s had taken off from Caen in France to attack the Poling Radar Station, followed by another Gruppe of Ju 87s bound for Ford.

The pilots had adjourned to their mess sat down with some relish to a pint of beer, recalled Urie. 'I had taken two sips when the telephone went: we were to take off as soon as possible.' The pilots galloped the quarter mile back to their aircraft. But as Urie breathlessly arrived at his Spitfire he found it up on jacks, the wheels being changed. Urie looked round. He was supposed to lead the squadron, he had to have an aircraft. Then his eyes fell on a Spitfire delivered only that morning, so new that its guns had not yet been harmonised with the sight. It would have to do. He grabbed his parachute and helmet, sprinted over to it, strapped in and started up. The Spitfire Mk1s of No. 602 Squadron roared into the air at 1415.[40]

Once airborne Urie found Ju 87s at Ford and tore into them. He had just fired at one Stuka and was pulling out of his attack when there were four loud bangs. He had been hit by an Me 109. He did not take evasive action because of the damage and as a result took more hits.

He returned to Westhampnett with no radio, flaps, brakes and wheels punctured tyres after his Spitfire was severely damaged in combat with Me 109s. His legs were also full of shrapnel, but he managed to pull off a safe landing. The aircraft lasted all of 27 minutes. The squadron lost two aircraft shot down and one damaged.

Flying as Red 3 in Villa Squadron, Sgt Andrew McDowall also took off from Westhampnett at 1415. Red Section was in the vanguard and Red Leader attacked the Ju 87s dive-bombing Ford. McDowall, however, spotted their escorts. 'I saw about 50 Me 109s circling above the Ju 87s in formation of three vics'. He headed for them, but a melee quickly ensued. 'As I climbed to attack these Me 109s four of them attacked me and forced me down to 500 feet, firing at me with cannon'.

The fighters were distinctively marked, he recalled. 'Spinners were painted blue and camouflage much the same as ours.'

McDowall got 'a long burst at one Me 109'. From 1,000 yards, he fired 2000 rounds in this 12 second stern attack and saw the enemy fighter crash into the sea.

After landing back at Westhampnett at about 1445, he reflected on the encounter and realised some limitations of his foe. 'In my opinion, Me 109s cannot beat Spitfires in right-handed turns because they can't turn inside you in stern attacks'. Also he observed that he didn't see any of them fire at him for more than five seconds and believed they have only five seconds worth of ammunition.[41]

Flt Lt Boyd was leading Blue Section and attacked the second formation of Ju 87s – but couldn't get there in time to stop them bombing the airfield but caught them as they left. He recalled: 'I singled out one and did a quarter attack and saw it crash into the sea. I shot at a second one and saw black smoke come out in large quantities from the engine'.[42]

On 18 August Biggin Hill came under fierce attack but 610 Squadron hurtled into the fray to stop the onslaught sending 15 aircraft. They took off to engage about 50 bombers and 50 fighters approaching the airfield from the south.

Sgt Parsons with Red Section attacked a Do 17 from behind putting the rear gunner out of action. He fired at the port engine which stopped running and carried out further quarter attacks, forcing the enemy aircraft down onto a field on Romney Marsh.

Auxiliary NCO pilot, Sgt Horatio Chandler climbed into the fight above Biggin Hill, he saw five Do 215s over Croydon and went on the attack. Firing long bursts at one Dornier, both the bomber's motors caught fire and it crashed five miles south of Croydon.[43]

As the Luftwaffe withdrew and the exhausted RAF pilots returned to their airfields, it became clear 610 Squadron had mounted a heroic defence of its home station. The unit submitted claims against 15 enemy aircraft – ten destroyed, one probably destroyed and four damaged, while suffering just two damaged Spitfires.[44]

That day 501 Squadron was at 15 minutes availability from dawn to 0830 when their aircraft took off for Hawkinge. An engagement took place in the Canterbury area in broken cloud and haze, and 501 became involved 'in a general dogfight'. It heralded a day which became very costly for the squadron.

Later all aircraft were ordered off the ground and were vectored to defend Biggin Hill which was being attacked. P/O Dafforn baled out but was injured. At 1650 seven Hurricanes took off for Hawkinge to patrol and they met a force of 50 enemy bombers and fighters. Red Section attacked and two Me 110s were shot down but Flt Lt Stoney was killed in the melee. Red Section was later ordered to night readiness.[45]

These were desperate times, but not every plane was sent up to fight. Some of 501's aircraft which took off that day were unserviceable fighters that could still make it into the air. They were sent on a 'survival scramble' getting the precious aircraft away from the incoming raiders.

The Hurricanes of 501 Squadron were halfway home from Hawkinge to Gravesend, when their controller vectored them to 'a very big raid coming in, 90, patrol Canterbury, Angels 20.' The

THE HARDEST DAYS, 13 AUGUST – 6 SEPTEMBER

Hurricanes climbed. A German fighter swooped down out of the sun firing at 'Hawkeye' Lee's Hurricane and quickly he felt his aircraft begin to fall apart around him.

> The first thing I knew there was a bang on the back and my leg shot up in the air. A bullet had hit me in the back of the leg. And immediately there was smoke and flames coming out from underneath the main tank.

The last time Lee had baled out was in France when he was almost killed by his own tailplane. This time he rolled the doomed Hurricane on to its back, pushed the stick forward, undid his belt, set his stopwatch, pushed himself out, and jumped. Soon he was in free fall. Lee had heard that the Germans had started shooting pilots escaping by parachute, so had decided he would free-fall for a minute before pulling the ripcord.

Lee tumbled head over heels and managed to glance at his stopwatch to make sure he'd been falling for a minute. The parachute opened and he drifted down, landing in a field near Whitstable. Suddenly, Lee recalled, 'an old chap jumped up from the corn with a military cap on and a gun which apparently he'd captured in Gallipoli himself from the Turks'. Lee's boot was soggy with his own blood. His back had been peppered with fragments of explosive bullet, so his shirt was also bloodstained. It was a hot day, and they were bound for base so he wasn't in uniform. The old man didn't believe him when he said he was British and marched him off at gunpoint. Then some soldiers of the London Irish arrived. Their officer accepted Lee's story, shook him warmly by the hand and took him to the local golf club bar for a refresher.[46]

Lee remembered a most British, bizarre situation: 'There I stood at the bar,' he recorded, 'wearing a Mae West, no jacket, and beginning to leak blood from my torn boot. None of the golfers took any notice of me – after all, I wasn't a member!'[47]

Lee had fallen victim to German fighter ace Gerhard Schöpfel who had a field day at 501's expense. Just before he despatched Lee, Sgt Donald McKay the former part-timer and bank clerk from Pontefract, too was shot down in flames. He managed to bale out but was burned. The fact that Schöpfel had managed to shoot down four Hurricanes in as many minutes sent shock waves through the squadron.[48]

Overall, Flt Lt Stoney and P/O Bland were killed, P/O Kozlowski and Sgts Lee and McKay were wounded and seven Hurricanes were lost in what was a disastrous day for 501.

No. 615 Squadron also had a devastating day as Kenley came under attack. Flt Lt Cromie was killed by a direct hit on the trench in which he was sheltering and LAC Holroyd was hit by shrapnel at the dispersal point and was killed instantly. LAC Tanner was seriously wounded by machine-gun fire. Twelve of their machines were quickly sent up and attacked the bombers and their escorting fighters.

Sqn Ldr Kayll attacked an Me 109 and saw smoke but was not able to see the crash somewhere near Sevenoaks. P/O Young attacked a Do 17 which he saw coming down in smoke just north of Tonbridge.

The overall results were one He 111, two Ju 88s and one Do 17 destroyed; one Me 109 probable; an Me 109, Ju 88, He 111 and Do 17 damaged. But there was a high price.

F/O Locker was in hospital suffering severe shock after landing his burning Hurricane at Croydon. Flt Lt Gaunce suffered burns after baling out from his flaming aircraft near Sevenoaks. Wounded in the legs after being attacked by fighters, P/O Hugo crashed his Hurricane and was in Orpington Hospital. Sgt Walley crashed at Morden Park Golf Course and was killed.

Overall, six of their Hurricanes were lost due to enemy action on the ground and five were written off due to action in the air.[49]

In the course of these and numerous smaller actions that day, 100 German and 136 British aircraft were destroyed or damaged in the air or on the ground. On no other day during the Battle of Britain would

THE HARDEST DAYS, 13 AUGUST – 6 SEPTEMBER

either side suffer a greater number of aircraft put out of action. It would become known as 'The Hardest Day'.

Following that hardest of days, there would be relief for some. For fellow Auxiliaries, No. 616 Squadron, this was the day of their move south. They flew to the Surrey station to relieve 64 Squadron who flew back to Leconfield.[50]

Hugh Dundas recalled, 616's move from Leconfield to Kenley was eagerly awaited, and the pre-war part-timers bade a hearty farewell to their Yorkshire home. It would be the beginning of a new era for the squadron and the grim reality of the battle raging in the south would soon hit them.

> Joy and jubilation marked our last hours at Leconfield. We did not know that they were also to be the last hours in which the squadron would exist in its old carefree form. Most of the original auxiliary pilots were still there – Teddy St Aubyn, leading the festivities in the mess at lunchtime; George April; Jack Bell, Ken Holden, Dick Hellyer, 'Buck' Casson, John Brewster – we had come through together from the earliest days of 616 Squadron and it never occurred to us that we should not continue together indefinitely. And so, we drank a little more than usual at lunchtime and went down to the airfield afterwards in a hilarious mood, eager to take off for Kenley and glory.

Their euphoria was soon dampened. 'When we landed at our new airfield our spirits were quickly subdued. Kenley had been heavily and successfully blitzed the day before. Much of the station lay in ruins. Wreckage of aircraft and motor transport spattered the periphery of the field. Newly filled craters dotted the landing ground'.

After the devastating attacks and losses that day, it was clear to Dundas the strain 615 Squadron and all at the station were feeling. He remembered the atmosphere in the officers' mess as 'taut and heavily overlaid with weariness. The station operations staff and the pilots of 615 Squadron, showed signs of strain in their faces and behaviour'. Dundas remembered vividly an outburst which confirmed the stress Kenley was under. 'The fierce rage of the station commander when a ferry pilot overshot the runway while landing a precious replacement Spitfire was frightening to behold'. Their arrival coincided with a couple of days' break in the battle and he recalled they sat at readiness throughout the long daylight hours from early morning to late evening.[51]

No. 601 were too given some rest. On 19 August, in exchange for No. 17 Squadron, 601 was withdrawn from the southern battle skies to Debden, just north of the inner ring of fighter stations' around London. F/S Harnden had reason to be proud of his auxiliary groundcrew while looking after the Hurricanes of No. 17 Squadron: 'When they came to us the pilots didn't seem to have any idea about getting away in less than two minutes and were absolutely amazed at the efficiency and enthusiasm of my lads, which was certainly a compliment from a regular squadron'.[52]

Four days earlier Churchill had visited the Fighter Command Ops room at Uxbridge. There in the circular gallery of Fighter Command's Ops Room he watched in silence as the WAAFs below him charted an approaching raid. Besides him, Air Chief Marshal Dowding, General Hastings (later Lord) Ismay, and Lord Beaverbrook, grave-faced in a crinkled blue serge suit, were silent, too. Ismay saw Churchill utterly absorbed in the scene before him.[53]

The wall display-panel showed Dowding's squadrons landing to refuel and waves of German raiders receding towards the coast. Barely saying a word, Churchill left the gallery, head bent in thought, shoulders squared, moving at speed. On the way back to Chequers, Ismay went to say something, but Churchill, cut him short, 'Don't speak to me, I have never been so moved.'

After a few minutes' silence, Churchill leant forward, his voice shaking with emotion, and said: 'Never in the field of human conflict was so much owed by so many to so few.' Ismay recalled 'At that, the words burned into my brain and I repeated them when I got home to my wife'.[54]

On the 20 August, those words formed a key part of a speech Churchill delivered to the House of Commons on the progress of the battle.

> The gratitude of every home in our Island, in our Empire, and indeed throughout the world, except in the abodes of the guilty, goes out to the British airmen who, undaunted by odds, unwearied in their constant challenge and mortal danger, are turning the tide of the world war by their prowess and by their devotion. Never in the field of human conflict was so much owed by so many to so few.

He added: 'All hearts go out to the fighter pilots, whose brilliant actions we see with our own eyes day after day'. Just as those words were burned into Ismay's brain – so they were for the nation from that day and have remained as potent since.[55]

The 22nd August was to be a day of surprises for 616 and Hugh Dundas.

After making little contact with the enemy, the early evening of 22 August, saw him and the pilots of 616 Squadron at Kenley looking forward to a night out.

'We were put on thirty minutes' notice and told that a little later we would be released until dawn next day'. The pilots had planned a night out in the West End of London and in the officers' mess they changed into their best uniforms. But their plans were dashed. 'No sooner were we ready to go than the Tannoy called us back to readiness. Cursing our luck, we drove round the perimeter track to dispersal, lugged our parachutes out to our planes, put on Mae West life jackets over our tidy tunics and awaited developments'. But as they waited they discovered there was to be no scramble. 'It turned out that the reason for our recall was a surprise visit to the station by the Prime Minister, Winston Churchill.' 'That', he admitted 'at least, made the sudden and enforced change in our evening plans seem worthwhile'. A procession of cars drove round the perimeter track and stopped outside their hut, where they lined up to meet the PM. But there was to be a further surprise. 'Just a few seconds after I had shaken hands with Churchill, Corporal Durham appeared on stage to produce one of his more spectacular performances. Racing out of the hut, he shouted to us to scramble'. Dundas recalled thinking as they sprinted out to their Spitfires and streamed down the runway in 'the fastest take-off of the squadron's history' that the whole performance had clearly been laid on for the Prime Minister's benefit. The evening's events soon took a turn for the worse. 'Unfortunately it was in that unexpected frame of mind that I flew along, "tail-end Charlie" in our formation of twelve'. They levelled out 12,000 feet above Dover and his mind was still on the night-out. 'I was still wondering whether there might yet be time to get into the fleshpots of London when the cannon shells from that unseen Messerschmitt ripped home and sent me spinning on my first face-to-face meeting with death.'

Violent explosions which shook his fighter were 'so unexpected, so shattering, their effect on my Spitfire so devastating, that I thought I had been hit by our own heavy ack-ack'. Thick and hot, white smoke filled the cockpit, and he could see nothing. He was pressed against the side of the cockpit by centrifugal force and knowing his aircraft was spinning 'panic and terror consumed me, and I thought, "Christ, this is the end."' Quickly, some rational thought returned. 'Then I thought, "Get out, you bloody fool; open the hood and get out." With both hands he tugged the handle where the hood locked on to the top of the windscreen. 'It moved back an inch, then jammed. Smoke poured out through the gap and I could see again. I could see the earth and the sea and the sky spinning round in tumbled confusion as I cursed and blasphemed and pulled with all my strength to open the imprisoning hood. If I could not get out

I had at all costs to stop the spin'. He pushed the stick hard forward, kicked on full rudder, opened the throttle. All had no effect. 'The earth went spinning on, came spinning up to meet me. Grabbing the hood toggle again, I pulled with all my might, pulled for my life, pulled, at last, with success. I stood up on the seat and pushed the top half of my body out of the cockpit. Pressed hard against the fuselage, half in, half out, I struggled in a nightmare of fear and confusion to drop clear but could not do so'. Somehow, he managed to get back into the cockpit, knowing the ground was very close. He tried again on the other side. 'Up, over – and out. I slithered along the fuselage and felt myself falling free. Seconds after my parachute opened, I saw the Spitfire hit and explode in a field below. A flock of sheep scattered outwards from the cloud of dust and smoke and flame'.

For a few moments all was quiet, but quickly the ground swung up fast and Dundas remembered to bend his knees and roll over and banged the quick release catch of his parachute harness. As he lay under a hedge at the side of a wood, his Spitfire lay burning 200 or 300 yards away. 'My left leg was sticky with blood and my left shoulder, badly dislocated, hurt abominably'.

He soon had company. 'A farmer with an old-fashioned hammer-gun stood over me and I thought his attitude none too friendly. Probably he did not much like having aeroplanes making holes in his fields and frightening his sheep'. Some people in khaki appeared and he was driven away in an army ambulance to the Kent and Canterbury Hospital. Later he discovered that he had been the subjected of an argument between the army Captain and Medical Officer (in khaki) of the Royal Artillery, and a local builder, Home Guard Commander and 'all-round bigwig'. The Home Guard Commander wanted to take him off to have a drink or two 'with his cronies, the former insisted that I was in no condition to be thus paraded and entertained and must be taken straight to hospital'. Fortunately for him the Medical Officer got his way.

The next morning Dundas learned the 'humiliating' truth: that he had been shot down by an Me 109 which he'd not even seen. It was a bracing, if unusual introduction to aerial combat over South-East England.[56]

John Dundas with 609 Squadron, wrote to his brother Hugh with his condolences on being shot down. 'Very sorry to hear that a 109 – or rather twelve of them – inflicted grievous bodily harm on you over Dover two days ago. Mummy sent me a wire yesterday, and you were mentioned as wounded in an 11 Group Intelligence Summary this morning. I haven't heard any details, but I do hope the damage isn't too bad. Write and tell me about it as soon as you're well enough to do so. Anyhow, you'll now get a nice spell of sick leave which I rather envy you.' He and 609 had a narrow escape, he said:

> The 109s nearly made hay with us over the Isle of Wight yesterday. They sent us off too late to do anything about the bombing of Portsmouth and too low to do anything about the myriads of 109s who were hovering around the scene and who, when they saw poor old 609 [Squadron] painfully clambering into the sun, came down on us. The result was that one of our machines was shot to hell, two more damaged and not one of us succeeded in firing a round. I was reduced to the last resort of a harassed pilot – spinning. It was humiliating. But fortunately, we didn't lose any pilots.[57]

On 23 August, although he and his fellow pilots had already celebrated the award Sgt James 'Ginger' Lacey was officially recognised for his extraordinary record built since the Battle of France in May. Awarded the Distinguished Flying Medal, his citation noted: 'He has displayed great determination and coolness in combat and has destroyed six enemy aircraft.' But there would be no rest for the decorated former pharmacist.

THE HARDEST DAYS, 13 AUGUST – 6 SEPTEMBER

Despite the honour the next day he flew eight times. The day's action began at 0935 when the squadron took off from Hawkinge and intercepted a formation of 30 Do 17s and Me 109s. They broke up the formation with many Dorniers jettisoning their bombs and fleeing east. Lacey, flying No. 2, saw his leader attack one of the bombers, and No. 3 in the last section broke right. Lacey attacked it head-on, from below, and saw it go into a dive with smoke coming out of an engine; then an Me 109 opened fire on him, and he had to abandon the bomber to deal with it.

Scrambled again at 1245, this time to the Ramsgate area, they found 50 Ju 88s, which had just bombed Manston with a fighter escort. Lacey saw one of the Ju 88s starting to dive and followed it, opening fire as it pulled up at 4,000 feet. The incendiary rounds from his Brownings struck both the bomber's engines and its rear turret. The upper rear gunner returned fire with a tracer. Suddenly its starboard engine cut out and fire stopped from the upper gunner. As Lacey turned to avoid colliding, the lower gunner opened fire and he moved slightly above but dead astern to avoid his fire and fired again. The pilot baled out and the bomber dived into the sea.

On Lacey's fourth flight of the day, 501 attacked a mixed force of Do 17s, Do 215s, and Me 109s near Graystone. Lacey had just put a burst into a Do 215, when 'there was a streak of vivid colour across his bows', a clang from somewhere in the Hurricane's nose, and he felt the aircraft pitch forward and down as its engine cut. He glided down to Lympne aerodrome and discovered that he had a bullet through the radiator. While fitters and riggers were patching his aircraft, he went to the mess for a quick meal; by the time he had eaten, the aircraft was fit to fly back to Gravesend. That day he had a Do 17 damaged and a Ju 88 destroyed.[58] By the following day, fellow 501 Squadron pilot and former reservist, Robert Dafforn had completed something of a purple patch that month. On 24 August he claimed a Ju 88 destroyed, but before that he claimed a Ju 87 destroyed on 12 August, a Do 17 destroyed and two Ju 87s damaged on the 15 and a Do 17 damaged on the 16th.[59]

No. 616 Squadron, by the 25 August, had suffered a series of heavy blows. Until mid-September Hugh Dundas was a spectator as the Battle of Britain reached its climactic stage in late August and the first weeks of September.

He recalled watching dogfights from the windows and terraces of the hospital he was in outside Canterbury. 'Every day more wounded pilots came in and they brought news from the squadron. And every day, I sat uselessly on the ground'. He heard of friends who had died and others who were wounded. On 25 August, George Moberley came to see him. Although born in Bombay, Moberley was educated at Ampleforth School, Yorkshire. After leaving school he was employed by Ruston & Hornsby, engine manufacturers in Lincoln and joined 609 Squadron in the summer of 1938 but transferred to 616 Squadron when it formed that November, being one of the first two officers to join.

He had been in action that morning, when he shot down an Me 109. George told Dundas how Sergeants Westmoreland and Waring; had been shot down that day. 'Then he talked to me about personal affairs, about his family and property. He told me that he wanted me to have his personal belongings if he were killed. I had a strong feeling that he had a premonition'.

If it was a premonition, it came true the following day when he was shot down in a dogfight south of Dover. He baled out at a very low altitude and his parachute couldn't open properly. He hit the sea close to shore and his body was recovered. In the same action Sgt Ridley was killed and Teddy St Aubyn was shot down and very badly burned. For days his life hung in the balance, and he was in hospital for several months.

The squadron, Dundas recalled, was taking a heavy toll. 'Roy Marples, Bill Walker and Sgt Copeland were also shot down and seriously wounded on that black day for 616 Squadron. Four days later Jack Bell was killed; he was badly shot up in combat and evidently, he himself was grievously wounded, for he tried to force land at West Malling but crashed and burned out on the airfield'.

In just eight days, 616 Squadron lost five pilots killed or missing and five others wounded and in hospital. 'About fifty per cent of the pilots', Dundas calculated, sadly 'who had flown down from Leconfield had gone'. Those left fought bravely on. In this they were inspired says Dundas by the leadership of the CO Denis Gillam. But on 2 September he too was shot down and injured. It was the final, knock-out blow. Without him the squadron was incapable of continuing the fight. And so, Dundas remembered, 'exactly fourteen days after our carefree and confident departure from Leconfield, 616 Squadron – what was left of it – was taken out of the line to re-form at Coltishall, near Norwich'.[60]

On 26 August, 602 Squadron was scrambled at around 1615 to 16,000 feet over Selsey Bill.

Sgt Andrew McDowall was flying as Red 2 and took off from Westhampnett at 1618. They soon encountered an enemy formation of 150 He 111s and Me 109s. He recalled in his combat report, 'I followed Red 1 and attacked [the] outside left He 111 of formation of E/A which had already began to turn south. Adopted full beam attack from sun, 2000 feet above'. The bomber then broke formation and dived towards cloud. McDowall continued 'Attacked again exactly same and saw port engine belch black smoke in clouds. Followed this E/A down through clouds and saw it crash on marshes west of Pagham.[61]

By 27 August, after fruitfully patrolling the east coast of Scotland since the beginning of the war, No. 603 (City of Edinburgh) Squadron moved south. Richard Hillary recalled their journey was not a smooth one and began some days before. 'We spent the night at Turnhouse, collected the two Spitfires and flew back to Montrose. The whole Squadron was moving down to Turnhouse. That was only Edinburgh, but with the German offensive in full swing in the south, it could mean only one thing. In a very few days we should be further south and in it. P/O Noel 'Broody' Benson was hopping up and down like a madman. "Now we'll show the bastards! Jesus, will we show 'em!"'

As they flew to Turnhouse using stones some children had spelt out on the road the words: 'Good Luck'. Hillary recalled as he headed south, he looked back. 'The children stood close together on the grass, their hands raised in silent farewell'.

But their departure was delayed. 'After kicking our heels for two days at Turnhouse, a reaction set in. We were like children with the promise of a trip to the seaside, broken because of rain'. The Duke of Hamilton, the Station Commander offered the squadron a couple of days grouse-shooting on his estate. After a day's shooting Hillary and Colin Pinckney retired early to bed and slept until 0200 when there was a bang at the door. They were handed a telegram, which read: 'SQUADRON MOVING SOUTH STOP CAR WILL FETCH YOU AT EIGHT OCLOCK DENHOLM.'

> For us, the war began that night. At ten o'clock we were back at Turnhouse. The rest of the Squadron were all set to leave; we were to move down to Hornchurch, an aerodrome twelve miles east of London on the Thames Estuary. Twenty-four of us flew south: of those twenty-four, eight were to fly back.

They landed at Hornchurch at about 0700 and were greeted with their 'first shock'. 'Instead of one section there were four Squadrons at readiness'. No. 603 Squadron were already in action and started coming in half an hour after Hilary and the new arrivals had landed. The smoke stains along the leading edges of the wings told that all the guns had been fired. 'They had acquitted themselves well,' he recalled 'although caught at a disadvantage of height'. Climbing down from his fighter, Brian Carbury said: 'You don't have to look for them. You have to look for a way out.'[62]

Based at Westhampnett with 602 was an RAFVR part-timer, Cyril Babbage. Born in the Shropshire market town of Ludlow in 1917, he worked in the family butchers' business after leaving school. He

THE HARDEST DAYS, 13 AUGUST – 6 SEPTEMBER

joined the RAFVR in October 1938 and after completing his training was posted to 602 Squadron.

On the 18 August, Babbage claimed a Ju 87 destroyed. The following day he shared a Ju 88 and on the 25th destroyed a Do 17 and an Me 110 and probably destroying an Me 109 on the 26th. The squadron took off at 1613 to intercept an enemy formation and saw around 150 He 111s, Do 17s and Me 109s approaching from the south. Attacking them at 15,000 feet over Selsey Bill, they split the formation in two, with one part heading south-west and the other south-east. Three He 111s were shot down, with one falling to Sgt Andrew McDowall. The squadron tally also included a Do 17 destroyed but after claiming a probable Me 109, Cyril Babbage was himself shot down, and after baling out, he was picked up by a rowing boat and landed alongside Bognor Pier. He was pictured being taken ashore at Bognor with the pier in the background having a section removed so the enemy could not use it for landing troops.

Discharged from Bognor Hospital two days later, he was driven back to the squadron by the CO, Sqn Ldr Johnstone. Babbage's clothes were still damp from his dip in the English Channel and he borrowed a coat from a hospital porter for the journey.[63]

At Hornchurch conditions were spartan for 603 Squadron, Richard Hillary recalled: 'Half a dozen of us always slept over at the Dispersal Hut to be ready for a surprise enemy attack at dawn. This entailed being up by four-thirty and by five o'clock having our machines warmed up and the oxygen, sights, and ammunition tested. The first Hun attack usually came over about breakfast-time and from then until eight o'clock at night we were almost continuously in the air. We ate when we could, baked beans and bacon and eggs being sent over from the Mess.'

They didn't have to wait long for to see the enemy. On the morning after their arrival they had their first contact. For Hillary it was a portentous moment.

> The voice of the controller came unhurried over the loudspeaker, telling us to take off, and in a few seconds we

> were running for our machines. I climbed into the cockpit of my plane and felt an empty sensation of suspense in the pit of my stomach. For one second time seemed to stand still and I stared blankly in front of me. I knew that that morning I was to kill for the first time. That I might be killed or in any way injured did not occur to me.

They ran into them at 18,000 feet, As Hillary remembered: 'Twenty yellow-nosed Messerschmitt 109s, about 500 feet above us'. As the Germans descended on them the eight Spitfires went into line astern and turned head on to the enemy. 'Brian Carbury, who was leading the Section, dropped the nose of his machine, and I could almost feel the leading Nazi pilot push forward on his stick to bring his guns to bear'. At that moment Carbury hauled hard back on his own control stick and led them over the Germans in a steep climbing turn to the left:

> In two vital seconds they lost their advantage. I saw Brian let go a burst of fire at the leading plane, saw the pilot put his machine into a half roll, and knew that he was mine. Automatically, I kicked the rudder to the left to get him at right angles, turned the gun button to 'Fire,' and let go in a four-second burst with full deflection. He came right through my sights and I saw the tracer from all eight guns thud home. For a second, he seemed to hang motionless; then a jet of red flame shot upwards and he spun out of sight.

For the next few minutes, he was too busy looking after himself to think of anything, but when, they were ordered back to base. Hillary allowed himself to relax slightly and to quickly reflect.

> It had happened. My first emotion was one of satisfaction, satisfaction at a job adequately done, at the final logical conclusion of months of specialized training. And then

I had a feeling of the essential tightness of it all. He was dead and I was alive; it could so easily have been the other way round; and that would somehow have been right too. I realized in that moment just how lucky a fighter pilot is. He has none of the personalized emotions of the soldier, handed a rifle and bayonet and told to charge. He does not even have to share the dangerous emotions of the bomber pilot who night after night must experience that childhood longing for smashing things. The fighter pilot's emotions are those of the duellist-cool, precise, impersonal. He is privileged to kill well. For if one must either kill or be killed, as now one must, it should, I feel, be done with dignity. Death should be given the setting it deserves; it should never be a pettiness; and for the fighter pilot it never can be.[64]

John Dundas wrote to his mother on 29 August, telling her he was happy his brother would have time to recover from his injuries 'So glad to hear that Hughie has got a fairly long leave'. He sounded an optimistic note and told also of 609's success the previous Sunday (25th). 'It almost looks as though – touch wood – August may peter out fairly quietly – only 2 1/2 more days to go now. Our last engagement was on Sunday, when we got in among a gaggle of Me 110 bombers and shot them down in considerable numbers. 609 shot down 13 of them and altogether 15 crashed on land near Warmwell the aerodrome in Dorset which they were trying to bomb and where 609 has spent quite a lot of time on and off. I felt very pleased about it because (a) we lost no one and (b) I was leading that time and managed to bring the chaps in against the leaders of the Jerry formation which broke up the raid completely. It was a most gratifying sight.[65]

On the morning of 30 August over North Foreland, Jim Lacey was in a similar fight – now with 30 or 40 Me 110s. He put two long bursts into one of them, saw it stagger into the low haze with smoke emerging from one engine and reckoned he had a 'probable' at least. No. 501 was soon in the air again, this time with the Controller ordering: 'Vector two-seven-zero. A hundred-plus Bandits approaching Dungeness.'

Flying as Yellow 2, Lacey attacked head-on the Me 110 which was leading a formation and opened fire at 400 yards. His combat report describes the engagement:

> Collision was imminent. So, I broke underneath and when I pulled up I saw that the Me 110 had left the formation and was going east with smoke coming from its port engine. Climbing, I found a He 111 just ahead, also going east, rather slowly, as though it had been damaged. I attacked, opened fire at 250 yards, and saw the undercarriage drop and the port engine catch fire. As I closed, long flames and thick black smoke made vision difficult. I had to break off, as I was attacked by several 110s. I continued fighting until I had no ammunition left.[66]

As the tally of this former reservist continued to grow, the conduct of others was recognised. The awards given that day gave a snapshot of the quality and scale of contribution by those pre-war part-time flyers. Among those awarded the DFC was Archie McKellar of 605 Squadron.

An auxiliary pilot of No. 615 Squadron, F/O Anthony Eyre, was awarded the DFC on this day too. After joining 615 Squadron in 1938, Eyre was deployed to France with the squadron in November 1939. He had destroyed two Me 109s on 19 May, and claimed an Me 109 destroyed and an Me 110 damaged on 11 June. On the 22nd he claimed an Me 110 destroyed and three damaged, and on 20 July an Me 109 destroyed and another damaged.[67]

His success continued in August and he claimed a Ju 87 destroyed on 14 August and then on the 15th he shared an Me 109. On the 20th he claimed a Do 17 destroyed, on the 26th an Me 109 and a Ju 88

THE HARDEST DAYS, 13 AUGUST – 6 SEPTEMBER

destroyed and an Me 109 probably destroyed, and on the 28th a Do 17 destroyed, an Me 109 probably destroyed and another damaged.

His citation told how 'This officer has shot down seven enemy aircraft, and inflicted damage on several others' praising his 'great coolness and presence of mind' and stating 'he has at all times shown great devotion to duty'.

Flt Lt Edward Smith of 610 Squadron also received the DFC. His citation lauded an officer who had 'led his flight with great success'; it highlighted Smith was the only member of his section to return from a patrol on 11 August and the next day, he was involved in an attack by twelve or more Messerschmitt 109. His aircraft was hit by two shells, damage being inflicted near the cockpit and petrol tanks. The squadron diary explained: 'His aircraft eventually caught fire and, although he himself was enveloped in flames, he successfully abandoned his aircraft and was rescued about eight miles out to sea. Flt Lt Smith has now destroyed six enemy aircraft. He has displayed great courage and leadership'.

One of 601 Squadron's most successful pilots, F/O Raymond Davis was also honoured that day. He was singled out as having 'personally destroyed six enemy aircraft, and severely damaged several others. He has shown great keenness and courage'.

On 3 September Richard Hillary became an ace but also looked death in the eye. Vectored to the Kent coast off Margate in Spitfire X4277, the patrol, led by Sqn Ldr 'Uncle' George Denholm, had been warned there were around 50 fighters. The Germans came straight at them 'like a swarm of locusts'. Quickly there was 'a blur of twisting machines and tracer bullets'. An Me 109 went down in a sheet of flame to his right, and a Spitfire hurtled past in a half-roll while Hillary weaved and turned to gain height. Then he caught sight of something.

'Just below me and to my left, I saw what I had been praying for – a Messerschmitt climbing and away from the sun'. He closed in to 200 yards, and from slightly to one side gave him a two-second burst: 'Fabric ripped off the wing and black smoke poured from the engine'. But the Me

109 didn't go down. 'Like a fool, I did not break away but put in another three-second burst. Red flames shot upwards, and he spiralled out of sight'. But there was no chance to even feel elated. 'At that moment, I felt a terrific explosion which knocked the control stick from my hand, and the whole machine quivered like a stricken animal. In a second, the cockpit was a mass of flames'. He tried to open the hood, but it wouldn't move. 'I tore off my straps and managed to force it back; but this took time, and when I dropped back into the seat and reached for the stick in an effort to turn the plane on its back, the heat was so intense that I could feel myself going. I remember a second of sharp agony, remember thinking "So this is it!" and putting both hands to my eyes. Then I passed out'.

When he came round, he was falling through the air. He pulled his rip cord and his parachute opened, slowing his rapid fall with a jerk. Falling into the sea with his parachute still attached, he tried to release it but his hands were badly burned with his skin in shreds. Floating on his back he assessed the situation. He was a long way from land and thought it unlikely anyone had seen him. The water felt colder and colder, even against his burnt skin. He looked down at his hands and realised he could not see them. He'd gone blind. The realisation then struck him that he was going to die. 'The manner of my approaching death appalled and horrified me, but the actual vision of death left me unafraid. I decided that it should be in a few minutes. I had no qualms about hastening my end'. Reaching up, he managed to unscrew the valve of his Mae West. 'The air escaped in a rush and my head went under water'. He reflected that 'it was said by people who have all but died in the sea that drowning is a pleasant death'. But he would not sink. He was so enmeshed in his parachute that he couldn't move. He lay back exhausted and started to laugh.

Sometime after, he remembered 'as in a dream' hearing somebody shout. Soon arms hauled him onto a boat and a brandy flask was pushed between his swollen lips. It was the Margate lifeboat. People had seen him come down and a search had been launched. Wrongly directed, they were about to give up when one of them saw his parachute.[68]

THE HARDEST DAYS, 13 AUGUST – 6 SEPTEMBER

To have some respite, 601 Squadron was to move to Exeter on 7 September, but the day before, the squadron fought one of its fiercest battles with 50 German fighters over Essex. Two 601 pilots were wounded and baled out and three others had to force-land. Two were killed. One was Raymond Davis, who was shot down by an Me 109 over Tunbridge Wells. Having only been awarded the DFC on 30 August, he crashed into a garden and the local man who first reached his body wrote to his wife, Ann, (the sister of Archibald Hope) to reassure her that Davis had not suffered. An ex-military man, he felt compelled to reassure them and wrote:

> I hope you will not mind receiving this letter from a stranger, one who saw the air battle in which your husband gave his life on Friday morning last, his plane falling in a cottage garden within a hundred yards of this house.
>
> I am able to tell you that he died in the air instantaneously as a result of two bullets through the brain, his machine afterwards breaking in two and falling.
>
> I was the first to enter the cottage garden and saw him sitting in his place, with his feet on the rudder bar and the belt still fastened round his waist, clearly showing that he had not moved again after being attacked. I placed a covering over him.

In order to be certain, Hubbard visited the hospital two days later, where he found Davis lying 'with a bunch of roses on his breast', and with the matron, he examined the fallen pilot's head and she agreed with him that death had indeed, been instantaneous.

> As a fighter of the last war, I pay homage to a fighter of today, and while I know that nothing I may say can be of any real comfort to you, I do ask you to think of him as soaring into the sky, on that glorious sunny morning, with a smile on

his lips and a song in his heart, to do battle for this England of ours, and then making the Supreme Sacrifice.

Eric W. Hubbard[69]

Flt Lt Carl Raymond Davis, DFC, had achieved nine victories and was one of the highest scoring former reservists of the Battle of Britain.

Flt Lt William Rhodes-Moorehouse, also with nine 'kills', had only six days earlier been awarded the DFC. Then he was accompanied by his wife Amalia, who was still grieving from the loss of her brother Dick Demetriadi. 'Willie' had been a mainstay of the squadron; the one who always paid the bills, who was in the Hurricane flight escorting Churchill to Paris, who was always there.

Both he and Davis were pre-war 'Legionnaires' and since the Borkum raid they had thrown themselves into every stage of the squadron's war effort with the same verve as they had into the peacetime mischief. He took off on patrol at 0850 and he too was shot down over Tunbridge Wells. The loss of these two was a searing blow for the 'Millionaires'.[70]

Fighter Command was battered but still fighting. As August drew to a close, the Luftwaffe stepped up its attacks, particularly on RAF airfields. The raids came over in such numbers that Operations Room controllers had trouble determining which deserved priority from the limited resources they had. The end of August, however, brought a promise of new beginnings for 604 Squadron. Flying the Blenheim Mk1 in the night-fighter role, like 600 Squadron, their Battle of Britain had been a very different affair to the squadrons equipped with the Hurricane and Spitfire, flying mostly in daylight. On 31 August, Flight Lieutenant Cunningham and Sergeant Rawnsley took with an unnamed operator off to work on what was variously called 'the Black Box' or 'the Gubbins'. This was an early version of 'Air Interception radar'. They were unsuccessful that night, but 604 and Cunningham, alongside their Auxiliary sister-squadron, No. 600 would soon become masters of this cutting edge technology.

THE HARDEST DAYS, 13 AUGUST – 6 SEPTEMBER

In the two weeks from 24 August to 6 September, British defences came close to collapse. The stress of combat encounters again and again through the day, every day from first light to nightfall drove Fighter Command's pilots to exhaustion. Air Chief Marshal Sir Hugh Dowding later wrote:

> A fresh squadron coming into an active Sector would generally bring with them sixteen aircraft and about twenty trained pilots. They would normally fight until they were no longer capable of putting more than nine aircraft into the air, and then they had to be relieved. This process occupied different periods according to the luck and the skill of the unit.
>
> The normal period was a month to six weeks, but some units had to be replaced after a week or ten days. By the beginning of September, the incidence of casualties became so serious that a fresh squadron would become depleted and exhausted before any of the resting and reforming squadrons was ready to take its place. Fighter pilots could still not be turned out by the training units in sufficient numbers to fill the widening gaps in the fighting ranks. Transfers were made from the Fleet Air Arm and from the Bomber and Coastal Commands but these pilots naturally needed a short flying course on Hurricanes and Spitfires and some instruction in formation flying, fighter tactics and interception procedure.[71]

Amid the growing losses, on 26 August, Churchill confided with the War Cabinet the gravity of the situation that faced them and how uncertain he was about the threat yet to come.

> The air battle now proceeding over Great Britain may be a decisive event in the war and must dominate all

other considerations. We cannot tell what new form the enemy's attack may take; nor what our losses will be; nor what damage will be done to our factories both of output and repair. We do not know with any certainty the size of the air force which the enemy may bring against us. It is certainly very much larger than our own.[72]

Just four days later, Churchill's blood would have run cold were he able to read the order issued from the Commander-in-Chief of the German army. Intended for the preparation of Operation *Sealion*, it read 'The Supreme Commander has ordered the services to make preparations for a landing in force in England. The aim of this attack is to eliminate the Mother Country as a base: for continuing the war against Germany.' The proposed method was: 'The Luftwaffe will destroy the British Air Force and armament production which supports it, and it will achieve air superiority. The navy will provide mine-free corridors and supported by the Luftwaffe will bar the flanks of the crossing sector'.[73]

Would September bring invasion? Would it bring further battering by the never-ending patrols, dogfights and losses? Would there be any relief?

BEGINNING OF THE BLITZ, 7 SEPTEMBER – 2 OCTOBER

6

Large-scale day and night attacks against London.

As well as the increased pressure on Fighter Command from the ceaseless attacks on their airfields, the Luftwaffe was also honing its tactics and mounting an ever-greater threat, as Dowding observed:

> When the Germans found that our fighters could deliver well-timed attacks on their bombers before the fighters could intervene or when our fighters attacked from above or below each move was met by a counter move on the part of the Germans so that in September fighter escorts were flying inside the bomber formations, others were below and a series of fighters stretched upwards to 30,000 feet or more. One squadron leader described his impression of the appearance of one of these raids. He said it was like looking up the escalator at Piccadilly Circus.[1]

On 7 September, after a fortnight of successfully attacking important RAF sector stations in the south-east, the Luftwaffe suddenly changed their tactics. That Saturday afternoon was, as the novelist William Sansom recalled: 'one of the fairest days of the century, a day of clear warm air and high blue skies'. Under that high blue sky 348 German bombers and more than 600 Messerschmitt fighters set off from northern France for England. Goering, who had arrived the day before in his personal train to take direct command of the mission, watched from the cliffs of Cap Gris Nez as his waves of his aircraft formed up over the Channel. At 1614, the first of them were over the English coast. Would this large bomber stream soon disperse to attack the usual targets – airfields, sector stations, and the like?

But as it flew west over Kent and Sussex the fleet remained intact, forming a block 20 miles wide, heading for London.

Fighters provided close escort support for the bombers and the sheer size of the German force meant many of the raids were successful in hitting targets in the capital. The Germans laid waste to large areas of the London docks, Woolwich Arsenal, Beckton gasworks, West Ham power station and the oil storage tanks at Thameshaven. A second wave caused more carnage in the densely populated streets of the East End. The fires from the burning buildings were perfect markers for the bombers which continued to come after dark fell. In raids through that dreadful night, the bombers would drop 337 tons of bombs on the capital, killing 448 Londoners.

The attack signalled a change in Hitler's strategy, away from attacking the Britain's fighters and their airfields and towards her cities. It would later become clear that 7 September was a day of miraculous release; although of course it didn't seem like it at the time. The German switch to attacking cities relieved pressure on Fighter Command and allowed some recovery from the losses they had experienced through August.

As Dowding later wrote: 'I could hardly believe the Germans would have made such a mistake ... it was a supernatural intervention ... [7 September] was really the crucial day.'[2]

AVM Keith Park, AOC 11 Group, would also recognise the importance of that day:

> On Saturday, September 7th, the enemy first turned to the heavy attack of London by day – perhaps because his timetable called for it, or because his Intelligence Staff were persuaded (on the example of Poland) that

our fighter defence was sufficiently weakened by the previous month's attacks. This change of bombing plan saved No. 11 Group Sector Stations from becoming inoperative and enabled them to carry on operations, though at a much lower standard of efficiency.[3]

Over the coming days and weeks, the impact of those raids on Fighter Command were clear too further down the chain. CO of 602 Squadron, Sqn Ldr 'Sandy' Johnstone, recalled his guilt on recognising the reprieve the bombing of London brought them. 'It's a terrible thing to say but it was an immense relief when we realised that they weren't coming for airfields again. They were going for London. I thought "sorry about this London" but it was the thing that saved us. By taking it, London gave the fighter chaps a chance to recover.'[4]

Relief or not – Fighter Command's effort continued unabated to stop the Luftwaffe attacks, wherever the target was. Having arrived at Croydon from Drem on 7 September, 605 were in action the following day. Flt Lts Edge and McKellar led attacks on large formations between Maidstone and Tunbridge Wells. They succeeded in turning the formation and it fled without dropping its bombs. The next day was quiet until 1700 when Archie McKellar flying Hurricane P3308 was at the vanguard of a 605 Squadron sortie against bombers bound for London and turned them back in the most spectacular way. The squadron diary told how it was a beautiful sunny day, and all was quiet until just before 1700 when 18 Hurricanes from the squadron took off from Croydon and ordered to Maidstone at 15,000 feet.

No. 605 Squadron was led by 'A' Flight (Red Section) at 10,000 feet followed by 'B' Flight in echelon stepped up to act as their escort. Near Farnborough, Kent, and approaching from the south-east a large enemy formation was observed, the squadron diary explained, headed west consisting of 17 He 111s flying in three Vics of five Sections, line astern, and two stragglers at 20,000 feet, with about 20 Me 110s slightly above and behind them and a large formation of about 50 Me

109s and He 113s [*sic*] weaving at 25,000 feet to 30,000 feet some four to six miles east of bombers.

As they climbed to attack the bombers the rear He 111 released two streams of red vapour, 'presumably as a signal for the fighter escort attack', for two Me 109s followed by another six Me 109s dived down on Yellow Section, which forced them to take evasive action and lose sight of the bombers. Some more Me 109s dived down on 'B' Flight which attack they evaded and carried on parallel to the bombers, preparing for a beam attack.

Then three more Me 109s fired upon 'B' Flight, Blue 1 (McKellar) destroyed the leader with a two second burst with a quarter head-on attack, the leader diving down in flames south of Croydon. 'B' Flight then recovered their parallel course to the bombers trying to get into position for a beam attack. As the flight was able to attack, the He 111s turned into them and McKellar ordered head on attacks.

McKellar with Blue 2 (Sgt Budzinski) protecting him from Me 109s who were diving down to attack, then opened fire from a slight dive at about 700 yards on the leader of the formation. Smoke and flames quickly issued from each wing. McKellar then fired on the leader's left-hand machine, and almost at the same moment the leading Heinkel exploded, a wing flew off the left-hand machine and the right-hand bomber rolled over on to its back and dived down in flames. In these frantic few seconds – all three were destroyed. The Paisley man shot down three He 111s with a single burst.

McKellar later said that it seemed the explosion of the leading Heinkel (which was near to the right-hand machine) must have caused the destruction of the right-hand machine as he had not fired at it. In this explosive encounter, McKellar used only 1,200 rounds of ammunition.[5]

The squadron diary added, 'By constant attack the enemy formation was broken up and prevented from attacking London'.

On 8 September 607 Squadron departed Usworth and flew south to Tangmere to take over from 43 Squadron. They were greeted with

BEGINNING OF THE BLITZ, 7 SEPTEMBER – 2 OCTOBER

scenes of a battered airfield and a battle-weary squadron. P/O Harry Welford recalled 'We arrived at a completely blitzed aerodrome and were greeted by the remains of 43 Squadron, some with crutches, others with their arms in slings and yet another with his head swathed in bandages, having had his face torn by an exploding cannon shell'.[6]

As if they needed any more proof of how close they were to the heart of the battle, soon after landing they were scrambled to patrol Shoreham at 15,000 feet.

The next day a big raid was directed against south London and its suburbs. The Durham squadron was scrambled, but it was to prove a costly encounter.

Attacking the bomber force over Mayfield, they were badly bounced by Me 109s, escorting the mixed bomber formation of around 60-70 Ju 88s and Do 17s flying north at around 15,000ft.

Sqn Ldr James Vick, leading the squadron, ordered Blue section to attack the bombers from underneath, the Hurricanes still in a climb, with Green section to protect the rear. The fighter escort had been seen above, and Red and Yellow sections climbed into the attack already at a disadvantage. The Me 109s, flying at around 19,000ft, on both sides and the rear of the bombers, saw them coming and pounced on them making 607 Squadron pay for their mistake.

During the ensuing dogfights P/O Drake flying Hurricane was shot down and killed along with P/O Parnell and P/O Lenahan, whilst Sergeants Lansdell, Spyer and Burnell-Philips were wounded.[7]

Welford recalled, 'We were well and truly bounced by Me 109s on that day: we lost six out of 12 aircraft; amongst these were my best friends Stuart Parnall and Scotty Lenahan and, as no more was heard of young George Drake, his death was presumed. We were shocked, we just could not take it all in. No one talked about it but we all hoped for news on George from some hospital or pub. No news came so we held back our sorrow. It was "You heard about Stuart and Scotty, rotten luck wasn't it?" and someone would add "…and young George Drake, bloody good blokes all of them."[8]

To replace pilots lost, transferred or exhausted, there was a steady stream of newly-trained aircrew. The boss of 602 (City of Glasgow) Squadron, 'Sandy' Johnstone recalled their youth and inexperience. 'The "veterans", if you could call them that – I was only 23 – could concentrate on fighting. The younger chaps had two battles to fight. They were fighting the Germans, and they had to battle to concentrate on simply handling their aircraft. It made them much more vulnerable to the enemy. We did our best for them. You tried to pair off an experienced chap with a newcomer. But one by one the experienced chaps were promoted to other squadrons or got shot out of the skies themselves. Newcomers sometimes were only there a couple of days.'

Some, he recalled, really stood out. 'There was a young sergeant named Sprague, a very serious lad. He was good. I knew he was good. I always took the new ones up before they went into battle to make sure they could at least fly the aeroplane'.[9]

Although newly posted, Mervyn Sprague was a pre-war reservist. From Richmond in Surrey, after leaving St Paul's School he worked in his father's accountancy firm but joined the RAF 'F' Reserve in May 1935 and in May 1938 he joined the RAFVR as a trainee pilot. After completing his training on the Spitfire, he joined 602 Squadron at Drem on 18 June. On 11 September, 602, was ordered on patrol with 213 Squadron. They encountered between 20-30 Dorniers and a further twenty Me 110s. No. 602 engaged the 110s south of Selsey Bill and Sprague was shot down and killed. His body was washed ashore almost a month later and he was buried at Tangmere. That April he had married Mary Cumming[10] and she would visit the airfield at Westhampnett after he was posted missing, gazing at the 'B' Flight huts waiting in vain for him to return.[11]

Amid this increased pressure, there was continued disagreement on tactics in Fighter Command. Caught in the tussle was 611 Squadron which was part of 12 Group's Duxford Wing. Led by Douglas Bader, it pitted his 'Big Wing' theory that large wings of many squadrons

BEGINNING OF THE BLITZ, 7 SEPTEMBER – 2 OCTOBER

flying together were more effective than smaller units fighting separately. The counterview, supported by Dowding and Park in particular, held that those smaller units were more agile and more quickly deployable to face an ever-changing threat.

On 11 September, 611 Squadron joined the Duxford Wing in taking on a vast German formation heading towards the capital.

They had left Digby at 0645 for satellite airfield Fowlmere and were despatched from there at 1530, going into position as a second squadron in the Wing formation. Ordered to patrol in southerly direction towards the Thames Estuary, the Spitfires of 611 formed up in three sections of four aircraft in lines astern. Then they saw them. The squadron diary told how '100 plus enemy aircraft were seen coming north towards the formation.' Consisting of 30 Do 215s and 'a number of He 111s at 18,000 feet', there was also 'a mass of Me 109s' stepped up at 20,00 feet and many more behind them at 24,000 feet. As reported by Dowding, this view was 'like looking up the escalator at Piccadilly Circus'. Pilots reported then that it was impossible to keep formation and that a general melee ensued. F/S Sadler – Yellow 4 – got separated from his section and attacked an Me 110, giving two long bursts, closing from 500 yards to 100 yards and using nearly all of his ammunition. The fuselage was seen to catch fire and the Me 110 was last seen losing height. It was noted by returning pilots that Me 110s were painted dark in colour and Me 109s were yellow from 'nose to cockpit'. The squadron landed at Duxford at 1620 to refuel and rearm.

The total claimed for 611 in the action was an Me 110 and Ju 88 destroyed and a He 111, one Me 110 and one Me 109 probable, which was off-set against considerable damage to Sgt Levenson's Spitfire while Sgt Shepherd was missing.[12]

We first met Barrie Heath of 611 Squadron in the skies over Dunkirk on 2 June. Flying in Spitfire IIa P7883 'Grahame Heath', which had been donated by his father G.F. Heath in memory of his son Grahame, Barrie's brother, he was reprimanded by the CO, Sqn Ldr

James McComb, for damaging his Spitfire on landing. Heath is said to have replied: 'this is my Spit and I'll fly it any bloody way I like'.[13]

He and his fellow pilots sometimes faced criticism of the 'Big Wing' tactic.

> People in 11 Group told us. 'We don't know what you buggers are doing in those great big balbos [large formations]. You'd do a damn sight better if you did some real fighting instead of going round in a huge formation being nothing but a bloody nuisance.' Normally, my response was 'Balls' or words to that effect.

Differences over the Big Wing remained pronounced and bitter and relations between 11 and 12 Group Commanders continued to be strained.[14]

As London suffered further raids from the Luftwaffe, like the one 611 confronted, nowhere was safe from attack. Amid low cloud and rain, 13 September saw 'Ginger' Lacey take off from Kenley in 501 Squadron's second patrol of the morning.

He had just returned from leave and volunteered to take off in search of a reported lone enemy raider. He spotted a He 111. 'I saw it, slipping through the cloud tops, half in and half out of cloud, making for the coast. I didn't know where I was, because I hadn't seen the ground since taking off. I dived down on him and got in one quick burst which killed his rear gunner. I knew he was dead, because I could see him lying over the edge of the rear cockpit'. The Heinkel dived into cloud, and as Lacey came up behind him, he throttled hard back and dropped into formation on him, in cloud.

> He turned, in cloud, two or three times, still making a generally south-easterly direction, and I'm quite certain he thought he had lost me or that I'd stayed above the cloud. Actually, I was slightly below and to one side.

You couldn't see very well, in cloud, through the front windscreen of a Hurricane, but you could see through the side quarter-panel and I was staying just close enough to keep him in sight through this. I stayed with him in all his turns. He made one complete circle and then carried on south-easterly.

Eventually the Heinkel eased its way up to the top and broke cloud, 'presumably to see I was still hanging around', Lacey recalled. 'Just as he broke cloud and I was dropping back into a position where I could open fire, the dead gunner was pulled away from his guns and another member of the crew opened up on me, at a range of, literally, feet. I remember a gaping hole appearing in the bottom of the cockpit'.

The entire radiator had been shot away, and he knew it was just a matter of time before the engine would seize, so he put his finger on the trigger and kept it there until his guns stopped firing. 'By that time he had both his engines on fire and I was blazing quite merrily too. I think it was a glycol fire rather than an oil fire, but what was burning didn't particularly interest me – I knew that I was burning and I was going to have to get out'. As soon as the guns ran out of ammunition, by which time the Heinkel was diving steeply through the cloud, he baled out. 'I came out of cloud in time to see my aircraft dive into the ground and explode. While drifting down, I saw various people running across the fields to where it had crashed. There was one man passing almost underneath me, when I was about 500 feet up, so I shouted. This chap stopped and looked in all directions, so I shouted again. "Right above you!". He looked up and I saw that he was Home Guard'. As he saw Lacey he raised his double-barrelled shotgun and took aim.[15]

Lacey eventually convinced the gun-toting LDV not to shoot after he led forth some 'Anglo-Saxon' expletives. When he got back to Kenley, he was told that the Heinkel he'd just shot down had bombed Buckingham Palace.[16]

On the same day, Archie McKellar received a DFC for actions off the north-east coast on 15 August.[17]

The 15 September was described by the 605 diarist as 'a beautiful sunny day'. But against that perfect blue sky ranged what he also described as 'enormous enemy bomber and fighter formations' which crossed the coast towards London morning and afternoon.

Just a week after their switch to big raids on London, the Germans chose this day to launch another massive assault, which they believed would crush Fighter Command and allow *Sealion* to proceed. But following the attacks of 7 September, Britain's defences had recovered, fighter production continued and operational pilot strength was the highest it had been since the start of the Battle of Britain.

The German offensive came in two waves, giving British aircraft time to refuel and rearm. Also, the usual diversionary manoeuvres were not employed so the British were able to deploy as many as 17 squadrons – in good positions – to meet the threat.

In the morning the fight took place around Croydon aerodrome and, it saw 605 Squadron doing well. Flt Lt Currant destroyed two Do 17s and damaged another, Sergeant Wright and Sgt Howes each destroying another. And Archie McKellar struck again, destroying two Me 109s.

In the afternoon three waves of enemy bombers and fighters approached from the south-east the first escorted by Me 109s and the second and third unescorted. Most of 605's attacks were upon the first formation around Maidstone. Again, the squadron tasted success. McKellar, was back in business, destroying a Do 17 and probably destroying a He 111. Flt Lt Currant destroying an Me 109, damaged two Do 17s and a He 111. Although he destroyed a Do 17, P/O Cooper-Slipper had a remarkable escape. His control was shot away and his aircraft hit a Do 17 amidships. His aircraft, minus port wing spiralled down, and he baled out landing unhurt other than small bruises near Marden. He returned to Croydon later in the

BEGINNING OF THE BLITZ, 7 SEPTEMBER – 2 OCTOBER

evening, apparently unshaken, with two German life jackets and a complete rubber boat, given to him by Maidstone police. The diary told of 'a very noisy night from AA fire and bombs whistling around. Two bombs landed within 200 yards of our sleeping quarters, neither yet exploded'.

Not content with his day's work, at 2310, McKellar took off for a night patrol with Sergeant Howes in bright moonlight and damaged, if not destroyed a He 111.[18]

We last met Ray Holmes when he got into trouble for low-flying over his native Wirral. Since then, he had completed his flying training and joined 504 (County of Nottingham) Squadron. They had moved to Hendon on 5 September from Catterick.

The squadron adopted the 'William Tell Overture' as their 'scramble' song as it happened to be playing when they were alerted once, and it was played thereafter whenever a scramble was called.

On the morning of Sunday, 15 September, Holmes' flight was brought to readiness at dawn. On this clear, bright day the conduct and actions of this former reservist would encapsulate the characterise the battle's pathos, heroism, verve and derring-do and its impact on ordinary people. Feeling scruffy after sitting at dispersal, Ray Holmes decided to have a bath.

Meanwhile, the squadron had some unusual visitors that morning. An American General and an Admiral came to the station and with them was a film crew aiming to capture 'the life of a fighter squadron'.

While Holmes lay in his bath, radar stations on the south coast registered contacts over the Dover Strait, and soon a formation of bombers with a heavy fighter escort appeared on their screens.

Within minutes, there was banging at the bathroom door. There was a flap on, and the squadron was called to readiness. It was 1100. Holmes leapt out of the bath and hurriedly pulled on his flying kit and barefoot ran out to the waiting Humber truck, the sound of the William Tell Overture filling the air as he clambered on.

Pulling his socks over still damp feet, the truck tore around the perimeter track to dispersal and the waiting Hurricanes.

Holmes collected his Mae West and flying boots from the dispersal hut and ran out to his machine – Hurricane P2725. Groundcrew had already started the Merlin engine and put the parachute harness in position. He settled into the cockpit and rammed his flying helmet over his still wet hair.

The 12 Hurricanes – six of 'A' Flight and six of 'B' Flight were away by 1120. One of the Americans watching the scramble took out his stopwatch when the call came and was impressed to note they were away in 4 minutes 50 seconds.

Ordered to patrol around North Weald at 15,000 feet, they joined with 257 Squadron. Then they were ordered to climb to 17,000 feet and were given a course to steer to the south-east to intercept a raid of 30-plus Dornier bombers heading for London. Holmes' position was guarding the rear of the formation and as he was flying into the sun, could see very little ahead. Then the call came from the CO, Sqn Ldr John Sample: 'Tally Ho!' – they had been spotted.

It was at moments like this that Holmes looked to his leader, Sample. The pre-war auxiliary was a flight commander in France before Dunkirk, and he inspired confidence.

We first met him in May when he was with 607 in France. Deployed to France with the squadron in November 1939, he was awarded the DFC and had become CO of 504 Squadron at Wick at the end of May on his return to Britain.

Sample turned, allowing the bombers to pass ahead of him and led the squadron into a quarter attack. One after another the Hurricanes chose their targets until Holmes, bringing up the rear, finally chose his. As he fired a burst he saw a blaze of return fire. Breaking, he dived away he frantically searched around an empty sky for the target. Then he spotted a tight formation of three Do 17s. He opened the throttle and overtook them on the port side. Opening fire at 400 yards his canopy was enveloped in black. Was it smoke or oil? 'Then', he recalled 'the windscreen cleared'. Suddenly the Dornier loomed large in front of him. 'I suddenly found myself going straight into his tail. So, I stuck my stick forward and went under him, practically grazing my head on his belly.'

Holmes had put both its engines out of action, which was why the Dornier had slowed down so suddenly. It began to glide downwards. Holmes opened fire on the second Dornier and saw a tongue of flame shooting out. Then he saw someone trying to escape from the stricken bomber. A white canopy appeared. He recalled 'Before I knew what had happened this bloody parachute was draped over my starboard wing. There was this poor devil on his parachute hanging straight out behind me... All I could do was swing the aeroplane left and then right to try to get rid of this man. Fortunately, his parachute slid off my wing and down he went.'

The third Dornier was on fire and heading for central London near Buckingham Palace. Holmes felt he must stop him. Oil was seeping over his windscreen but now from the inside. His Hurricane too had been hit. His engine was running rough, and the rev-counter started to surge. Time was running out. He had to avoid the Dornier's return fire and the only way to do that was a head-on attack. He overtook the lone bomber and turned to make his frontal attack. Hurtling straight at it he pressed the fire button. Nothing came out. He had run out of ammunition. There was only one thing for it. In that moment it became clear what he must do. His fighter was crippled, but his foe had to be stopped. He decided to ram. 'His aeroplane looked so flimsy, I didn't think of it as solid and substantial. I just went on and hit it for six.'

Now sweating, he aimed his port wing at the nearest side of the Dornier's twin tail. There was a slight shudder as his wing hit it and sliced through the tail section which fell away. It had worked. But after thinking he had survived unscathed; his Hurricane began to dive. He tried to pull back on the stick, but nothing happened. He picked up speed and plunged vertically down. He had to get out. He pulled back the hood and unfastened his safety harness. Trying to climb out he realised he was still connected by his radio lead. He unplugged it but his parachute became snared on something in the cockpit. With his eyes closed against the onrushing air and biting cold, he kicked against the control column. The doomed Hurricane did him one last favour and lurched into a spin and he was catapulted out into the air. Flying backwards, as if in final salute, the Hurricane's tail fin struck his shoulder. Hurtling downwards, he grasped desperately for the 'D' ring to open his parachute. His right arm, paralysed by the strike on the fighter's tail couldn't pull it. He guided the limp hand by the wrist with his left hand and tugged his arm across his body. The canopy exploded above him.

As he plunged down, he looked up and saw the Dornier spinning too, earthwards minus its tail. It landed on Victoria Station, with the tail section hitting a rooftop in the Vauxhall Bridge Road.

Unbeknown to Holmes, the aerial drama had been watched by crowds of Londoners. Pointing excitedly up, they watched as the Hurricane, parachute and Dornier fell out of the sky.

Holmes drifted down and approached electric cables over railway lines near Victoria Station. Missing these, he landed on the roof of some flats on Ebury Bridge Road. Having had his boots torn off when his parachute opened, he slid in his stockinged feet down the steeply raked tiles and dropped down onto the road. Two young women watched him from the neighbouring garden. In the euphoria of survival, he leapt over the fence and kissed them both. 'I hope you don't mind,' he said 'I'm so pleased to see you'. Inside the flats he telephoned his squadron to tell them where he was.

A Home Guard Sergeant appeared at the flats and invited Holmes to come and see his Hurricane, now lying in crater at a nearby crossroads. A crowd had gathered where the Hurricane had crashed, and they cheered as Holmes approached and patted him on the back. He collected a souvenir – part of a nameplate from the engine. A reporter appeared, and as a fellow journalist, Holmes told him about his job before the war when he had joined the RAFVR as a part-timer. Holmes asked the reporter to send a message for him to his father – also a reporter for the Press Association. 'Tell Dad I'm okay, will you?', he asked. He then went to the Orange Brewery on Pimlico Road for a medicinal drink.

He was then taken to nearby Chelsea Barracks where he was examined by an army doctor. They sent for a taxi to take Holmes back to Hendon but before leaving he was told there was a lady at the gate who wanted to speak to him. 'Was it you that came down in that plane?' she asked. He replied it was. She held out a tin of 50 cigarettes. 'Will you take these as a present?' she asked. The gift was generous. 'No, I couldn't possibly', he replied. 'Please do' she answered. 'My baby was outside in his pram. They're for making your plane miss my baby.' Holmes was so touched by her gesture, he didn't say that he'd been unaware of her or her baby from 17,000 feet, nor did he have the heart to tell her he didn't smoke.[19]

There is some controversy, however, as to whether Ray actually intended to hit the Dornier, indeed in his combat report, he made no mention of deliberately ramming the bomber. But whether intentional or not, his heroic action, and incredible survival, are one of the iconic actions of the Battle of Britain which took place on that pivotal day.

In what was a remarkable day for No. 504 Squadron, Now Flt Lt William Royce damaged a Do 17 while F/O Michael Rook shared in the destruction of another Do 17. 'Mickey' Rook was born in Edwalton, Nottinghamshire and attended Oakham School and Uppingham School from 1929 to 1933. Rook joined 504 Squadron in 1938 and following the outbreak of war completed his training, arriving at 6 OTU Sutton Bridge in April 1940 and converted to Hurricanes. He then rejoined 504 Squadron in France and returned to England with it that May. He was to make three claims during the Battle of Britain, including a Me 110 destroyed and probably a second on the 27 September and on 6 October he shared a Me 109. He was promoted to command the squadron in March 1941.

More remarkably still, both these Auxiliary flyers had brothers in the same squadron. Williams's brother, Michael 'Scruffy' Royce, flying Hurricane L1913 on 15 September, was hit over London but was able to returned to Hendon. 'Mickey' Rook's brother Anthony joined 504 in early 1937. He claimed a Me 110 destroyed and shared another on 27 September.

What Holmes didn't know was that the Do 17 had already been attacked, by another auxiliary squadron, No. 609.[20] The Observer and Gunner had both been killed and the aircraft was abandoned by the pilot and the remaining members of his crew. Although claimed by a number of pilots – it was credited to Canadian 609 Squadron pilot Keith Ogilvie. John Dundas wrote in the 609 Squadron diary, 'One portion of this Dornier is reported to have reached the ground just outside a Pimlico public house to the great comfort and joy of the patrons'. The diary credited Ogilvie with destroying it, adding '(with two other pilots)'. Any joy at this success was tainted when it was confirmed that Pilot Officer Geoffrey Gaunt, one of the pre-war part-timers had been killed in the action.[21] Gaunt, Dundas added, 'was a good pilot...but even more as a man is his loss deeply regretted'.

The death of his old school friend affected David Crook deeply. He later wrote 'For me it was the biggest loss that I ever experienced. I could not believe that such a vital spark was now extinguished for ever and that I would never see him again.'

He added, 'We had known each other all our lives and been at school together for about twelve years, and after that we were in the same squadron'.

He remembered the 'grand times we have had together...those glorious summer days we spent rock climbing on Scafell and Doe Crag, or sailing unskilfully but with endless amusement in the dinghy on Windermere'.

Uncannily, Crook had spoke to Gaunt just a week or two before about a worry he had about his friend. 'I said to him one evening that if anything were to happen to him, I should feel rather responsible because he was an only son, and I had persuaded him to join the RAF with me'.

Gaunt would have none of it. 'He replied that he would always be grateful to me for my persuasion, because the year that he had spent in the RAF since the beginning of the war had been the best year of his life and he wouldn't have gone into the Army for anything and missed all this glorious fun'.[22]

No. 501 joined the battle over Heathfield, at 1400. Lacey, flying Red 3, said in his combat report that they intercepted a raid flying north-west at 16,000 feet. He attacked from slightly below, head-on, throttling back to 150mph so that the approaching speed would not be too great. He opened fire, himself, at 400 yards, pulling his Hurricane's nose up as his target approached until he went over from vertical and stalled into a right-hand spin. By the time he had regained control and climbed to 17,000 feet there were no other aircraft in sight. Calling Red Leader, he was told to meet them at 15,000 feet just north of Brighton. Lacey recalled. 'After the squadron had been split up, and I was trying to rejoin, I was, as usual, showing a lot more interest in where I'd been than in where I was going; because the danger always came from behind. I kept looking over my shoulder to make certain there was nothing coming in behind me. As I brought my head round from one shoulder to look over the other I saw that I was doing what amounted to a head-on attack on twelve yellow-nosed 109s. My immediate reaction was to push the stick forward and dive to hell out of it.' Instead he destroyed one and severely damaged another, but was set on by their ten companions: 'The others were thoroughly annoyed about the whole business and this time I did have to dive out of it.'

The third hostile wave of the day was at the coast soon after 1900. That evening the air over the south-east filled with aircraft. At about 2000 Jim Lacey shot down two more of the enemy – an Me 109 and a He 111.[23]

The day had seen momentous struggles again in the skies over the south-east, but this time the outcome was clear. German bomber formations were smashed, making accurate bombing impossible. Although bombs were dropped on London, Portland and Southampton, little damage was done. Some of the fighting in the skies was visible from the ground and the dogfights between the RAF and the Luftwaffe – like Ray Holmes' epic tussle above central London – were closely followed during the battle.

The Germans suffered their highest losses since 18 August. It was obvious to both sides that German tactics had failed, and the Luftwaffe had not gained the air supremacy they needed for *Sealion* to be launched. Of course, this did not mean the end of the battle – far from it. But the 15 September was seen as an overwhelming and decisive defeat for the Luftwaffe. For this reason, this date is celebrated in the United Kingdom as Battle of Britain Day.

Thus, by mid-September 1940, it was clear to senior German leaders that the Luftwaffe's campaign to break the RAF to allow Operation *Sealion* (*Unternehmen Seelöwe*) had not yet been successful. Colonel General Franz Halder, head of the Army General Staff, wrote in his diary on 14 September recording Hitler's assessment of the 'Problem of Britain' at a conference held that afternoon. 'A successful landing followed by occupation would [end] the war in short order' Hitler had said, and saw the invasion of Britain as 'essential'. Despite this, he asserted that the 'execution *[of Operation* Sealion] is not tied to any particular date' but it was recognised that 'enemy fighter forces have not yet been completely eliminated' and therefore 'the prerequisites for Operation *Sealion* have not yet been completely realised'. At this conference the next target date for *Seelöwe* was set for 27 September. However, if the invasion was to be mounted on this date, then forces were to be alerted 10 days before, on 17 September.

When 17 September arrived it was decided not to proceed, the operation being postponed 'until further notice'.[24]

While part of the Duxford Wing, 611 Squadron also operated from their home county in Lancashire and frequently tackled raiders striking the docks at Liverpool. On 21 September, P/O D.A. Adams

BEGINNING OF THE BLITZ, 7 SEPTEMBER – 2 OCTOBER

flying Spitfire P7923 out of Ringway sighted a Dornier 215, which weaved desperately to escape the attentions of his Spitfire. Its manoeuvres were in vain, and Adams shot it down near Hoylake. The Wirral town was not far from where local reservist Ray Holmes had had his low-flying incident at the start of the war. Genteel Hoylake with its golf course was a world away from the destructive raids visited on Liverpool and towns in the North-West and whose suffering had grown in the previous weeks – just as it had in the south.[25] A couple of days later, the squadron received its first honour when Flt Lt William Johnson Leather was awarded the DFC. His citation read, 'This officer has conducted many convoy patrols under very adverse weather conditions. Many times, when the weather has been unfit for a section he has flown alone in an effort to engage the enemy. On one occasion he shot down a Junkers 88 a hundred miles out to sea. Over Dunkirk he destroyed a Messerschmitt 109 and in September 1940, he shot down two Dornier 215s. Flight Lieutenant Leather has led his flight, and frequently his squadron, with skill and courage'. Commissioned on 14 May 1936, he was the first Auxiliary officer of 611 Squadron and the first to be awarded his wings with the squadron at Speke.[26]

On 24 September, Flt Lt Findlay Boyd was awarded the DFC. His citation told how he had: 'led his flight into action on all possible occasions and by his initiative and accurate shooting has personally destroyed nine enemy aircraft. He has displayed cool judgment and a keen desire to engage the enemy irrespective of the odds against him'.

Two days later Boyd was to score two victories which highlighted his innate skill as a fighter pilot.

In his combat report, he told how he was Blue 1 and took off from Westhampnett at 1603 and was confronted by a swarm of attackers.

> I saw 30/40 enemy bombers approaching Southampton from SW at 15,000 feet. I then asked control if I should

attack bombers as I saw no enemy fighters there, but was ordered to continue patrol to engage fighters. I attacked about 12 Me 109s 2,000 feet below and a dog fight ensued. I selected the first Me 109 of a bunch of four in line astern, attacked quarter out of sun, and knocked large pieces off. Black smoke came out of engine cowling. I last saw this enemy aircraft diving almost vertically and believe that this was destroyed. I was then attacked myself and broke off vertically downwards to 10,000 feet. I then saw another Me 109 apparently alone about 13,000 feet heading south. I climbed into stern position and attacked dead astern from 30 degrees below. I broke off to right then turned to see what had happened and saw E/A upside down and saw pilot fall out; did not see parachute. I was then attacked by another Me 109 and fought back, eventually getting into quarter astern. Attack delivered in turn and again got large trail of thick black smoke out of underside of engine. I then climbed back to 25,000 feet over the Needles and seeing nothing more to engage and oxygen having run out, I returned to base and landed.[27]

In total he expended just 460 rounds and fired for 3, one-second bursts, close-up at no more than 150 yards. For that measured and modest outlay, he despatched one Me 109 destroyed and scored another probable.

No. 602 Squadron's historian, Wg Cdr Hector Maclean, lauded Boyd's skill as a fighter pilot and that, 'Like Baron Richthofen and Mick Mannock, the two aces of the Great War who ran up the highest score of victories for their respective sides, Findlay regarded a fighter aeroplane as a gun platform. In the air, Findlay tended to wait for his opportunity. Then he would move in with rapid and devastating effect'.[28]

BEGINNING OF THE BLITZ, 7 SEPTEMBER – 2 OCTOBER

Another 602 Squadron pilot who was honing his deadly craft was Sgt Andrew McDowall, and the 30 September was to be a memorable one for him when he destroyed at least two enemy bombers. Although he had flown on two sorties already that day, it was late afternoon before he embarked on an intense and violent encounter. His section was ordered to patrol over Selsey Bill and flew to three miles east of Bembridge where they found a formation of 12 Ju 88s at 11,000 feet. He had become an ace on 11 September when he destroyed an Me 110 near Selsey Bill and his stalking of a luckless foe on this afternoon showed his skill and confidence as a fighter pilot. 'I was Green 1 and took off from Westhampnett at 1547. I was the last Spitfire to attack because I waited to see if any Me 109s were present. I picked out a straggler on port side and tail end of enemy formation, and went into cloud and flew (overtaking) till I could see shadow of E/A above me, then came out on tail of E/A 50 yards behind, throttling as I did so. Opened fire while actually flying slower than E/A. Saw this E/A break into pieces in air and dive into sea 7 miles from Selsey Bill'. Another Ju 88 would not make it home and would add to the Galloway NCO pilot's tally. 'After watching my first E/A crash into the sea, I climbed up again and saw a second Ju 88 appear out of the cloud with one engine stopped and the propeller feathered. E/A saw me, when about 500 yards off and tried to climb back into the cloud. I fired at the one motor which was still working and stopped it. E/A then stalled and dived straight into the sea.' As well as these two Ju 88s, there is mention of a 'probable' Ju 88 as well. The diary told how the squadron destroyed four Ju 88s, had two probables and one damaged. It had been a successful afternoon.[29]

P/O Peter Burnell-Phillips came to be a reservist in a most circular way. Born in Richmond, Surry, he joined the RAF on a short service commission in February 1936. On completion of his training, he was posted first to 54 Squadron and then to 65 Squadron. But after flying low over Crowborough for a bet, he was obliged to resign his commission in February 1939. Undaunted, he joined the RAFVR in April, and was called up that October, now as a Sergeant and posted to 607 Squadron. He saw his first action during the Luftwaffe's attacks from Norway on the north-east of England on 15 August, and subsequently during September when the unit moved south. On 9 September, his Hurricane, P2912, was hit and he was wounded in the ankle, force-landing at Knockholt when the damaged engine seized. On 26 September, he forced a Do 17 to crash into the sea by making mock attacks after his ammunition had been exhausted. The afternoon of the same day, his squadron engaged large formations of German aircraft bound for Southampton, heading for the aircraft factories at Woolston. The Hurricanes of 607 Squadron were among those scrambled.

The squadron diary described how combats took place over the Isle of Wight and Portsmouth, at sea, 6-12 miles south of the Needles between 1550 and 1630. Two Sections and one Flight took off at different times and eventually joined up as a Squadron with Flt Lt Blackadder leading. They were vectored to Southampton where AA fire drew their attention to the presence of enemy aircraft. About 50 to 60 enemy aircraft in all, possibly Do 17s or Me 110s, were seen at 12,000-15,000 feet, flying in mass formation slightly below and to the right of the Hurricanes. Enemy aircraft were diving down on the various targets in and around Southampton. The Squadron went into sections line astern and made a head-on diving attack, which developed into a beam quarter attack. Afterwards the Squadron broke up and carried out a number of individual attacks on two separate enemy formations, one going out to sea and another coming inland. Each formation consisted or 40 bombers accompanied by fighters, positioned above and behind'. Their own losses were recorded as F/O Bowen baled out but returned to base from Kaylthorpe, on the Isle of Wight. Enemy losses were one Do 215 and one Me 109 destroyed in sea and one Ju 88 damaged.

Flight Lieutenant Francis Blackadder recalled, 'We were ordered to Southampton. Just as we reached it the Hun was diving down to bomb the Supermarine works. We came down on top of them in a head-on attack, some say right through the balloons, the Hun disappeared to the south towards Portsmouth and we were split up'. adding, 'Sergeant Cunnington and I spied another large formation of bombers up to meet'. They had fighter escort and they carried out a beam attack.[30] Burnell-Phillips was awarded a DFM on 1 November, and was commissioned again during the month.[31]

The groundcrews of 602 Squadron exemplified the hard work and commitment of the mechanics and fitters who kept the aircraft in the air through the summer and autumn of 1940.

When the fighters were on the ground, they were not just out of combat, they were vulnerable to attack. The quicker they could be turned around, the quicker they could fight the enemy and be back in their natural element – the sky. Much depended upon how rapidly this servicing could be done.

The chronicler of 602 Squadron, F.G. Nancarrow, declared that:

> The Glasgow crews were past-masters at the art. A Spitfire would come roaring into the tarmac, and almost before the air-screw had stopped turning, a group of lads in blue overalls would be clambering over it like an army of ants. As the pilot jumped out and puffed a welcome cigarette while telling his story to an Intelligence officer, the servicing team would set about their individual jobs in the shortest space of time. It was teamwork to perfection.
>
> The mobile petrol wagon would swing into line and, like the tentacles of an octopus, the multi-pipe lines sprouting from the tank would be clamped into the fuel inlets. And as the spirit was pumped at high pressure into the bowels of the fighter, others of the team would be hauling out ammunition boxes from the wing sections and refilling with yards of bullet-laden belt. So it went on for four or five hectic minutes, re-fuelling, re-armouring,

checking guns, oil levels, and a dozen-and-one other odds and ends.³²

LAC Jeff Brereton was a Mechanic/Fitter who joined 605 (County of Warwick) Squadron at the end of the month, and he gave an insight into life as groundcrew at this time.

'The auxiliaries were well-trained and were very proud of their squadron and had a special dispensation that they were allowed to wear the county badge of a bear and a ragged staff in the lapel of their uniforms'.

He recalled there was a groundcrew of two people with each aircraft, a Flight Mechanic–Engine and a Flight Mechanic–Airframe, 'who the pilot relied upon a great deal, particularly in helping him to taxi down the rough ground of the field and through a gap in the fence onto the main airport for take-off'.

It would be clear the aircraft had been in scrapes when they returned. 'Aircraft were often returning with their airframe covered in bullet holes. They would quickly set to work in repairing the damage. 'The ground crew had the job of cutting a piece of canvas to cover the damage and had two tins of quick drying synthetic camouflage paint, which was used to attach the canvas to the aircraft'. There was only one petrol tanker and oil bowser, so it was quite a rush to get the aircraft serviced in time for the next take off. Often the aircraft took off while the paint was still drying, and it was also common to see an airman stretched out across the tail plane helping to keep the rear wheel down on the ground.³³

On the first day of October, two DFCs were gazetted for two prominent Auxiliaries who had led their squadrons through the battle and were steeped in the Auxiliary tradition of volunteer service from before the war.

The end of the month would bring the impressive tally of one 603 Squadron pilot to a close with the Scottish unit. James 'Black' Morton was one of those who had a hand in shooting down the

BEGINNING OF THE BLITZ, 7 SEPTEMBER – 2 OCTOBER

first enemy aircraft over the UK of the war back in mid-October. On 30 September, he destroyed an Me 109, scored a probable 'kill' on another damaged a third one and shared in the destruction of yet another luckless Me 109. Shot down on 5 October he was badly burned and did not return to duty until the following August.[34]

Sqn Ldr Archibald Hope had been 'A' Flight Commander during 601 Squadron's time in France. August had seen frantic activity and on 11 August he claimed two probable Ju 87s; on the 13th two probable Ju 88s and damaged another, on the 15th shared a Ju 88 and damaged another; and on the 16th destroyed an Me 110 and got a probable Ju 87. Promoted to Acting Squadron Leader on 19 August he then took command of the squadron.

Alexander 'Sandy' Johnstone of 602 (City of Glasgow) Squadron had also enjoyed much success since taking part in those first combats over the Firth of Forth in October 1939. Johnstone shot down a He 111 at night on 25 June, shared a probable Ju 88 on 1 July and damaged a Do 17 on the 3rd. He had been commanding 'B' Flight until 12 July but he was promoted to Acting Squadron Leader on the 13th and took command of 602 on the 17th.

He claimed a Ju 88 destroyed on the 19th, an Me 109 and an Me 110 destroyed on the 25th, and a He 111 destroyed and another damaged on the 26th. He shot down an Me 110 on 4 September, got a probable Me 109 and damaged a Ju 88 and a He 111 on 7 September, shared a Do 17 on the 9th, destroyed a Ju 88 and the day before damaging another (on the 30th).[35]

Sandy Johnstone was awarded the DFC on 1 October and his aunt,[36] Mrs Jean Cook, later wrote to her nephew, telling him of the excitement caused by news of his award of the DFC.

> My dearest Sandy,
> You have no idea the excitement you have caused by having your photograph in the papers [when he received the Distinguished Flying Cross]. I am told the villagers

feel a sort of reflected glory. The little boy next door is very disappointed that it is only your head and shoulders that is showing. I believe Jeannie had bought five Bulletins [a Glasgow newspaper which printed the photograph]. Mrs Patterson phoned from Greenock to say how pleased she was about your honour. We are all terribly proud of you. I hear your mother spent a whole day at the phone. I wish you would come north so that we can have a look at you.

With all my love, dear,
Yours, Jean[37]

There would be further honours for 602 Squadron a few days later. On 8 October Sgt Andrew McDowall was awarded the DFM. Throughout September, his tally had steadily grown, with an Me 109 on the 9th, an Me 110 on the 11th, a probable Do 17 on the 15th and a Ju 88 destroyed on the 30th. His citation told how 'This airman has led his section on many occasions and has destroyed at least six enemy aircraft, one of which he destroyed in a brilliant head-on attack at night [in July while still in Scotland]. His capable leadership has contributed largely to the many successes of his section'.[38]

Dowding later reflected that a turning point could be seen by the end of the month. He concluded that this was the most critical stage the Battle of Britain.

> On the 15th September the Germans delivered their maximum effort, when our guns and fighters together accounted for 185 aircraft. Heavy pressure was kept up till the 25th September, but, by the end of the month, it became apparent that the Germans could no longer face the bomber wastage which they had sustained, and the operations entered upon their fourth phase, in which a proportion of enemy fighters themselves acted as bombers.[39]

BEGINNING OF THE BLITZ, 7 SEPTEMBER – 2 OCTOBER

On 2 October, following the mounting losses of vessels that were being caused by RAF Bomber Command's attacks on invasion shipping, Hitler directed that preparations hitherto made for *Sealion* should be 'largely dismantled'. Ten days later it was decided to defer the invasion until spring 1941. Although it continued to figure in German planning until 1942, it had in reality been relegated to the status of a deception operation aimed at pinning down British forces in the UK.[40]

The German strategy had, like their formations, been disrupted, broken up and made less and less effective. But this did not mean the attacks would cease. October would bring further trials as the bombing of London continued. Fighter Command's struggle would also continue – with its pre-war part-timers of the AAF and RAFVR now fewer in number. But now the balance had shifted and those times of dire crisis it seemed had passed, but the dangers Fighter Command faced each day had not.

FIGHTER-BOMBER AUTUMN, 3 – 31 OCTOBER

Smaller scale daylight fighter-bomber attacks while large-scale night attacks continued mainly against London.

This final phase of the Battle of Britain was also saw the continuation of what came to be called the 'Blitz' on the capital and against other cities and towns of Britain and which lasted until May 1941.

As the RAF shot down more and more of the slow and vulnerable bombers, the Luftwaffe changed tactics. Some of the Me 109s the RAF now encountered were equipped for a new kind of mission. At the end of September an instruction was issued to fit some of the fighters with bomb racks. Coming over the coast at high altitude, these high-flying 'Snappers' as they were day called, were difficult to intercept.[1]

On 7 October at Croydon, the day dawned fine and bright. It would be a momentous day among many that autumn for 605 Squadron and Archie McKellar, on 29 September was made Acting CO. On 2 October, a signal was received confirming McKellar's promotion to Squadron Leader and . The next day the squadron was released for the first time since they arrived at Croydon and they celebrated with an 'excellent dinner' at The Greyhound in Croydon. The squadron made three sorties that day. In the first one a patrol lifted off at 0935 and they encountered seven Me 109s over London. One was damaged by McKellar, one by Sergeant Wright and one by P/O Muirhead. The latter was shot down and baled out near Deptford returning two hours later unhurt.[2]

The next patrol, the diarist noted, 'was remarkable for the success of Sqn Ldr McKellar'. A dogfight took place between Westerham and Maidstone during which 'Shrimp' McKellar had the most extraordinary impact.

Scrambled at 1245, McKellar was leading 'Turkey Squadron', following fellow Auxiliaries No. 501 Squadron and was told to patrol around Sevenoaks. Before the enemy was sighted, 605 had to contend with the aggressive attentions of another RAF patrol when several Spitfires came down as if to attack them. 'As they were coming up in a necessarily threatening manner, I broke the Squadron up to do evasive tactics. This flight of Spitfires was most troublesome and I would like to register a strong protest', McKellar later wrote in his report.

Shortly after this Control informed him that there were bandits approaching from the south-east and from the east, and that they were very near them 'at Angels 15 to 25'. The wily McKellar kept his Squadron 'into the sun as much as possible'.

His former boss, Wing Commander Walter Churchill summed up the fine pitch of performance the Scotsman had brought himself and the squadron to. 'Always he was thinking of the squadron, how to improve them and weld them into a finer team. In the end he achieved such a high degree of understanding that he had only to give a flick of his wings and the boys knew at once what he wanted and would automatically take up position'.³ There then is the sense of a leader and fighter pilot at the top of his game. 'Shortly after this I noticed 15 Me 109s at approximately Angels 18 near Biggin Hill, followed by about 50 at various heights'. Battle was then joined when at McKellar's command, Turkey Squadron followed him and dived to attack the swarms of German fighters.

He dived down on the 15 Me 109s at 18,000 feet and after firing saw a bomb being dropped from his target, pieces flew off from its wings and dense white smoke or vapour pour from him and went into 'a most violent outside spin', he recalled, adding, 'This enemy aircraft was seen by Yellow 3 to crash in flames in a field north of the railway between Brasted and Westerham'. In his mirror he could see another Me 109 coming up to attack him. 'I therefore turned sharply to the right and found myself just behind and slightly below an Me 109'. He opened fire and could see his rounds hitting home. 'It burst into flames almost at once and went diving down over the inverted somewhere East of Biggin Hill'.

Perhaps cowed by this bravura display and no doubt at the edge of their endurance, the enemy was beginning to turn tail, but McKellar was not finished with them yet.

> As I again had an Me 109 trying to come on my tail, I spiralled down to about 15,000 feet and by now there appeared to be Me 109s straggling all over the sky heading South East. I followed one, pulled my boost control [giving more fuel and power] and speedily made up on him. I gave him a burst from dead astern and at once his radiator appeared to be hit as dense white vapour came back on me and as I was rather close, my windscreen was all fogged up.

This rapidly cleared and he gave him another burst. The machine erupted into flames and fell into a wood near a quarry west of Maidstone. He then noticed another luckless Me 109 'nipping in and out of clouds'. His evasion failed to hide him from the laser-like vision of McKellar. 'I followed him, still with boost pulled, attacked him from astern and saw his machine catch alight and the pilot bale out'. It crashed near Ashford. By this point he had fired all his ammunition and returned to Croydon at 1410. But 605 did not have it all their own way in this brief but brutal encounter and P/O English was shot down near Westerham and killed.

The attacks were delivered between 1320 and 1340. In just 20 short minutes, McKellar despatched four enemy fighters. Doubtless some of his foes might many years later applaud such a display of consummate and deadly skill in the air. But at that moment all of them were in grave danger as the diminutive Scotsman found his mark again and again.[4]

While McKellar was sending enemy fighters plummeting earthwards – it's fitting that his rival as the highest scoring reservist Ace of the Battle of Britain – Sergeant James 'Ginger' Lacey was one of the pilots of 501 Squadron accompanying 605 Squadron that afternoon. And while Lacey's tally that day didn't match that of McKellar, he did account for one Me 109. 'I was flying as Yellow 2, he recalled, when No. 501 Squadron intercepted two Me 109s at 23,000 feet and attacked them. I saw five Me 109s diving to attack us from behind and turned round behind the rear aircraft, opening fire at 150 yards'. He got in a short burst before he turned out of his sights and saw glycol pouring out from his centre radiator. 'I followed him round the turn and managed to get in a short burst at about 100 yards range…and the enemy aircraft went into a vertical dive turning slowly round to the right. It dived straight into a cloud still revolving slowly and I did not see it again.'[5]

Another former part-timer flying with 501 Squadron that day was Ken Mackenzie. Born in Belfast in 1916, Mackenzie was clearly something of a natural pilot, obtaining his civil 'A' licence as a teenager. He joined the RAFVR in 1939 while studying technical engineering at Queen's University, Belfast. Called up on 19 December, after completing his studies he was posted to 501 Squadron, in September 1940.[6]

The Ulsterman had opened his account three days before when he shared in the destruction of a Ju 88. The next morning McKenzie revealed further enhancements to their guns needed to make them more lethal. It hinted how quickly he was learning from encounters like the previous day's. 'I was still concerned regarding the 303 guns and again tried to get the 'Chiefy' Armourer to reharmonise mine down to a two foot diameter circle at 200 yards, I was convinced that had they been so sighted we could have clobbered that 88 once and for all instead of nibbling at undoubtedly very robust engines with 'buck shot'. The Ju 88 was a notoriously strong aircraft and difficult to shoot down, certainly if not from close range. Though I had got the port engine from about 80 yards, my burst of fire was too short owing to my high closing speed and I should have throttled back to be able to get in a sustained burst, I made a mental note for next time. In discussion, we all agreed that the best way to get an 88 was to clobber the front crew compartment where all the crew were, if one could do so, either head on, or from astern above.

The following day he was scrambled at 1145, he attacked an Me 109 which flew across his path. 'I reefed hard round, nearly blacking out to get a full deflection shot at him from 100 yards' and saw 'strikes visible all over him'. Smoke came from the exhaust, it slowed and began to dive. 'When just off Margate, I followed him at 600 yards down over the sea, closing fast'. He went to 100 yards and gave him a long burst from dead astern. The stricken fighter dived into the sea in a cloud of spray.

There were celebrations that night Ken recalled. 'That evening we betook ourselves to the Greyhound Inn, East Croydon, where the manager was very pro RAF and the steaks were like baby calves'. Their hosts treated them 'right royally' but the hospitality went further than plying them with food and drink. 'Sometimes when it came to paying we would find that someone had met the bill for us, a most kind gesture but embarrassing'.

On the afternoon of 7 October, the encounters dissolved into dogfights and Mackenzie followed an Me 109 as it entered cloud at 6,000 feet. He recalled, the fighter emerged at right angles and turned towards the sea. 'With a superb height advantage, I half rolled after him giving the Hurricane everything it had got. Closing fast astern I hit him fair and square under the radiator and under the engine from 150 yards, he slowed rapidly, lost height and ditched off Hythe'.

He'd scored a fine victory, but still with ammunition and fuel left, he climbed to 23,000 feet and patrolled between Dover and Folkestone. At about 1330, he spotted eight Me 109s coming across the coast from the east about 1,000 feet above him. 'With ample speed in hand I pulled up into a loop under them and half-rolled onto the last three when the fourth came into sight a little ahead and slightly above me. Obviously they had not seen me, or so it seemed. He was so close I gave him a quick burst in the belly from about 200 yards, noting many strikes around the radiator and under the cockpit. He took violent evasive action and half rolled into a dive and nearly hit me in doing so. It took me a few seconds to recover and dive after him, by which time he had drawn away to about 800 or 900 yards with glycol streaming from his radiator.

As the Me 109 dived towards Folkestone, Mackenzie followed and opened fire at 100 yards but after a few seconds his guns stopped. Undaunted, he continued the chase. 'I was determined that he should not get away as the pilot would undoubtedly be picked up by their efficient rescue service and live to fight another day. Having got him to this state he had to be finished off somehow and quickly before we were too close to France'. Mackenzie described what happened next as 'like doing close formation practice but with a difference'.

With that he manoeuvred his Hurricane. 'I flew alongside him, round him, signalled him to ditch; he never looked up but seemed slumped over his control column. I lowered my undercarriage thinking to knock his tail off with it, but it slowed me down so much that I lost ground. Raising it, I formated on the port side and in an impulse smacked my starboard wing tip down on his port tail plane, it broke off, I pulled up to the left as he plunged in and about three or four feet of my wing tip flew into the air, he partially sank without opening the canopy'.

He wasn't able to see what happened next as he spotted two Me 109s which attacked him from above and behind. Now the hunter was suddenly the hunted. 'I shot down to within a few feet of the sea, jinking madly to left and right, up and down. With no ammunition left I was a sitting duck'. They eventually landed hits on his radiator and armour plating, but as they approached

Folkestone they broke off and McKenzie forced landed on a hill north of the town'.

After his first success just days before, the CO Sqn Ldr Henry Hogan had said 'Congratulations Mac, you're a mad bugger... glad to have you with us!' Those words seemed even more fitting after this unorthodox victory.[7]

During a later patrol, 605 Squadron, scrambled at 1540 and McKellar led the six aircraft to 27,000 feet and encountered four Me 109s near Biggin Hill. McKellar destroyed one with Sergeants Wright and Budzinski and P/O Passy dispatching another between them.[8]

On that day, McKellar joined a very select club. Because he had notched up five in one day, he became a very rare 'Ace in a Day'.

RAF historian, Chaz Bowyer saw McKellar's success 'was primarily due to his exceptional eyesight and ... his outstanding marksmanship in air-to-air shooting. Undoubtedly his constant obsession with physical fitness meant his mind and body were always at a peak of alertness, able to react with lightning swiftness to every shift of situation when engaged in combat.[9] The month would see many former part-time volunteers – now aces gain recognition for their continued success.

On 22 October, John Dundas of 609 Squadron was awarded the DFC. He had proved his pedigree as a fine fighter pilot many times that summer and into the autumn before these actions. Flying as Yellow Leader, on 15 September he was on patrol over Rye when he sighted 25 Do 215s in 'compact formation' flying south at the same height as them. Two bombers detached themselves from the formation as Red Section launched their attack. It was to be a fatal mistake. Dundas selected one and went after it opening fire at 350 yards, he closed to 150 yards, attacking from dead astern and slightly above. At first the Dornier returned fire and Dundas was hit twice. Then his attacks began to tell on the enemy aircraft. 'Pieces started to fall off and flames came from the starboard wing and engine'. After breaking away he saw the Dornier fall away and some of the crew escaped by parachute. He also made a short attack on a second Do 215 which crashed inland.

On 24 September, a formation from 609 Squadron was approaching the coast on its way to patrol over Swanage at 15,000 feet when it was told bandits had turned north-east towards Southampton at 20,000 feet. The enemy consisted of 10 Do 17s at 14,000 feet and a rear formation of 12-15 Me 110s at 17,000 feet about 3 miles behind. The Controller ordered 609 to attack the bombers.

Dundas had what the Intelligence Officer described in his report as 'an exhilarating dogfight with an Me 110'. He told how Dundas was able to hold his climb and turn inside him. Giving the German a long burst at short range after he had straightened out, Dundas sent him spinning into the sea. He also damaged another. Dundas also paid tribute to accuracy of the anti-aircraft fire saying that it was 'very helpful in locating the enemy aircraft'.

He followed this with a Do 17 destroyed near Bristol on the 25th, an Me 109 destroyed and a Do 17 damaged off the Isle of Wight on the 26th, and an Me 110 destroyed on the following day off Portland.[10]

On 7 October, six miles north of Warmwell around 1630, he was flying as Blue 2 in Spitfire R6915 and hurtled towards a circle of about 15 Me 110s. 'I did a beam attack flying straight across the circle', he recalled in his combat report. He found a straggler with no protection astern and went in for the kill, firing for 12 seconds closing to 180 yards. Smoke streamed from the German's port engine, glycol spewed out and the starboard engine then emitted smoke. The wounded Me 110 dived and climbed slightly in a desultory effort to evade its pursuer. It seemed to be done and dusted and Dundas went in to finish him off from below and the quarter but was hit himself 'by an explosive cannon shell from astern'. He recalled, 'My aircraft spun and I was obliged to force land at Warmwell.' He didn't see his attacker but nevertheless claimed as destroyed the Me 110 which he saw gliding down at 14,000 feet 5 miles north of Weymouth. 'With both motors out of action', he wrote 'I am sure it could not have reached France'.

Another sortie on 15 October saw him flying as Blue Leader on patrol at 14,000 feet flying west over Christchurch. He saw 'at least three vics of Me 110s' had flown over their heads about 5,000 feet above them and 'an unspecified number of Me 109s'. Climbing south-west they tried to reach the enemy and they were clearly silhouetted against 9/10ths white cumulus cloud. Suddenly, Blue 3 – David Crook gave a warning on the R/T and then Dundas saw them. 'Three yellow-nosed Me 109s broke away about 50 yards to starboard and below'. It looked like they were in trouble. 'They had just executed an attack from astern and above and had a lot of excess speed on us'. The Germans opened fire. But the 609 pilots were lucky. Only one of their section was hit and then, as they discovered later, by just one bullet. 'Their aim must have been very poor', he recalled.

Breaking away he tried to reform 'B' Flight at 12,000 feet but without success and his transmitter began to fade. Deciding to climb up alone, he spotted a circus of 15-20 Me 110s at 18,000 feet near Christchurch. Making short beam attacks, he gave two short bursts, allowing double deflection closing from 300–100 yards. He saw no results. Having to break away to avoid other enemy fighters above him, he was chased 'for some time' by two Me 109s which he eventually lost. Later he discovered as he was the only pilot in the action to attack an Me 110, he felt entitled to claim the one which crashed in Christchurch Bay, although he admitted 'I did not at the time observe any results.'[11]

Dundas' citation for his DFC read: 'This officer has displayed great courage and determination and has destroyed six enemy aircraft, of which five have been shot down within the last two weeks. He has shown outstanding leadership throughout'.

FIGHTER-BOMBER AUTUMN, 3 – 31 OCTOBER

Although officially gazetted on 22 October, John was given the medal earlier in the month as he modestly told his mother in a letter written on 6 October. He had news on a new boss too. 'Good news! When I got back here I found I'd got B Flight and have been given the DFC. The Station Commander had the ribbon tucked away in a drawer in his desk and produced it immediately, so I am now wearing it and feeling rather a fool. Not that it's worth much these days. Our CO. S/Ldr Darley, has been sent to Exeter as Station Commander and we have a new CO called Robinson, no relation of H's [brother Hugh] ex-CO. I like him on first impression. He's young, energetic and rather offhand. Also he's a crack pilot. Darley's got the DSO and McArthur, now in hospital, the DFC. So 609 is getting some recognition at last.[12]

While this book is about the part-time flyers who flew with Auxiliary squadrons – themselves both Auxiliary and RAFVR - mention must be given of some of those RAFVR pilots who went on to serve with regular squadrons. Two of the most successful of these pilots during the Battle of Britain were Eric Lock and Bob Doe. A farmer's son, Eric Lock was born in Bayston Hill, Shrewsbury in 1919 and after leaving school in 1933 he worked helping his parents on the farm and with their quarrying business. Being more mechanically minded, Eric preferred to work at the quarry. Working with the lorries here saw Eric develop a passion for driving and speed.

This passion inspired him to save five shillings to pay for an experience flight with Sir Alan Cobham's 'Flying Circus' at nearby Prees Heath. A later chance meeting with aviator Amy Johnson at a gliding club on the Long Mynd in the Shropshire hills further cemented a growing interest in flying.

After his 18th birthday Lock joined the RAF Volunteer Reserve in February 1939. He began weekend flying and soon displayed a real talent in the air by 3 March he had flown solo.

When war broke out Lock was called to full-time service and went to 6 FTS at Little Rissington. He was posted to 41 Squadron, then based at Catterick, flying Spitfires.

His first victory in came on 15 August when he destroyed an Me 110 near Seaham Harbour in County Durham. He had to wait until the squadron was sent south to Hornchurch early in September for further victories. And then his tally grew quickly. On 5 September Lock claimed an Me 109 destroyed and one probable off Maidstone. Incredibly, within, within half an hour he was airborne again and claimed two He 111s destroyed and another Me 109, giving him a total of four aircraft destroyed and one probable in one day.

The next day, Lock claimed a Ju 88, with two more Me 109s on 9 September. On 11 September he claimed a Ju 88 and an Me 110. On 14 September, he claimed two Me 109s off the coast between Dover and Deal and on 15 September, Lock destroyed an Me 109 and a Do 17.

In two patrols on the 18 September, he claimed one Me 109 destroyed and two more probables, and two days later he claimed a 'He 113' [probably an Me 109] and a Hs 126 as destroyed.

Awarded the DFC on 1 October, he was in action again on 5 October when in three patrols he destroyed one Me 109s plus two probables. On the 9th he claimed one Me 109 destroyed and two more as probable. On 11 October he again claimed an Me 109 destroyed while patrolling with 92 and 66 Squadrons.

Final victories within the battle came with an Me 109 destroyed on 20th and one probable on 25 October. Lock, who'd later join 611 Squadron, destroyed 21 enemy aircraft during the Battle of Britain. He was awarded a Bar to the DFC on 22 October.[13] His citation read:

> In September, 1940, whilst engaged on a patrol over the Dover area, Pilot Officer Lock engaged three Heinkel He 111s, one of which he shot down into the sea. Immediately afterwards he engaged a Henschel 126 and destroyed it.

He has displayed great courage in the face of heavy odds, and his skill and coolness in combat have enabled him to destroy fifteen enemy aircraft within a period of nineteen days.

Another RAFVR pilot who saw success was Bob Doe. Fascinated by flying from an early age, he devoured the Biggles books of W.E. Johns and by the late 1930s, he was working as an office boy in the News of the World. He was 18 on 10 March 1938 and having read about the RAFVR – 'the best flying club in the world' – he was keen to apply as soon as possible. Applicants were required to apply to Hendon. Bob, however, working in Fleet Street in central London was not far from the heart of UK aviation, so he decided on a direct approach.

'The Air Ministry in those days was at the end of Kingsway, just above Bush House and just below Fleet Street, and one lunchtime I walked in to the Air Ministry and said, I want to be a pilot please.'

A sympathetic officer heard his case and he was invited to apply. Having successfully passed an entrance exam he was told to report to Hanworth aerodrome, a grass airfield also known as London Air Park. His tutor, Louis Rowley, had flown with Alan Cobham's Flying Circus.[14]

He was accepted for a short service RAF commission in January 1939 and was posted to 234 Squadron in November of that year on completion of training.

Between August and October 1940, he became one of the top-scorers of the Battle of Britain with 14 victories, including three Me109s shot down on 4 September. At the end of September he was posted to 238 Squadron and was one of the few pilots successfully to fly both Hurricanes and Spitfires during the battle.

His part in the battle ended on 10 October, when he was shot down over Warmwell, baling out of his Hurricane with wounds to his leg and shoulder.[15]

Bob was awarded a DFC on 22 October and his citation told how he had 'displayed great courage in the many patrols undertaken by his squadron and has destroyed nine enemy aircraft. He has shown outstanding dash and an eagerness to engage the enemy at close quarters.' A Bar was added to this on 26 November, the citation his continued bravery and verve in taking the fight to the enemy: 'On one occasion he dived vertically through a strong protective formation of fighters and attacked two four engine enemy aircraft. He has destroyed a total of 14 hostile aircraft.'[16]

Another honour – this time for a pre-war auxiliary – was for Flt Lt James Bazin. As well as many victories in France, he claimed a Do 17 destroyed and damaged another on 15 September, and on the 30th he destroyed a Ju 88 and probably a second. Bazin, who had been shot down once in France, crash-landed at Hurn on 5 October when his engine failed and was later awarded the DFC on 25 October. The citation stated that he had destroyed ten enemy aircraft, most of which were in France.[17]

There was further distinction for 609 Squadron on 21 October, when it became the first Spitfire squadron to achieve 100 confirmed aerial victories. Flt Lt Howell and P/O Hill attacked a Ju 88 which was bombing Old Sarum airfield and after a chase 'above and below tree-top height' the enemy aircraft crashed. A portion of the rudder was salvaged 'inscribed with the Swastika' as a memento of this auspicious 'kill'.[18]

Written following a request by Churchill, Air Chief Marshal Hugh Dowding completed the 'Battle of Britain Despatch' in the summer of 1941. In it he conceded that any decision on the dates of the Battle is in part subjective. He did not specify an end date, only stating that it 'may be said to have ended when the Fighter and Fighter-Bomber raids died down'. His comparative table of operations and casualties ends on 31 July 1941. Nevertheless, Sebastian Cox, the Head of the Air Historical Branch puts it succinctly: 'the official dates of

FIGHTER-BOMBER AUTUMN, 3 – 31 OCTOBER

the Battle are now set in stone, literally in the case of some of the Memorials, and run from 10 July to 31 October 1940'.[19]

But before that date of 31 October was reached, two of the highest-scoring reservists increased their tally further still.

Sqn Ldr Archie McKellar destroyed an Me 109 and damaged another over Mayfield, with another Me 109 destroyed in the Redhill area are on the 27th. Sergeant James 'Ginger' Lacey, meanwhile destroyed an Me 109 10 miles north of Beachy Head on the 26th, and on the 30th he damaged another Me 109 in the Maidstone area.

McKellar's former squadron – 602 were still battling raids over the south coast, but the autumn weather was taking its toll on men and the airfield. Even this late in October attacks continued, and on the 27 October, 602 was in action again against a raid on Portsmouth by Ju 88s escorted by Me 109s. By the end of the month the airfield was a sea of mud, especially in the vicinity of the dispersal huts and this was causing problems for the Squadron. The wet, cold conditions were to take their toll on the pilots and the squadron diary records a shortage of pilots in November due to cold and influenza, with the airfield also suffering badly with the grass being torn up.[20]

There was no dramatic finale to the Battle of Britain. It ended not with a bang. On 21, 23 and 24 October, Fighter Command suffered no casualties in combat. The 29th saw the last significant daylight battle and one in which the RAF scored a major victory against the 'Snappers' who were outnumbered, broken up and sent scuttling home, leaving 11 of their number destroyed.[21]

The last day of October saw low cloud and drizzle with minor attacks across the Channel. Suffering disproportionate losses by day, with not enough fighters to protect them, the German strategy now changed to bomb Britain into submission by night rather than to crush the RAF. The RAF stood undefeated. This was enough. With the former part-timers from the Auxiliary Air Force and the RAF Volunteer Reserve, the RAF had won.

EPILOGUE

The official end of the Battle of Britain, of course did not mean the attacks from the Luftwaffe stopped and nor did the sorties by Fighter Command. Archie McKellar took off at 0740 on 1 November leading a patrol near Faversham at 25,000 feet. At about 0815 Me 109 fighter-bombers crossed the coast heading for Canterbury and were intercepted by McKellar's Hurricanes. They turned and dived on the Germans but after a short, sharp engagement, the other pilots lost sight of McKellar. An eye-witness later saw his Hurricane circling Woodlands Manor, Adisham, apparently searching for somewhere to land.

After several circuits the aircraft suddenly flicked on to its back and ploughed, inverted, through some trees. It finally came to rest against the wall of the manor house. In the cockpit, McKellar was dead.

The squadron diary recorded the dreadful news and paid tribute their fallen leader. 'A sad day for the Squadron, as S/L McKellar was killed during the morning patrol. His charming personality, his generosity, his wit and vivaciousness will be missed not only by the Squadron but by all with whom he came into contact.' His loss was also marked by his former squadron, No. 602 (City of Glasgow).[1]

Buried at New Eastwood Cemetery in Thornliebank, East Renfrewshire on 6 November, his funeral was attended by hundreds of people and there were scores of wreaths. Sir Archibald Sinclair, Secretary of State for Air delivered the eulogy and described how

EPILOGUE

Mckellar flew 'with daring resolve' and was 'regarded with the greatest admiration and affection by his officers' adding he had proved proving himself 'a leader amongst leaders'.² He was killed just hours after the official end of the Battle of Britain and as a result Archie, one of the RAF's most successful fighter aces during the battle, is not listed on the Battle of Britain roll of honour in Westminster Abbey.

McKellar was awarded a posthumous DSO on 16 November 1940 for his 'outstanding courage and determination' in leading his squadron and received a Mention in Despatches on 1 January 1941. His decorations were presented to his father by HM King George VI at Buckingham Palace in early 1941.

With his cool head and indomitable courage, the reservist who was a plasterer by day and a pilot at the weekends became the scourge of the Luftwaffe. In total, he destroyed 17 enemy aircraft during the Battle of Britain. (All information on 'kills' given here is taken from the rigorous analysis of Christopher Shores' and Clive Williams' from *Aces High: A Tribute to the Most Notable Fighter Pilots of the British and Commonwealth Forces in WWII* and of Kenneth G Wynn in Men of the Battle of Britain. I acknowledge that other sources vary the tallies for these pilots.)

For 609 Squadron, there was also an honour when David Crook was awarded the DFC on 1 November 1940. His citation, the cutting of which is neatly pasted into his logbook, told that he had 'led his section with coolness and judgement, and has destroyed six enemy aircraft besides damaging several more.' However, he was to meet his end as the embers of the battle glowed. On 10 November, Crook became an instructor in various units until 18 December 1944 when on a high-level photographic sortie he was seen to dive into the sea near Aberdeen. His body was never found. He destroyed five enemy aircraft during the Battle of Britain.

John Dundas was part of a patrol scrambled at 1550 on 28 November. Meeting a formation of Me 109s, he was heard by the Controller and the new CO, Sqn Ldr Robinson to say over the radio

'I've finished an Me 109 – Whoopee!' to which Robinson was heard to reply 'Good show, John,' after which nothing further was heard or seen of him.

The diarist told it was thought possible that he might have been responsible for bringing down the German Ace, Major Helmut Wick who was reported in the German press to have been killed in action at the time off the Isle of Wight and that his friend had immediately disposed of the British pilot who brought down Wick's Me 109. He continued

> Flight Lieutenant John Charles Dundas the last of the 'A' [Auxiliary] Officers to leave the Squadron, joined it at Yeadon in May 1938, and was one of the more brilliant of the younger journalists of the *Yorkshire Post*. From 31 May to 28 November 1940, he accounted for the following, 13½ Destroyed; 7 Damaged. 4 Probable. Grand Total 24½ all in. His courageous example and breezy personality are sorely missed.[3] Shores and Williams credit him with 10 victories.

After his brother John was reported missing, Hugh Dundas went to visit 609 Squadron and he wrote in his diary. 'John's CO, Michael Robinson, and all his squadron, were very kind and their sympathy was very obvious and very sincere, but they held out little hope'. He later went to collect John's effects. 'I collected the Lagonda [John's car] from Wallop and packed all John's belongings into the back.' He wrote a few weeks later, 'I think that hardly a day has gone by since then when I have not thought of John.'[4]

Another casualty of the battle was the man who arguably led the RAF to victory. As a result of disagreements over tactics, particularly over the 'Big Wing' and some think due to his abrasive style which upset Churchill, among others, Dowding was controversially removed from command on 24 November

EPILOGUE

and was replaced by Big Wing advocate Air Marshal Sholto Douglas.

Here is what became of some of those other aces who have filled these pages:

James 'Ginger' Lacey of 501 Squadron scored 18 victories during the battle, received a Bar to his DFM on 26 November and was commissioned the following January. He joined 602 Squadron at Kenley in March 1942 and later went to Boscombe Down to test rocket weaponry. Posted to India in June 1943, he spent the rest of the war in East Asia, flying Hurricanes, Thunderbolts and Spitfires. He was posted to 17 Squadron as CO in November 1944 and led them to the end of the war in Asia and then to Japan in March 1946. He retired from the RAF in 1967 and died in May 1989.

As well as the victories already mentioned in October, on the 25th Ken Mackenzie claimed a Me 109 destroyed, another shared and another damaged. On the same day he was awarded the DFC and his citation described his audacious attacking of an enemy by slapping its tail with his wing tip, saying 'His skill and gallantry have been of the highest order.[5]

He destroyed Me 109s on the 27th, 29th and the 30th, bringing his tally in the battle to six enemy aircraft destroyed.

Later shot down and captured, he was transferred to Stalag Luft III at Sagan of Great Escape fame. His final years in the RAF were spent in Africa and was invited to join the newly independent Zambian Air Force as deputy commander. Mackenzie died in June 2009 aged 92.[6]

Findlay Boyd of 602 Squadron, with nine 'kills' in the Battle of Britain, was given command of 54 Squadron in December 1940 and 12 months later went to Kenley as Wing Leader. Awarded the DSO in April 1942, the citation stated that he'd destroyed 22 enemy aircraft. Posted to the Far East, he commanded 293 Wing in Burma and left the RAF in 1945. Post-war Boyd flew charter flights for Scottish Aviation, later became a pig farmer, then a fisherman before moving to Skye, where he kept the Ferry Inn at Uig. He died in February 1975 at the home of his old 602 Squadron friend, George Pinkerton.[7]

Sgt Andrew McDowall, also of 602 Squadron, would add to his already sizeable tally in October all coming in three days at the end of the month. On 27 October he destroyed a Ju 88 and another probably destroyed. Two days later in a frantic encounter he claimed two Me 109s destroyed. He followed this with an Me 109 destroyed on the 30th before the end of the battle.

Credited with destroying 10 aircraft in the Battle of Britain, Andrew McDowall was commissioned in November 1940 and received a Bar to his DFM on 17 December.

Posted to 245 Squadron in April 1941 as a Flight Commander. By July he was OC 'B' Squadron at 52 OTU Debden and took command of 232 Squadron in April 1942. In July 1944 McDowall made history when he took command of another auxiliary unit, 616 (South Yorkshire) Squadron at Manston and led them in becoming the RAF's first jet squadron, flying the Meteor. Leaving the RAF in 1945, he joined Rolls-Royce as a test pilot, later going on to work for Glosters testing Meteors being sold to foreign air forces. He died in October 1981 in Derby.'[8]

With seven victories in the battle, by December 1941, William 'Billy' Clyde of 601 Squadron, now a Squadron Leader, was one of only two original 601 members remaining by that time. After suffering from colitis and gallbladder infections, when he left hospital, he was appointed Deputy Director (Air) for the Combined Chiefs of Staff in Washington. After the war ended, he returned to Johnson & Johnson, but his failing health in the late 1940s saw him settle happily in Acapulco. He died in March 1985.[9]

Joseph Kayll of 607 and 615 Squadrons notched up at least seven victories (at least four of these were from the Battle of France) and was posted to Fighter Command HQ. He returned to operations in June 1941 as Wing Commander Flying at Hornchurch. The following month he was shot down over northern France and was captured and sent to

EPILOGUE

a PoW camp. He escaped in September 1942, but was recaptured and later transferred to Stalag Luft III in May 1943. He was head of the Escape Committee which oversaw the 'Wooden Horse' escape. Freed in May 1945, Kayll was released from the RAF as a Wing Commander and received a Mention in Dispatches in December 1945 and an OBE in June 1946.

Kayll returned to the family timber business and led the reformation of 607 Squadron as a fighter squadron after the war. He died in March 2000.[10]

Following the Battle of Britain, Hugh Dundas was given command of 56 Squadron flying Typhoons, where he was to remain for nearly a year. In November 1942 he was promoted to Wing Commander and went to North Africa. Awarded a DSO in March 1944, in October he was promoted to become one of the youngest Group Captains in the RAF with four aircraft destroyed throughout the war and four shared victories during the Battle of Britain. He received a Bar to his DSO in March 1945, leaving the RAF in January 1947 to become air correspondent with the *Daily Express*. He remained a member of the now 'Royal' Auxiliary Air Force, joining 601 Squadron and in June 1948 replaced Max Aitken as CO, serving with the unit until 1950. In 1960 he joined Rediffusion Ltd in 1961, becoming Chairman by the 1970s, then serving as Chairman of Thames Television Ltd until 1987. Made a CBE in 1977, he was knighted in 1987, holding many charitable appointments, and being High Sheriff of Surrey in 1989. He died in July 1995.[11]

Being badly burned when he was shot down, Richard Hillary became one of the first of Sir Archibald McIndoe's plastic surgery 'Guinea Pigs' at East Grinstead. During his recovery he wrote his book, The Last Enemy, quoted here which was to become a wartime classic. Able only to be deployed in night fighters, he undertook conversion training. But while flying a Blenheim in poor weather after dark on 8 January 1943, his aircraft crashed and he and his navigator were killed. He is credited with destroying five enemy aircraft during the Battle of Britain - all between 29 August and 3 September.[12]

After spending some months in hospital after being shot down and badly injured on 15 August 1940, in 1941 John McGrath was posted to the Operations Room at Exeter, becoming the youngest Fighter Interceptor Controller in the service. He later commanded a Ground Control Intercept unit, being promoted to Flight Lieutenant in December. Posted to HQ Fighter Command in 1944, he remained there until November 1945 and was released from the service in January 1946 as a Squadron Leader, having led the RAF fighters in the Victory Parade flypast on 17 September 1945. Following demobilisation, he rejoined the family firm until 1971, when he became Managing Director of Bowater Travel. He died on 17 June 1981.[13]

Having destroyed six enemy aircraft during the battle in 1941 'Sandy' Johnstone became Controller at Turnhouse, but in September he was posted to the Middle East to Beirut and then became Sector Commander at Haifa, Palestine and later posted to Malta as a controller. In 1943 he became Wing Commander Flying at a Hurricane OCU and in August 1944 he went to France with General Eisenhower's HQ. The year later he was sent to the USA with the RAF Delegation in Washington. He then held a number of senior positions including Director of Personnel at the Air Ministry and Air Commodore, Commonwealth Air Forces, during the Indonesian Confrontation. He returned to the UK in July 1965 to become an Air Vice-Marshal, and AOC 18 Group, doubling as Air Officer Scotland. He retired in 1968 with a CBE and died in 2000.[14]

Ronald 'Ras' Berry destroyed seven enemy aircraft during the battle, including three on 31 August. He took command of 81 Squadron at Turnhouse. In November he flew to North Africa at the start of the Operation 'Torch' landings. During this campaign he claimed a number of victories and was awarded a Bar to his DFC and a DSO in 1943. He became OC Training Wing with 53 OTU at Kirton-in-Lindsey in 1943 and later commanded RAF Acklington. He held a series of Fighter and Bomber Command posts reaching the rank of Air Commodore. He retired in 1969, having been made an OBE in 1946 and a CBE in 1965. He died in 2000.[15]

EPILOGUE

With 11 victories credited to him during the Battle of Britain (although all of them within the battle were with 253 Squadron, which he took command of on 5 September 1940), Gerry Edge was awarded a DFC on 13 September but was shot down on the 26th suffering burns. On recovery he was posted back to 605 Squadron on 29 November as Commanding Officer. Posted to the Middle East in 1941, he later took command of 84 Group Control Centre, taking this unit to France after the Normandy Invasion, and subsequently into Germany.[16]

Anthony Eyre claimed six victories during the Battle of Britain in addition to two enemy aircraft destroyed before the battle. He became a flight commander in December and commanding officer in February 1941, but he was rested in April. In March 1942 he became Wing Leader at North Weald and on his first sweep on 8 March he was shot down over northern France and spent the rest of the war as a PoW at Stalag Luft III. He returned at the end of the war, but was killed in February 1946 when his Tempest crashed near RAF St Athan.[17]

Early in 1941 Jim Bazin left 607 Squadron and became a Controller in the 14 Group Operations Room. In January 1944 following a course on four-engined aircraft, he attended 16 (Bomber) OTU on Lancasters, and in June of that year was appointed commanding officer of 9 Squadron, flying 25 bombing sorties including one against the battleship Tirpitz in Norway. He was awarded a DSO in September 1945, but had already left the service in May, with the end of the European war. He resumed his profession as an engineer and also rejoined 607 Squadron in November 1946 and was the unit's Officer Commanding from 1949–51. He died in 1985.[18]

Although inevitably the high-scoring aces take the limelight, all of those pre-war part-timers played their part. They did this through those peacetime days with silver biplanes, training and japes; the coming of war; the sporadic encounters of the phoney war; the chaos of the Battle of France and evacuation and Dunkirk and the frantic, relentless days of July and August 1940. Swept by furious seas, Fighter Command fought to keep its head above water throughout August. But September brought relief. Suddenly the waters calmed just enough to take breath. The reservists whose exploits have filled these pages then helped turn that monstrous tide in September and October.

After the battle, Air Chief Marshal Sir Keith Park, AOC 11 Group reflected: 'Without the Auxiliaries we would not have defeated the Luftwaffe in 1940'.[19] Similarly, the invaluable contribution of the Volunteer Reserve was summed up by Dowding when, in his desperate need for pilots in August 1940, he was reported to have exclaimed 'Thank God for the RAFVR'.[20]

This reflection on the huge contribution of those part-timers to the eventual victory in the battle the importance to the RAF as a whole and was also echoed many years later by the now Air Vice Marshal 'Sandy' Johnstone.

> It is fair to say, too, that the Royal Air Force came of age as a result of this battle. Before 1940 the RAF had been striving hard to convince 'The Powers That Be' of its worth as an independent Service, but there had been many who continued to maintain that it was an unnecessary extravagance and that military air matters could better be handled by the military. But the public had now been able to see for itself how much it owed to inspired planning and execution by men able to devote their whole time to the air defences of their country. It also established once and for all that members of the Auxiliary and Reserve forces were more than able to play their full part alongside the Regular squadrons. After all, more than a third of all aircrew taking part in the battle had been 'part-time aviators' before the outbreak of the war.[21]

As the battle progressed their numbers gradually reduced and the AAF squadrons numbers were 'leavened' by regular recruits replacing the

EPILOGUE

pre-war part-timers who were either being killed or were moved on to non-flying duties.

As the war went on that leavening continued, however, the squadrons of the AAF in particular, remained a focus of pride for the achievements of the pre-war part-timers and their geographical identity. Many continued to be supported by local groups, especially by their County Territorial Associations.

In his fascinating investigation of Auxiliary success in the Battle of Britain, Christopher Shores paid tribute to the Auxiliary squadrons for their contribution to eventual victory in the Battle of Britain.

> Since success in aerial combat contains a mixture of innate skill, training, experience, opportunity and downright luck, it is perhaps a good indication of the AAF's state of training and experience that no less than 57.7% of those engaged in the Battle of Britain were able to submit confirmable claims.

He added another important question is how the AAF units had performed in comparison with the rest of Fighter Command's squadrons. 'The answer here', he said 'is stunningly well'. Out of sixty squadrons and units taking part in the battle, Nos. 602 and 603 Squadrons were the second and third highest scoring respectively. No. 501 Squadron was placed fifth, No. 609 Squadron seventh, 601 Squadron eleventh and 610 Squadron fourteenth. To have six squadrons amongst the fourteen most successful was without any doubt a most extraordinary performance.[22]

There is another important contribution. The distinctive ethos and spirit which would be inculcated to those new, largely regular recruits which leavened the auxiliary squadrons I believe cannot be underestimated. Heritage and pride in a unit's identity are vital motivating factors and crucial in bonding new joiners to the common cause and cementing a fighting unit together. One which will quickly and instinctively work together and support each other in hard times and laugh together in the good.

As the squadrons went on to fight in the wider war, they achieved many great things – developing airborne radar (600 and 604 Squadrons), pioneering Typhoon operations (609 Squadron) and being the first to operate RAF jets in 1944 (616 Squadron) – to name just a few.

That pride and ethos remain. Almost all of those auxiliary squadrons which took part in the Battle of Britain operate still today. Now they fulfil very different roles to their counterparts in 1940. Only No. 616 Squadron provides aircrew today, but the others – 501, 504, 600, 601, 602, 603, 605, 607, 609 and 611 Squadrons recruit men and women from across the UK from a wide variety of backgrounds. They are trained – as they were before the war at weekends, in the evening and at annual camp. With this training they support RAF operations in the UK and around the world. They are drivers, cooks, technicians, intelligence analysts, photographers, RAF Regiment gunners, RAF Police, HR specialists, and more. All do this work, as those pre-war part-timers did, in their spare time. Some choose a role very different to their day-job. Others, like nurses, cyber or media specialists are recruited to bring their talents from civilian life to the military. Whatever their background, they all bring distinct skills and experience to the table which makes their contribution to the wider force all the more valuable.

The Royal Auxiliary Air Force celebrated its centenary in 2024. Branded 'RAuxAF100 – 100 years of Volunteer Reserve Service' it marked the Auxiliary and RAFVR histories of part-time service for the RAF. There was much reflection on the distinguished history of this part-time arm of the world's oldest Independent Air Force. Through all the many achievements of those part-timers – those in the Battle of Britain stand out because of their importance in saving Britain in its moment of utmost peril. This was perhaps their 'Finest Hour'. However, in giving up their spare time to serve their country and the RAF they remain, in another of Churchill's enduring phrases 'twice the citizen'.

ENDNOTES

Introduction

1. https://www.rafmuseum.org.uk/research/online-exhibitions/history-of-the-battle-of-britain/introduction-to-the-phases-of-the-battle-of-britain/

Prologue

1. Crook, David, *Spitfire Pilot: A Personal Account of the Battle of Britain*, Spitfire Publishers 2018 p92
2. Shores, Christopher; Williams, Clive, *Aces High: a Tribute to the Most Notable Fighter Pilots of the British and Commonwealth Forces in WWII*. Grub Street, 2001, p358
3. Crook, David, *Spitfire Pilot: A Personal Account of the Battle of Britain*, Spitfire Publishers 2018 p10
4. 600squadronassociation.com/history-of-the-royal-auxiliary-air-force/
5. Harwood, Derrick, 'The History of our Reserves', MOD Directorate of Media and Communications, 2014, p18
6. Shores, Christopher, RAF Historical Society Seminar - *Reserve Auxiliary Forces* - Journal-29A, p47-51
7. Crook, David, *Spitfire Pilot: A Personal Account of the Battle of Britain*, Spitfire Publishers 2018 p10

8. Ross, David M.S.; Blanche, Bruce J. Sqn Ldr; Simpson, William (2003a). *The Greatest Squadron of Them All: The Definitive History of 603 (City of Edinburgh) Squadron, RAuxAF. Vol. 1: Formation to 1941*. Grub Street, p180
9. Collier, Richard, *Eagle Day: The Battle of Britain*, Cassell, 1966, p86
10. Crook, David, *Spitfire Pilot: A Personal Account of the Battle of Britain*, Spitfire Publishers 2018 p10
11. Dundas, Hugh, Flying Start, A Fighter Pilot's War Years, Pen and Sword, 1988, p14

Chapter 1: The AAF, the RAFVR and the Coming of War

1. Jefford Wg Cdr, Jeff, RAF Historical Society Seminar – *Reserve Auxiliary Forces* – Journal-29A, p11
2. 600squadronassociation.com/history-of-the-royal-auxiliary-air-force/
3. Moulson, Tom, *The Millionaires' Squadron – The Remarkable Story of 601 Squadron and the Flying Sword*. Pen and Sword Aviation, 2014, p25
4. Templewood, Viscount (Sir Samuel Hoare), *Empire of the Air – The Advent of the Air Age – 1922-29*. Collins, London, 1957
5. White, Ian, *If You Want Peace, Prepare For War. A History of No. 604 (County of Middlesex) Squadron RAuxAF, in Peace and in War*. London, 2005, pp8-9
6. Raymond Davis family archive. Courtesy of Carolyn Horton
7. Deighton, Len, *Fighter – The True Story of the Battle of Britain*. Jonathan Cape, 1977, p40
8. Ross, David M.S.; Blanche, Bruce J. Sqn Ldr; Simpson, William (2003a). *The Greatest Squadron of Them All: The Definitive History of 603 (City of Edinburgh) Squadron, RAuxAF. Vol. 1: Formation to 1941*. London: Grub Street, p2
9. Dixon, Robert, *607 Squadron: A Shade of Blue*. The History Press Ltd, 2008

ENDNOTES

10. Dundas, Hugh, *Flying Start, A Fighter Pilot's War Years.* Pen and Sword, 1988, p12
11. Dixon, Robert, *607 Squadron: A Shade of Blue.* The History Press Ltd, 2008
12. Mansell, Dr A., *Professionals, Amateurs and Private Armies. Pilot Entry Portals in the RAF Expansion of 1934 to 1939* Proceedings of the RAF Historical Society Number 11, 1993, pp55-62
13. https://www.key.aero/article/who-was-first-fly-over-everest
14. White, A., *If You Want Peace, Prepare For War. A History of No. 604 (County of Middlesex) Squadron, Royal Auxiliary Air Force*, p18
15. Jefford Wg Cdr, Jeff, RAF Historical Society Seminar – Reserve Auxiliary Forces – Journal-29A, pp1-22
16. Ibid, pp22-3
17. https://www.rafmuseum.org.uk/research/online-exhibitions/taking-flight/historical-periods/inter-war-flying-training/
18. Mansell, Dr A., The Royal Air Force Volunteer Reserve 1936-1939, RAF Historical Society Seminar – Reserve Auxiliary Forces – Journal-29A, p31
19. Dixon, Wg Cdr Alex, *The Royal Air Force Volunteer Reserve – Memories, RAF Innsworth, Gloucester*, 1997, p24
20. Mansell, Dr A., *Professionals, Amateurs and Private Armies. Pilot Entry Portals in the RAF Expansion of 1934 to 1939* Proceedings of the RAF Historical Society Number 11, 1993, p32
21. Wynn, Kenneth G, Men of the Battle of Britain, Gliddon Books, 1989 p17
22. Townshend-Bickers, Richard, *Ginger Lacey Fighter Pilot*, Pan, London, 1962, p25
23. Ibid, pp26-7
24. Holmes, Ray, *Sky Spy – From Six Miles High to Hitler's Bunker*, 1989, Airlife, pp1-4
25. Townshend-Bickers, Richard, *Ginger Lacey Fighter Pilot*, Pan, London, 1962, pp28-9

26. Townshend-Bickers, Richard, *Ginger Lacey Fighter Pilot*, Pan, London, 1962, pp28-34
27. Holmes, Ray, *Sky Spy – From Six Miles High to Hitler's Bunker*, 1989, Airlife, pp5-11
28. Dundas, Hugh, *Flying Start, A Fighter Pilot's War Years*, Pen and Sword, 1988, pp12-13
29. Faber, David, *Munich: The 1938 Appeasement Crisis*, Pocket Books, London, 2009, pp356-7
30. AIR-27-222
31. Dixon, Robert, *607 Squadron: A Shade of Blue*, The History Press Ltd, 2008
32. https://www.chch.ox.ac.uk/cathedral/war-memorials/flight-lieutenant-john-charles-dundas
33. Shores, Christopher; Williams, Clive, *Aces High: a Tribute to the Most Notable Fighter Pilots of the British and Commonwealth Forces in WWII*. London: Grub Street, 1994, p695
34. https://www.chch.ox.ac.uk/cathedral/war-memorials/flight-lieutenant-john-charles-dundas
35. Goss, Chris, *Brothers in Arms: The Story of a British and a German Fighter Unit, August to December 1940*, Air World, 2020 p28
36. https://www.rafmuseum.org.uk/research/online-exhibitions/history-of-the-battle-of-britain/expansion-at-last/
37. EMPIRE AIR DAY DISPLAYS (ACCIDENTS) – 'House of Commons Debates – 28 July 1937 vol 326 cc 3095-100'. Hansard, 28 July 1937. Retrieved 4 August 2014, https://hansard.parliament.uk/commons/1937-07-28/debates/d94995f3-a1c7-48f5-abe1-b28ed23b5b21/EmpireAirDayDisplays(Accidents)
38. Dickson, Wg Cdr Alex, RAFVR Memories, HQPTC, RAF Innsworth, 1997, p24
39. Hillary, Richard, *The Last Enemy*, Pan, London, 1960, pp285-6
40. Dixon, Robert, *607 Squadron: A Shade of Blue*, The History Press Ltd, 2008

41. Dundas, Hugh, *Flying Start, A Fighter Pilot's War Years*, Pen and Sword, 1988, p13-14
42. *Manchester Guardian*, 22 August 1939
43. Jennings, W. Ivor, "The Emergency Powers (Defence) (No. 2) Act, 1940". Modern Law Review, 1940, p132
44. Dundas, Hugh, *Flying Start, A Fighter Pilot's War Years*, Pen and Sword, 1988, pp15-16
45. Battle of Britain Monument – bbm.org.uk/airmen/Clyde.htm
46. Sword, Keith, *British Reactions to the Soviet Occupation of Eastern Poland in September 1939*. The Slavonic and East European Review, Vol. 69, No. 1 (Jan., 1991), pp. 81-101.
47. Dickson, Wg Cdr Alex, RAFVR Memories, HQPTC, RAF Innsworth, 1997, p24

Chapter 2: Phoney War and Battle of France

1. Townshend-Bickers, Richard, *Ginger Lacey Fighter Pilot*, Pan, London, 1962, p38
2. AIR-27-2087-1
3. Dundas, Hugh, *Flying Start, A Fighter Pilot's War Years*, Pen and Sword, 1988, pp15-17
4. Townshend-Bickers, Richard, *Ginger Lacey Fighter Pilot*, Pan, London, 1962, pp35-6
5. Hillary, Richard, *The Last Enemy*, Pan, London, 1960, p68
6. Dundas, Hugh, *Flying Start, A Fighter Pilot's War Years*, Pen and Sword, 1988, p17
7. Holmes, Ray, *Sky Spy – From Six Miles High to Hitler's Bunker*, 1989, Airlife, pp45-6
8. Ferguson, Aldon P., Hamlin, John, *Beware! Beware!: The History of 611 (West Lancashire) Squadron Royal Auxiliary Air Force*, Airfield Publications, 2004 p18
9. Ferguson, Aldon P, Barrie Heath, *This is Your Life*, 2018

10. Dundas, Hugh, *Flying Start, A Fighter Pilot's War Years*, Pen and Sword, 1988, pp17-18
11. Ross, David M.S.; Blanche, Bruce J. Sqn Ldr; Simpson, William, *The Greatest Squadron of Them All: The Definitive History of 603 (City of Edinburgh) Squadron, RAuxAF. Vol. 1: Formation to 1941*. London: Grub Street, 2003, p55
12. Bowman, Martin W., and Masters, David, *RAF Fighter Pilots in WWII*, Pen and Sword, 2020, Ch11
13. Shores, Christopher; Williams, Clive. *Aces High: a Tribute to the Most Notable Fighter Pilots of the British and Commonwealth Forces in WWII*. London: Grub Street, 1994, p1329
14. Bowman, Martin W., and Masters, David, RAF Fighter Pilots in WWII, Pen and Sword, 2020, Ch11
15. Ibid, p1846
16. Ross, David M.S.; Blanche, Bruce J. Sqn Ldr; Simpson, William, *The Greatest Squadron of Them All: The Definitive History of 603 (City of Edinburgh) Squadron, RAuxAF. Vol. 1: Formation to 1941*. London: Grub Street, 2003, p57
17. https://www.scottishlegal.com/articles/gillian-mawdsley-in-memoriam-squadron-leader-patrick-gifford-dfc-castle-douglas
18. Ross, David M.S.; Blanche, Bruce J. Sqn Ldr; Simpson, William, *The Greatest Squadron of Them All: The Definitive History of 603 (City of Edinburgh) Squadron, RAuxAF. Vol. 1: Formation to 1941*. London: Grub Street, 2003, p137
19. Ibid, p151
20. Ibid, pp61-66
21. AIR-27-2073
22. Nancarrow, F.G., *Glasgow's fighter squadron: 602 Squadron RAF*. London and Glasgow: Collins, 1942, p22
23. AIR-27-2079
24. Ross, David M.S.; Blanche, Bruce J. Sqn Ldr; Simpson, William, *The Greatest Squadron of Them All: The Definitive History of*

ENDNOTES

603 (City of Edinburgh) Squadron, RAuxAF. Vol. 1: Formation to 1941. London: Grub Street, 2003, p70
25. Ibid, p75
26. Nancarrow, F.G., *Glasgow's fighter squadron: 602 Squadron RAF*. London and Glasgow: Collins, 1942, p23
27. https://rauxaf.org/vignettes-first-blood-to-the-auxiliaries/
28. AIR-27-2073
29. Dixon, Robert, *607 Squadron: A Shade of Blue*, The History Press Ltd, 2008
30. Kayll, Wg Cdr Joe, *Defending Northern Skies 1915–1995 24 October 1995*, The Royal Air Force Historical Society at The University of Newcastle, p132
31. AIR-27-2093
32. AIR-27-2079
33. Ibid
34. Cameron, Dugald, *Glasgow's Own: Visual Record of the Men and Machines of 602 (City of Glasgow) Squadron, Royal Auxiliary Air Force, 1925-57,* Squadron Prints Ltd, 1987
35. Moulson, Tom, *The Millionaires' Squadron – The Remarkable Story of 601 Squadron and the Flying Sword*, Pen and Sword Aviation, 2014, p63
36. Shores, Christopher; Williams, Clive, *Aces High: A Tribute to the Most Notable Fighter Pilots of the British and Commonwealth Forces in WWII*. London: Grub Street, 1994, p1084
37. Kayll, Wg Cdr Joe, *Defending Northern Skies 1915–1995 24 October 1995*, The Royal Air Force Historical Society at The University of Newcastle, p133
38. AIR-27-2093
39. AIR-27-2123
40. Kayll, Wg Cdr Joe, *Defending Northern Skies 1915–1995*, 24 October 1995, The Royal Air Force Historical Society at The University of Newcastle, p133
41. AIR-27-2087

42. AIR-27-2109
43. AIR-27-2058
44. Onderwater, Hans, *Gentlemen in Blue: The History of No. 600 (City of London) Squadron Royal Auxiliary Air Force*, Pen & Sword, 1997, p113
45. AIR-27-2058
46. Onderwater, Hans, *Gentlemen in Blue: The History of No. 600 (City of London) Squadron Royal Auxiliary Air Force*, Pen & Sword, 1997, p113
47. AIR-27-2058
48. AIR-27-2082
49. AIR-27-2068
50. AIR-27-1949
51. AIR-27-1949
52. https://winstonchurchill.org/resources/speeches/1940-the-finesthour/blood-toil-tears-sweat/
53. Shores, Christopher; Williams, Clive, Aces High: A Tribute to the Most Notable Fighter Pilots of the British and Commonwealth Forces in WWII. London: Grub Street, 1994, p1328
54. Shores, Christopher; Williams, Clive, *Aces High: A Tribute to the Most Notable Fighter Pilots of the British and Commonwealth Forces in WWII*. London: Grub Street, 1994, p614
55. Battle of Britain Monument - bbm.org.uk/airmen/RoyceWB.htm
56. AIR-81-476
57. Francis Blackadder diary via Dixon, Robert, 607 Squadron: A Shade of Blue, The History Press Ltd, 2008
58. AIR-27-2068
59. AIR-27-1963
60. AIR-27-2093
61. AIR-27-2102
62. AIR-27-2068

ENDNOTES

63. AIR-27-2903
64. AIR-27-2093
65. AIR-27-1963
66. AIR-27-2087
67. Shores, Christopher; Williams, Clive, *Aces High: A Tribute to the Most Notable Fighter Pilots of the British and Commonwealth Forces in WWII*. London: Grub Street, 1994, p714
68. AIR-27-2106
69. AIR-27-2087
70. AIR-27-2106
71. AIR-27-2102
72. AIR-27-2068
73. AIR-27-2126
74. Ferguson, Aldon P., Hamlin, John, *Beware! Beware!: The History of 611 (West Lancashire) Squadron Royal Auxiliary Air Force*, Airfield Publications, 2004, p16
75. AIR-27-2109
76. Battle of Britain Monument, bbm.org.uk/airmen/Stoddart.htm
77. AIR-27-2109
78. AIR-27-2102
79. Ferguson, Aldon P., Hamlin, John, *Beware! Beware!: The History of 611 (West Lancashire) Squadron Royal Auxiliary Air Force*, Airfield Publications, 2004, p25
80. https://winstonchurchill.org/resources/speeches/1940-the-finest-hour/we-shall-fight-on-the-beaches/
81. AIR-27-2109
82. Michael Appleby logbook
83. AIR-27-2074
84. AIR-27-1949
85. AIR-27-2087
86. Bowman, Martin W., and Masters, David, RAF Fighter Pilots in WWII, Pen and Sword, 2020, Ch11

87. Shores, Christopher; Williams, Clive, Aces High: A Tribute to the Most Notable Fighter Pilots of the British and Commonwealth Forces in WWII. London, Grub Street, 1994, p1084
88. https://winstonchurchill.org/resources/speeches/1940-the-finesthour/their-finest-hour/

Chapter 3: Battle of Britain Phase 1, 26 June – 16 July

1. Dowding, Air Chief Marshal, *Despatches on the Conduct of the Battle of Britain*, August 1940
2. Deighton, Len, *The Battle of Britain*, Jonathan Cape, 1980, p114
3. Shores, Christopher; Williams, Clive, *Aces High: A Tribute to the Most Notable Fighter Pilots of the British and Commonwealth Forces in WWII*. London: Grub Street, 1994, p623
4. Gelb, Norman, *Scramble – A Narrative History of the Battle of Britain*, Michael Joseph, 1986, pp35-6
5. Dempster, Derek and Wood, Derek, *The Narrow Margin*, Hutchinson, 1961 (A Summer for Heroes), p11
6. Deighton, Len, *The Battle of Britain*, Jonathan Cape, 1980, pp110-1
7. Dixon, Robert, 607 Squadron: A Shade of Blue, The History Press Ltd, 2008
8. AIR-27-2079
9. Ross, David M.S.; Blanche, Bruce J. Sqn Ldr; Simpson, William (2003a). *The Greatest Squadron of Them All: The Definitive History of 603 (City of Edinburgh) Squadron, RAuxAF. Vol. 1: Formation to 1941*. London: Grub Street, p140
10. AIR-27-2074
11. Ibid
12. Shores, Christopher; Williams, Clive, *Aces High: A Tribute to the Most Notable Fighter Pilots of the British and Commonwealth Forces in WWII*. London: Grub Street, 1994, p511

ENDNOTES

13. AIR-27-2126
14. AIR-27-2079
15. Shores, Christopher; Williams, Clive, *Aces High: A Tribute to the Most Notable Fighter Pilots of the British and Commonwealth Forces in WWII*. London: Grub Street, 1994, p394
16. Roskill, S.W.; Butler, J.R.M (ed.). *War at Sea. History of the Second World War United Kingdom Military Series. Vol. I*, HMSO London, 1954, pp323-324
17. https://www.key.aero/article/battle-britain-80-610-squadron
18. Crook, David, *Spitfire Pilot: A Personal Account of the Battle of Britain*, Spitfire Publishers 2018 p30
19. Ibid, p33
20. AIR-27-2102
21. Crook, David, *Spitfire Pilot: A Personal Account of the Battle of Britain*, Spitfire Publishers 2018 p31
22. AIR-27-2123
23. AIR-27-2123
24. https://winstonchurchill.org/resources/speeches/1940-the-finest-hour/war-of-the-unknown-warriors/
25. Trevor-Roper, Hugh, *Hitler's War Directives; 1939–1945*. Edinburgh: Birlinn. 2004, p74-79

Chapter 4: Battle of Britain Phase 2, 17 July – 12 August

1. Deighton, Len, *The Battle of Britain*, Jonathan Cape, 1980, p109
2. Vital Speeches of the Day, Vol. VI, pp617-625
3. Shores, Christopher; Williams, Clive, *Aces High: A Tribute to the Most Notable Fighter Pilots of the British and Commonwealth Forces in WWII*. London: Grub Street, 1994, p1151
4. Craig, Phil; Clayton, Tim, *Finest Hour: The Story of the Battle of Britain*, Hodder & Stoughton, 2000, p230
5. Townsend-Bickers, Richard, *Ginger Lacey Fighter Pilot*, Pan, London, 1962, pp77-8

6. Craig, Phil; Clayton, Tim, *Finest Hour: The Story of the Battle of Britain*, Hodder & Stoughton, 2000, pp231-2
7. Battle of Britain Monument – bbm.org.uk/airmen/Sylvester.htm
8. Craig, Phil; Clayton, Tim, *Finest Hour: The story of the Battle of Britain*, Hodder & Stoughton, 2000, pp231-2
9. AIR-27-1949
10. Craig, Phil; Clayton, Tim, Finest Hour: The story of the Battle of Britain, Hodder & Stoughton, 2000, pp231-2
11. Shores, Christopher; Williams, Clive, *Aces High: A Tribute to the Most Notable Fighter Pilots of the British and Commonwealth Forces in WWII*. London: Grub Street, 1994, p1679
12. Wynn, Kenneth G, Men of the Battle of Britain, Gliddon Books, 1989 p17
13. AIR-27-2106
14. Wynn, Kenneth G, Men of the Battle of Britain, Gliddon Books, 1989 p17
15. Shores, Christopher; *Williams, Clive, Aces High: A Tribute to the Most Notable Fighter Pilots of the British and Commonwealth Forces in WWII*. London: Grub Street, 1994, p1447
16. AIR-50-166-73
17. Townsend-Bickers, Richard, *Ginger Lacey Fighter Pilot*, Pan, London, 1962, p80-2
18. Shores, Christopher; Williams, Clive, *Aces High: A Tribute to the Most Notable Fighter Pilots of the British and Commonwealth Forces in WWII*. London: Grub Street, 1994, p1327
19. Townsend-Bickers, Richard, *Ginger Lacey Fighter Pilot*, Pan, London, 1962, p82
20. Sarkar, Dilip, The Few: The Story of the Battle of Britain in the Words of the Pilots, Amberley 2012, p95
21. AIR-27-2102
22. Ziegler, Frank H., *The Story of 609 Squadron: Under the White Rose*. London: Macdonald, 1971, p116

ENDNOTES

23. Sarkar, Dilip, *The Few – The Story of the Battle of Britain in the Words of the Pilots*, Amberley, 2012, p96
24. Michael Appleby logbook
25. Sarkar, Dilip, *The Few – The Story of the Battle of Britain in the Words of the Pilots*, Amberley, 2012, p86
26. Crook, David, *Spitfire Pilot: A Personal Account of the Battle of Britain*, Spitfire Publishers 2018, p55
27. Shores, Christopher; Williams, Clive, *Aces High: A Tribute to the Most Notable Fighter Pilots of the British and Commonwealth Forces in WWII*. London: Grub Street, 1994, p1322
28. Ziegler, F.H., *The Story of 609 Squadron – Under the White Rose*, London, 1971, p39
29. AIR-27-2068
30. Shores, Christopher; Williams, Clive, *Aces High: A Tribute to the Most Notable Fighter Pilots of the British and Commonwealth Forces in WWII*. London: Grub Street, 1994, p1003
31. Ibid, p1526
32. https://601squadron.com/men-of-601-squadron/a-through-e/demetriadi-dick/
33. Shores, Christopher; Williams, Clive, *Aces High: A Tribute to the Most Notable Fighter Pilots of the British and Commonwealth Forces in WWII*. London: Grub Street, 1994, p1527
34. Bishop, Patrick, *Battle of Britain*, Quercus, 2010, pp152-3
35. Moulson, Tom, *The Millionaires' Squadron – The Remarkable Story of 601 Squadron and the Flying Sword*, Pen and Sword Aviation, 2014, p88
36. https://601squadron.com/men-of-601-squadron/s-through-w/smithers-julian-langley/
37. https://601squadron.com/men-of-601-squadron/a-through-e/dickie-william-gordon/
38. https://601squadron.com/men-of-601-squadron/a-through-e/demetriadi-dick/

39. AIR-50-165-24
40. AIR-27-2058
41. Deere, Group Captain Alan C., *Nine Lives*, Hodder And Stoughton Ltd, 1959, p118
42. AIR-27-2082-21
43. Townsend-Bickers, Richard, *Ginger Lacey Fighter Pilot*, Pan, London, 1962, pp87-9
44. AIR-27-1949
45. Townsend-Bickers, Richard, *Ginger Lacey Fighter Pilot*, Pan, London, 1962, pp87-8
46. AIR-27-2123
47. Shores, Christopher; Williams, Clive, *Aces High: A Tribute to the Most Notable Fighter Pilots of the British and Commonwealth Forces in WWII*. London: Grub Street, 1994, p1679
48. AIR-27-2102-15
49. Crook, David, *Spitfire Pilot: A Personal Account of the Battle of Britain*, Spitfire Publishers 2018, p55
50. AIR-27-2102
51. Ziegler, Frank H., *The Story of 609 Squadron: Under the White Rose*. London: Macdonald, 1971, p123

Chapter 5: Battle of Britain Phase 3, 13 August – 6 September

1. Deighton, Len, *The Battle of Britain*, Jonathan Cape, 1980, p131
2. AIR-50-165-6
3. AIR-50-165-24
4. AIR-50-165-18
5. Moulson, Tom, *The Millionaires' Squadron – The Remarkable Story of 601 Squadron and the Flying Sword*, Pen and Sword Aviation, 2014, p90

ENDNOTES

6. Shores, Christopher; Williams, Clive, *Aces High: a Tribute to the Most Notable Fighter Pilots of the British and Commonwealth Forces in WWII*. London, Grub Street, 1994, p630
7. AIR-50-165-7
8. AIR-50-165-24
9. AIR-27-2068 and AIR-27-2102
10. Crook, David, *Spitfire Pilot: A Personal Account of the Battle of Britain*, Spitfire Publishers 2018, p55-9
11. Shores, Christopher; Williams, Clive, *Aces High: A Tribute to the Most Notable Fighter Pilots of the British and Commonwealth Forces in WWII*. London: Grub Street, 1994, p1703
12. Crook, David, *Spitfire Pilot: A Personal Account of the Battle of Britain*, Spitfire Publishers 2018, p59
13. AIR-27-2102
14. Collier, Richard, *Eagle Day: The Battle Of Britain: August 6-September 15, 1940*, Cassell, Orion, 1999, p66
15. Johnstone Air Vice Marshal, Sandy, Spitfire Into War, Grafton Books, London, 1988
16. Deighton, Len, The Battle of Britain, Jonathan Cape, 1980, p135
17. Collier, Richard, Eagle Day: The Battle of Britain, Cassell, 1966, p70
18. AIR-27-2102
19. AIR-50-171-24
20. Deere, Group Captain Alan C., *Nine Lives*, Hodder And Stoughton Ltd, 1959, p121 & p137
21. Onderwater, Hans, *Gentlemen in Blue: the History of No. 600 (City of London) Squadron Royal Auxiliary Air Force*, Pen & Sword, 1997, p127
22. Ibid, p42
23. AIR-27-2087
24. AIR-50-169-92
25. AIR 27-2087

26. Bowyer, Chaz, Fighter Pilots of the RAF, 1939–1945. London: William Kimber & Co Ltd., 1984, p96
27. Bowman, Martin W., and Masters, David, RAF Fighter Pilots in WWII, Pen and Sword, 2020, Ch11
28. Welford, Harry, The Unrelenting Years 1916–1946, BJ&M Promotions, p108
29. Dixon, Robert, 607 Squadron: A Shade of Blue, The History Press Ltd, 2008
30. https://www.thegazette.co.uk/London/issue/34932/supplement/5219
31. Shores, Christopher; Williams, Clive, *Aces High: A Tribute to the Most Notable Fighter Pilots of the British and Commonwealth Forces in WWII*. London: Grub Street, 1994, p1322
32. Shores, Christopher; Williams, Clive, Aces High: A Tribute to the Most Notable Fighter Pilots of the British and Commonwealth Forces in WWII. London: Grub Street, 1994, p544
33. Battle of Britain Monument – bbm.org.uk/airmen/FightforSight.htm
34. Dundas, Hugh, Flying Start, *A Fighter Pilot's War Years*, Pen and Sword, 1988, pp43-45
35. AIR-50-165-7
36. Nancarrow, F.G., Glasgow's fighter squadron: 602 Squadron RAF. London and Glasgow: Collins, 1942, p49
37. Gelb, Norman, *Scramble – A Narrative History of the Battle of Britain*, Michael Joseph, 1986, p160
38. Hough, Richard and Richards, Denis, *Battle of Britain*, Pen and Sword Military, 2007 p191
39. Moulson, Tom, *The Millionaire's Squadron – The Remarkable Story of 601 Squadron and the Flying Sword*, Pen and Sword Aviation, 2014, p93
40. Price, Alfred, *Battle of Britain – The Hardest Day*, Book Club Associates, 1979, p116
41. AIR-50-166-9
42. AIR-50-166-73

ENDNOTES

43. AIR-27-2106
44. Bailey, David J., *610 (County of Chester) Auxiliary Air Force Squadron, 1936–1940*, Fonthill Media, 2019
45. AIR-27-1949-11
46. Craig, Phil; Clayton, Tim, *Finest Hour: The story of the Battle of Britain*, Hodder & Stoughton, 2000, pp249-52
47. Moulson, Tom, *The Millionaire's Squadron – The Remarkable Story of 601 Squadron and the Flying Sword*, Pen and Sword Aviation, 2014, p97
48. Watkins, David; Listemann, Phil (2007). *No.501 (County of Gloucester) Squadron, 1939–1945: Hurricane, Spitfire, Tempest*. France, Philedition, p19
49. AIR-27-2123
50. AIR-27-2126
51. Dundas, Hugh, Flying Start, *A Fighter Pilot's War Years*, Pen and Sword, 1988, p46
52. Moulson, Tom, *The Millionaires' Squadron – The Remarkable Story of 601 Squadron and the Flying Sword*, Pen and Sword Aviation, 2014, p95
53. Collier, Richard, *Eagle Day: The Battle of Britain, Cassell, 1966,* p96
54. Hastings, Max, *Finest Years: Churchill as Warlord 1940–45*, HarperPress, 2009, p98
55. https://winstonchurchill.org/resources/speeches/1940-the-finest-hour/the-few/
56. Dundas, Hugh, *Flying Start, A Fighter Pilot's War Years*, Pen and Sword, 1988, pp47-8
57. Gelb, Norman, *Scramble – A Narrative History of the Battle of Britain*, Michael Joseph, 1986, pp175-6
58. Townsend-Bickers, Richard, *Ginger Lacey Fighter Pilot*, Pan, London, 1962, pp90-1
59. Shores, Christopher; Williams, Clive (1994). Aces High: a Tribute to the Most Notable Fighter Pilots of the British and Commonwealth Forces in WWII. London, Grub Street, p615

60. Dundas, Hugh, *Flying Start, A Fighter Pilot's War Years*, Pen and Sword, 1988, pp49-50
61. AIR-50-166-73
62. Hillary, Richard, *The Last Enemy*, Pan, London, 1960, p110
63. Shores, Christopher; Williams, Clive, *Aces High: A Tribute to the Most Notable Fighter Pilots of the British and Commonwealth Forces in WWII*. London: Grub Street, 1994, p292
64. Hillary, Richard, *The Last Enemy*, Pan, London, 1960, pp110-12
65. Dundas, Hugh, Flying Start, A Fighter Pilot's War Years, Pen and Sword, 1988, p202
66. Townsend-Bickers, Richard, *Ginger Lacey Fighter Pilot*, Pan, London, 1962, p96
67. Shores, Christopher; Williams, Clive, *Aces High: A Tribute to the Most Notable Fighter Pilots of the British and Commonwealth Forces in WWII*. London: Grub Street, 1994, p736
68. Hillary, Richard, The Last Enemy, Pan, London, 1960, p9
69. Courtesy of Carolyn Horton/Raymond Davis Family Archive
70. Moulson, Tom, *The Millionaires' Squadron – The Remarkable Story of 601 Squadron and the Flying Sword*, Pen and Sword Aviation, 2014, p103
71. Gelb, Norman, *Scramble – A Narrative History of the Battle of Britain*, Michael Joseph, 1986, pp174-5
72. Ibid p166
73. Ibid p198

Chapter 6: Battle of Britain Phase 4, 7 September – 2 October

1. Gelb, Norman, Scramble – A Narrative History of the Battle of Britain, Michael Joseph, 1986, p226
2. Stansky, Professor Peter, *The First Day of the Blitz: 7-Sep-40*. Yale University Press, 2007, p136
3. AIR-2-7355

ENDNOTES

4. Johnstone, Air Vice Marshal Sandy, *Spitfire Into War*, Grafton Books, London, 1988
5. AIR-50-169-191
6. Welford, Harry, The Unrelenting Years 1916–1946, BJ&M Promotions, p112
7. Dixon, Robert, 607 Squadron: A Shade of Blue, The History Press Ltd, 2008
8. Welford, Harry, The Unrelenting Years 1916–1946, BJ&M Promotions, p112
9. Johnstone, Air Vice Marshal Sandy, *Spitfire Into War*, Grafton Books, London, 1988
10. Battle of Britain Monument – bbm.org.uk/airmen/Sprague.htm
11. Johnstone, Air Vice Marshal Sandy, *Spitfire Into War*, Grafton Books, London, 1988
12. AIR-27-2109
13. Ferguson, Aldon P., Hamlin, John, Beware! Beware!: The History of 611 (West Lancashire) Squadron Royal Auxiliary Air Force, Airfield Publications, 2004
14. Gelb, Norman, *Scramble – A Narrative History of the Battle of Britain*, Michael Joseph, 1986, p225
15. Townshend-Bickers, Richard, Ginger Lacey Fighter Pilot, Pan, London, 1962, p 103-5
16. Watkins, David; Listemann, Phil, *No.501 (County of Gloucester) Squadron, 1939–1945: Hurricane, Spitfire, Tempest*. France: Listemann, 2007, p22
17. AIR-27-2087
18. AIR-27-2087
19. Holmes, Ray, *Sky Spy – From Six Miles High to Hitler's Bunker*, 1989, Airlife, p94-101
20. Ziegler, Frank H., *The Story of 609 Squadron: Under the White Rose*. London: Macdonald, 1971 p144
21. Goss, Chris, Brothers in Arms: *The Story of a British and a German Fighter Unit, August to December 1940*, Air World, 2020 p93

22. Crook, David, *Spitfire Pilot: A Personal Account of the Battle of Britain*, Spitfire Publishers 2018, p84-6
23. Townsend-Bickers, Richard, *Ginger Lacey Fighter Pilot*, Pan, London, 1962, pp105-7
24. *Bravery, Sacrifice, Freedom*, Battle of Britain 70 publication, Royal Air Force with Newsdesk Media, p167
25. Frayn-Turner, John, The Bader Wing, Airlife 1999, p120
26. https://www.thegazette.co.uk/London/issue/34964/page/5900/data.pdf
27. AIR-50-166-137
28. MacLean, Charles Hector, Fighters in Defence: Memories of the Glasgow Squadron, 1999, Squadron Prints
29. AIR-50-166-73
30. Sarkar, Dilip, The Few: The Story of the Battle of Britain in the Words of the Pilots, Amberley 2012, p251-2
31. Shores, Christopher; Williams, Clive, *Aces High: A Tribute to the Most Notable Fighter Pilots of the British and Commonwealth Forces in WWII*. London: Grub Street, 1994, p497
32. Nancarrow, F.G., *Glasgow's Fighter Squadron: 602 Squadron RAF*. London and Glasgow: Collins, 1942, p31
33. https://rafa.org.uk/blog/2020/09/30/battle-of-britain-flightmechanic/
34. Ross, David M.S.; Blanche, Bruce J. Sqn Ldr; Simpson, William (2003a). The Greatest Squadron of Them All: The Definitive History of 603 (City of Edinburgh) Squadron, RAuxAF. Vol. 1: Formation to 1941. London: Grub Street, p273
35. Shores, Christopher; Williams, Clive, Aces High: A Tribute to the Most Notable Fighter Pilots of the British and Commonwealth Forces in WWII. London: Grub Street, 1994, p1067
36. Ibid
37. Gelb, Norman, Scramble – A Narrative History of the Battle of Britain, Michael Joseph, 1986, p151

ENDNOTES

38. London Gazette, No. 34945, 8 October 1940
39. Dowding, Air Chief Marshal Hugh, *Battle of Britain Despatch*, Air Power Review
40. *Bravery, Sacrifice*, Freedom, Battle of Britain 70 publication, Royal Air Force with Newsdesk Media, p167

Chapter 7: Battle of Britain Phase 5, 3–31 October

1. https://www.rafmuseum.org.uk/research/online-exhibitions/history-of-the-battle-of-britain/the-battle-of-britain-phase-five/
2. AIR-27-2087
3. Bowman, Martin W., and Masters, David, *RAF Fighter Pilots in WWII*, Pen and Sword, 2020, Ch11
4. AIR-50-169-92
5. AIR-50-162-34
6. Shores, Christopher; Williams, Clive, *Aces High: A Tribute to the Most Notable Fighter Pilots of the British and Commonwealth Forces in WWII*. London: Grub Street, 1994, p1279
7. Mackenzie, Wg Cdr K.W., Hurricane Combat, William Kimber, 1987, p48-50
8. AIR-27-2088-19
9. Bowyer, Chaz, Fighter Pilots of the RAF, 1939-1945, William and Kimber, 1984, p108
10. AIR 27-2102-19
11. AIR-50-177-253 24
12. Dundas, Hugh, Flying Start, A Fighter Pilot's War Years, Pen and Sword, 1988, p204
13. Shores, Christopher; Williams, Clive (1994). Aces High: a Tribute to the Most Notable Fighter Pilots of the British and Commonwealth Forces in WWII. London, Grub Street, p1171
14. Doe, Helen, Fighter Pilot: The Life of Battle of Britain Ace Bob Doe, Amberley, 2016 p26-36

15. Shores, Christopher; Williams, Clive, Aces High: A Tribute to the Most Notable Fighter Pilots of the British and Commonwealth Forces in WWII. London: Grub Street, 1994, p656
16. https://www.thegazette.co.uk/all-notices/content/100648
17. Shores, Christopher; Williams, Clive, Aces High: A Tribute to the Most Notable Fighter Pilots of the British and Commonwealth Forces in WWII. London: Grub Street, 1994, p330
18. AIR 27-2102-19
19. Dowding, Air Chief Marshal Hugh, *Battle of Britain Despatch*, Air Power Review, Vol 18 Iss 2, introduction by Sebastian Cox
20. AIR-27-2074
21. 'Bravery, Sacrifice, Freedom', Battle of Britain 70 publication, Royal Air Force with Newsdesk Media, p158

Epilogue

1. AIR-27-2074
2. Bowyer, Chaz (1984). Fighter Pilots of the RAF, 1939–1945, William Kimber & Co, p98
3. AIR-27-2102
4. Dundas, Hugh, Flying Start, A Fighter Pilot's War Years, Pen and Sword, 1988, p65
5. The London Gazette. 25 October 1940. p. 6194.
6. Wynn, Kenneth G, Men of the Battle of Britain, Gliddon Books, 1989 p61
7. Wynn, Kenneth G, Men of the Battle of Britain, Gliddon Books,1989, p12
8. Shores, Christopher; Williams, Clive, Aces High: A Tribute to the Most Notable Fighter Pilots of the British and Commonwealth Forces in WWII. London: Grub Street, 1994, p1319

ENDNOTES

9. Shores, Christopher; Williams, Clive, Aces High: A Tribute to the Most Notable Fighter Pilots of the British and Commonwealth Forces in WWII. London: Grub Street, 1994, p553
10. Battle of Britain Monument – bbm.org.uk/kayll
11. Battle of Britain Monument – bbm.org.uk/DundasHSL.htm
12. Shores, Christopher; Williams, Clive, Aces High: A Tribute to the Most Notable Fighter Pilots of the British and Commonwealth Forces in WWII. London: Grub Street, 1994, p988
13. Ibid p1322
14. Ibid p1067
15. Wynn, Kenneth G, Men of the Battle of Britain, Gliddon Books, 1989, p10
16. Shores, Christopher; Williams, Clive, Aces High: A Tribute to the Most Notable Fighter Pilots of the British and Commonwealth Forces in WWII. London: Grub Street, 1994, p713
17. Wynn, Kenneth G, Men of the Battle of Britain, Gliddon Books, 1989, p30
18. Shores, Christopher; Williams, Clive, Aces High: A Tribute to the Most Notable Fighter Pilots of the British and Commonwealth Forces in WWII. London: Grub Street, 1994, p330
19. https://rauxaf.org/force-history-1939-to-1945/
20. Mansell, Dr A., The Royal Air Force Volunteer Reserve 1936-1939, RAF Historical Society Seminar – Reserve Auxiliary Forces – Journal-29A, p36
21. Johnstone, Air Vice Marshal Alexander 'Sandy', *75 Eventful Years – A Tribute to the Royal Air Force 1918-1993*, Tony Ross (ed, p23)
22. Shores, Christopher, RAF Historical Society Seminar – Reserve Auxiliary Forces - Journal-29A, p49-50

BIBLIOGRAPHY

Websites, newspapers and miscellaneous publications:
Battle of Britain Monument - bbm.org.uk
RAF Museum - www.rafmuseum.org.uk/research
Royal Auxiliary Air Force Foundation - rauxaf.org
International Churchill Society - winstonchurchill.org
601 (County of London) Squadron Historical Database -601squadron.com
Manchester Guardian
RAF Historical Society, Journal 29 - Reserve Auxiliary Forces
RAF Historical Society, Journal 11, Professionals, Amateurs and Private Armies. Pilot Entry Portals in the RAF Expansion of 1934 to 1939
London Gazette
Hansard

The National Archive:
Operations Record Books in series AIR-27 at the National Archive, from AIR-27-1948 to AIR-27-2126. These are of the following squadrons: 501, 504, 600, 601, 602, 603, 604, 605, 607, 609, 610, 611, 615 and 616.
Combat reports in series AIR-50 at the National Archive, from AIR-50-162-34 to AIR-50-177-253.

Books:
Bailey, David J., 610 (County of Chester) Auxiliary Air Force Squadron, 1936-1940, Fonthill Media 2019

BIBLIOGRAPHY

Bishop, Patrick, Fighter Boys, Harper Collins, 2003

Brickhill, Paul, Reach for the Sky, Fontana, 1954

Bowman, Martin W., and Masters, David, RAF Fighter Pilots in WWII, Pen and Sword, 2020

Bowyer, Chaz, Fighter Pilots of the RAF, 1939–1945, William Kimber & Co, 1984

Bravery, Sacrifice, Freedom, Battle of Britain 70 publication, Royal Air Force with Newsdesk Media

Cameron, Dugald, Glasgow's Own: Visual Record of the Men and Machines of 602 (City of Glasgow) Squadron, Royal Auxiliary Air Force, 1925-57, Squadron Prints Ltd, 1987

Collier, Richard, Eagle Day: The Battle of Britain, Cassell, 1966

Coombs, L.F.E., The Lion Has Wings: The Race to Prepare the RAF for World War II, 1935-1940. Airlife, 1997

Craig, Phil; Clayton, Tim, Finest Hour: The Story of the Battle of Britain, Hodder, 2001

Crook, David, Spitfire Pilot: A Personal Account of the Battle of Britain, Spitfire Publishers 2018 (First published in June 1942 by Faber and Faber, updated and expanded edition published September 2018)

Deere, Group Captain Alan C, Nine Lives, Hodder and Stoughton Ltd, 1959

Deighton, Len, The Battle of Britain, Jonathan Cape, 1980

Delve, Ken; Pitchfork, Graham, South Yorkshire's Own: 616 Squadron RAF. Doncaster Books, 1990

Dempster, Derek and Wood, Derek, The Narrow Margin, Hutchinson, 1961

Dickson, Wg Cdr Alex, RAFVR Memories, HQPTC, RAF Innsworth, 1997

Dixon, Robert, 607 Squadron: A Shade of Blue, The History Press Ltd, 2008

Doe, Helen, Fighter Pilot: The Life of Battle of Britain Ace Bob Doe, Amberley Publishing 2016

Dowding, Air Chief Marshal, Despatches on the Conduct of the Battle of Britain, August 1940

Dundas, Hugh, Flying Start, A Fighter Pilot's War Years, Pen and Sword, 1988

Ferguson, Aldon P., Hamlin, John, Beware! Beware! The History of 611 (West Lancashire) Squadron Royal Auxiliary Air Force, Airfield Publications, 2004

Frayn-Turner, John, The Bader Wing, Airlife, 1999

Freeman, Sqn Ldr AF, The Post-War Royal Auxiliary Air Force. Royal Air Force Reserve and Auxiliary Forces, RAF Historical Society, 2003

Gelb, Norman, Scramble - A Narrative History of the Battle of Britain, Michael Joseph, 1986

Goss, Chris, Brothers in Arms: The Story of a British and a German Fighter Unit, August to December 1940, Air World, 2020

Hastings, Max, Finest Years: Churchill as Warlord 1940–45, HarperPress, 2009

Halstead, Ivor, Wings of Victory - A Tribute to the RAF, The Right Book Club, 1941

Hillary, Richard, The Last Enemy, Pan, London, 1960

Holmes, Ray, Sky Spy - From Six Miles High to Hitler's Bunker, Airlife, 1989

Hough, Richard and Richards, Denis, Battle of Britain, Pen and Sword Military, 2007

Hunt, Leslie, Twenty-One Squadrons: The History of the Royal Auxiliary Air Force, 1925-1957, Garnstone Press, 1972

Jefford, Wing Commander CG MBE BA., Reserve Auxiliary Forces - Air Force Reserves 1912 to Munich, RAF Historical Society Seminar, 2003

Johnstone, Air Vice Marshal Sandy, Spitfire into War, Grafton Books, London, 1988

Kayll, Wg Cdr Joe, Defending Northern Skies 1915–1995, 24 October 1995, The Royal Air Force Historical Society

BIBLIOGRAPHY

Lepine, Mike, Voices of The Battle of Britain 80th Anniversary 1940 – 2020, Sona Books 2020

Mackenzie, Wg Cdr K.W., Hurricane Combat, William Kimber, 1987

MacLean, Charles Hector, Fighters in Defence: Memories of the Glasgow Squadron, 1999, Squadron Prints

Mansell, Dr A., Professionals, Amateurs and Private Armies. Pilot Entry Portals in the RAF Expansion of 1934 to 1939 Proceedings of the RAF Historical Society Number 11, 1993

Mansell, Dr A., The Royal Air Force Volunteer Reserve 1936-1939, RAF Historical Society Seminar – Reserve Auxiliary Forces – Journal-29A

Moulson, Tom, The Millionaire's Squadron - The Remarkable Story of 601 Squadron and the Flying Sword, Pen and Sword Aviation, 2014

Nancarrow, F.G. (1942). Glasgow's fighter squadron: 602 Squadron RAF. London and Glasgow: Collins.

Onderwater, Hans (1997). Gentlemen in Blue: the History of No. 600 (City of London) Squadron Royal Auxiliary Air Force and No. 600 (City of London) Squadron Association, 1925–1995. London: Pen & Sword Books Ltd. ISBN 0-85052-575-6.

Overy, Richard, The Battle of Britain - Myth and Reality, Penguin, 2000

Philpott, Wg Cdr Ian M, The Royal Air Force - An Encyclopaedia of the Interwar Years - Volume 1, Pen and Sword Aviation, 2005

Price, Alfred, Battle of Britain - The Hardest Day, Book Club Associates, 1979

Price, Alfred, The Legendary Spitfire Mk I/II 1939-41, Osprey 1996

Price, Alfred, The Battle of Britain, Arms and Armour Press, 1990

Ross, David M.S.; Blanche, Bruce J. Sqn Ldr; Simpson, William (2003a). The Greatest Squadron of Them All: The Definitive History of 603 (City of Edinburgh) Squadron, RAuxAF. Vol. 1: Formation to 1941. London: Grub Street Publishing. ISBN 1-904010-49-0.

Roskill, S.W.; Butler, J.R.M (ed.). War at Sea. History of the Second World War United Kingdom Military Series. Vol. I, HMSO London, 1954

Sarkar, Dilip, The Few – The Story of the Battle of Britain in the Words of the Pilots, Amberley, 2012

Shores, Christopher; Williams, Clive, Aces High: A Tribute to the Most Notable Fighter Pilots of the British and Commonwealth Forces in WWII. London, Grub Street, 1994

Stansky, Professor Peter, The First Day of the Blitz: 7 Sep-40. Yale University Press, 2007

The Battle of Britain August-October 1940, Ministry of Information, 1941

Templewood, Viscount (Sir Samuel Hoare), Empire of the Air - The Advent of the Air Age - 1922-29, Collins, London, 1957

Terraine, John, The Right of the Line, The Royal Air Force in the European War 1939-1945, Hodder And Stoughton, 1985

Thetford, Owen Aircraft of the Royal Air Force 1918-58. Putnam, 1958

Townshend-Bickers, Richard, Ginger Lacey Fighter Pilot, Pan, London, 1962

Trevor-Roper, Hugh, Hitler's War Directives; 1939–1945. Edinburgh: Birlinn. 2004

Watkins, David; Listemann, Phil, No.501 (County of Gloucester) Squadron, 1939–1945: Hurricane, Spitfire, Tempest, 2007

Welford, Harry, The Unrelenting Years 1916–1946, BJ&M Promotion, 1997

Wilkinson, Louise, Freeman, Sqn Ldr Tony, The Royal Auxiliary Air Force - Commemorating 100 years of service. Air World - Pen and Sword, 2023

Wilkinson, Louise, The Territorial Air Force - The RAF's Voluntary Squadrons, 1926– 1957. Air World - Pen and Sword, 2020

Wynn, Kenneth G, Men of the Battle of Britain, Gliddon Books, 1989

White, Ian, If You Want Peace, Prepare For War. A History of No 604 (County of Middlesex) Squadron RAuxAF, in Peace and in War, 604 Squadron Association, 2005

Ziegler, Frank H. (1971). The Story of 609 Squadron: Under the White Rose. London: Macdonald. ISBN 0-356-03641-3.

INDEX

Groups:
9 Group 68
10 Group 68, 98, 102, 132
11 Group 67–8, 81, 98, 132, 146, 162–3, 168, 210
12 Group 33, 67, 166, 168
13 Group 67, 12
14 Group 67, 209

Squadrons:
1 Squadron 31, 98
19 Squadron 30, 53–4
32 Squadron 56, 76
41 Squadron 198
43 Squadron 44, 47, 164–5
65 Squadron 53, 181
81 Squadron 208
92 Squadron 56, 60, 198–9
111 Squadron 22, 44, 47, 86
213 Squadron 166
500 (County of Kent) Squadron 3
501 (County of Gloucester) Squadron xviii, 3, 22, 29, 46–7, 63–4, 86, 90–1, 105, 138, 147, 168, 189, 191, 198, 205, 212–13
502 (Ulster) Squadron 3, 9
503 (City of Lincoln) Squadron 3, 9
504 (County of Nottingham) Squadron xviii, 3, 9, 21, 47, 49, 50, 72, 171–2, 212, 175
600 (City of London) Squadron xiv, xvii, 3, 4, 31, 31, 44, 45, 54, 56, 93, 104, 125–6, 158, 212
601 (County of London) Squadron xiv, xix, 3–6, 26–7, 41, 45, 48–9, 50, 55, 100–103, 113, 115, 118–19, 130–1, 134, 142, 155, 157, 185, 207–208, 212
602 (City of Glasgow) Squadron xi, xiv, 3–4, 8, 22, 35–9, 41, 63–4, 68, 72–5, 93, 123, 134–6, 149, 151, 163, 166, 181–3, 186, 194, 201–202, 205–206, 211–12
603 (City of Edinburgh) Squadron xiv, xvii, xviii, xix, 3, 6, 14, 21–2, 32, 35–8, 39–40, 48, 72–4, 85, 149, 150–1, 179, 184–5, 211–2

604 (County of Middlesex)
Squadron 4–5, 9, 45, 105, 124, 158, 212
605 (County of Warwick)
Squadron 4, 24, 30, 43–4, 51–5, 61, 63–4, 68, 126, 129, 154, 163, 170, 184, 188–91, 194, 209, 212
607 (County of Durham)
Squadron 2, 4, 6, 17–18, 24, 39, 40, 42–3, 48–50, 72, 129, 164–5, 172, 182, 206–207, 209, 212
609 (West Riding) Squadron xv–xvi, xvii, xxii, 9, 19–20, 28, 30, 44, 50, 54, 60, 63, 69, 76, 80–81, 83, 95–96, 98–100, 109–111, 113, 119–22, 124, 146, 148, 153, 176, 194–7, 200, 203–204, 211–12
610 (County of Chester)
Squadron 6, 9, 11, 30, 41, 45, 52, 54, 58, 76, 91–3, 108–109, 137–8, 155, 211
611 (West Lancashire)
Squadron 9, 33–34, 44, 54, 55–60, 69, 166–8, 178–9, 212
612 (County of Aberdeen)
Squadron xvii, 9
613 (City of Manchester)
Squadron 9
614 (County of Glamorgan)
Squadron vii, xii, 9
615 (County of Surrey)
Squadron xx, 9, 42–3, 50, 55, 64, 81–2, 108, 140–2, 149, 154, 206
616 (South Yorkshire)
Squadron xiv, xxii, 4, 7, 9, 16, 30, 32–4, 52–5, 74, 132, 141, 143, 148–9, 206, 212

Abbeville 90
Adams, F/O Dennis Arthur 58, 178
Adler Tag 112
Adlerangriff 112
Agazarian, F/O Noel le Chevalier 29, 96
Aitken, Sqn Ldr (The Hon) John William Maxwell 27, 41, 48–9, 113, 131, 207
Appleby, P/O Michael 20, 63, 76, 95–7, 100, 122, 124
Aquitania 27
Arras 50–1, 100, 130
Auchinleck, Lt Gen Claude 123
Aysgarth School 16

Babbage, Sgt Cyril Frederick 150–1
Bader, Sqn Ldr Douglas 166
Baker, LAC 44
Bazin, Flt Lt James Michael 24, 48, 200, 209
Beaverbrook, Lord 27, 48, 142, 208
Belgium 44, 48–50
Ben Lomond 24
Berlin 85

INDEX

Berry, P/O Ronald 73, 208
Bétheniville 45, 47
Birkenhead Advertiser 11–12
Bisdee, P/O John Derek xvi–xvii, 69, 95
Blackadder, Flt Lt William Francis 48, 72, 129–30, 181–2
Blenheim, Bristol 41, 44–5, 49–50, 101–102, 104–105, 124, 158, 207
Blitzkrieg 61
Bognor 126, 134, 151
Boulogne 50–1
Boyd, Flt Lt Robert Findlay 36, 75, 134, 137, 179–80, 205
Brereton, LAC Jeff 184
Brewster, P/O John 141
Bristol xvii, 195
British Expeditionary Force 41–2, 49–52, 61–4, 69, 86
Brooke, Lt-Gen Alan 123
Browning 31
Brussels 48–9
Buchanan Arms, Drymen 24
Budzinski, Sgt Jan 164, 194
Burnell-Phillips, P/O Peter 130, 165, 181–3

Caister, P/O James Russell 74
Cambrai 49–50
Casson, P/O Lionel Harwood 'Buck' 141
Chamberlain, Neville 18–19, 24, 28, 46, 124

Chandler, Sgt Horatio Herbert 11–12, 91–2, 108, 138
Channel Islands 64, 87
Cherbourg 64, 98, 102
Christchurch 19, 196
Churchill, Winston xii, xix–xx, 42, 46, 55, 61, 63–5, 81, 83, 86, 122, 129, 142–4, 158–9, 189, 200, 204
Cleaver, F/O Gordon 'Mouse' 101–102, 130–1
Cloves, Flight Sergeant 19–20
Clyde, Flt Lt William Pancoast 26–7, 54–5, 113–14, 207
Clydesdale, Marquis of 4, 8
Cockburnspath 37
Collard, F/O Peter 82, 108
Cooper-Slipper, F/O Thomas Paul Michael 51–2, 170
Cornwall 84
Cowdenbeath 37
Croix de Guerre 47
Cromer 41
Crompton, F/O Ralph Kenyon 58–9
Crook, P/O David Moore xv–xviii, xxi, 20, 28, 76, 78–80, 96, 98, 109–11, 119, 121, 124, 176, 196, 203
Crowborough 181
Currant, P/O Christopher Frederick 'Bunny' 51, 128–9, 170
Czechoslovakia 17, 20, 24

Dalkeith 37
Danielson, F/O Peter John 51, 53
Danzig 20, 24, 27
Davis, Flt Lt Carl Raymond xi, 5, 41, 102, 118, 134, 155, 157–8
Deere, Flt Lt Alan 72, 104, 125–6
Demetriadi, F/O Richard Stephen 'Dick' 101–103, 158
Demon, Hawker 5, 21
Denholm, Sqn Ldr George Lovell 6, 36, 73–4, 150, 155
Denmark 43
Dickie, P/O William Gordon 102–103
Do 17 xiv, 43, 46–7, 49, 52–4, 64, 73–4, 81, 85, 90–2, 94, 96, 102–103, 124–5, 129–30, 138, 140, 147–8, 151, 154–5, 165, 170, 172, 175–6, 182, 185–6, 195, 198–200
Doncaster 7, 9, 15–16, 27, 30
Dore, Wing Commander 5
Dorset 18, 80, 98, 102, 153
Douglas-Hamilton, Sqn Ldr Douglas 8
Dover 50, 52, 81–2, 89, 91, 94–5, 101, 109, 144, 146, 148, 192, 198, 208
Dowding, Air Chief Marshal Hugh xii, 38, 60–1, 66–8, 94–5, 103, 123, 142, 159, 161–2, 167, 186, 200, 204, 210
Drummond-Hay, F/O Peter 76, 79

Dundas, F/O John Charles 18–20, 54, 74, 81, 96–7, 109, 111, 120, 122, 124–6, 153, 175–6, 194–7, 203–204
Dundas, P/O Hugh 4, 7, 16, 24, 26, 30, 32, 34, 74, 132, 141–6, 148–9, 204, 207
Dunkirk 51–9, 63–4, 66, 69–70, 76, 80, 86, 91, 100–101, 130–1, 167, 172, 179, 209
Dunning-White, P/O Peter William 100

Eastleigh 30, 92
Edge, Sqn Ldr Gerald Richmond 43, 51, 96, 129, 163, 166, 181, 209
Edinburgh xix, 6, 35, 38, 72, 149
Edinburgh, HMS 37
Ellis, Sqn Ldr John 52, 54, 109
Else, Sgt Peter 92
Empire Air Day 21–2
Eyre, F/O Anthony 154, 209

Fighter Command xii, 38, 62, 66–8, 71, 85, 104, 111–12, 124, 134, 142, 158–9, 161–3, 166, 170, 187, 201–202, 206, 208–209
Firth of Forth 37, 39 40, 48, 73, 126, 185
Fiske, P/O William Meade Lindsley 'Billy' 102
Flamingo, de Havilland 55, 63, 81
Folkestone 56, 92, 192–4

INDEX

France 18, 20, 23–5, 27, 41–2, 44–51, 54–5, 60, 62–4, 66, 69, 71–2, 75, 86, 90, 102–104, 118, 136, 139, 146, 154, 161, 172, 185, 193, 196, 200, 206, 208–209

Gallipoli 139
Gardner, Charles 81–2
Gardner, Sgt Bernard George Derry 108–109
Gaunce, Flt Lt Lionel Manley 'Elmer' 108, 140
Gauntlet, Gloster 21, 33
Gayner, F/O John Richard Hensman 82
Germany 17–18, 21, 22–3, 25–8, 41–4, 64, 84, 124, 160, 209
Gifford, Sqn Ldr Patrick 'Patsy' 36–7, 39–40, 48
Gillam, Flt Lt Denys Edgar 149
Gillan, F/O James 102–103
Gilroy, F/O George Kemp 74
Gladiator, Gloster 21, 39–40, 42–3
Glasgow 35–6, 72, 85, 135, 183, 186
Gore, F/O William Ernest 24, 72
Gravelines 50–1
Grosvenor, Lord Edward Arthur 1–4

Halifax, Lord 18–19, 197
Hamilton, Duke of 150
Hamme-Mille 48
Hampden, Handley Page 33
Harrogate 19
Harrow, Handley Page 46
Harrow School 90, 100, 130, 147
Hart, Hawker 58–9
Haslemere 114
Hawkings, Sgt Redvers Percival 102
Hayes, P/O Norman 44–5
Hazebrook 51
He 111 36, 40–52, 54, 56, 63–4, 73–4, 85–6, 90–1, 93–4, 96, 100, 102, 118, 124, 129–31, 136, 140, 149, 151, 154, 164, 167–8, 170, 177, 185, 198
He 113 109, 118–19, 130, 164, 198
He 115 48, 57
Heath, Flt Lt Barrie 34, 54, 58, 167–8
Hillary, F/O Richard Hope 22–3, 29, 32, 149–52, 155, 207
Hilbre Island 33
Hind, Hawker 19–21, 36, 59
Hitler, Adolf 17–18, 20, 25, 27, 51, 65, 83–5, 178, 187
Hoare, Sir Samuel 2–3
Holden, F/O Kenneth 53, 141
Holmes, Cpl John 44–5
Holmes, Sgt Raymond Towers xiv, 12–17, 33, 171–6, 178–9
Hood, HMS 37
Howes, Sgt Harold Norman 170–1

Hugo, P/O Petrus Hendrik 82, 108, 140
Hull 29, 73
Hunter, LAC 19
Hurricane, Hawker 21, 24, 30–3, 42–3, 47–8, 50–3, 71, 76, 81–2, 86–7, 89–90, 92, 98, 101–103, 105–106, 108, 113, 115–17, 119, 122–3, 130, 135, 138–40, 142, 147, 158–9, 163, 165, 169, 172–5, 176, 182, 192–3, 199, 202, 205, 208

Isle of Wight 84, 97, 102, 104, 109, 134, 146, 182, 195, 204
Ismay, General Sir Hastings 142–3

Johnstone, Sqn Ldr Alexander Vallance Riddell Johnstone 'Sandy' 72–3, 123, 134, 151, 163, 166, 185, 208, 210
Jones, P/O Robert Eric 57
Ju 52 45
Ju 87 49, 50–1, 58–60, 77–9, 82, 87, 89, 95, 101, 105–107, 119–22, 124, 131, 134–7, 147–8, 151, 154, 185
Ju 88 37–8, 52–3, 73–5, 102, 107, 113–14, 124–5, 130, 136, 140, 147, 151, 154, 165, 167, 180–2, 184–6, 191, 198–200, 206

Kanalkampf 67, 75–6
Kayll, Sqn Ldr Joseph Robert 6, 24, 40, 42–3, 55, 64, 140, 206–207

Kelvinside Academy 36, 72, 135
Kerr, F/O Gerald Malcolm Theodore 54
Kerr-Wilson, F/O John 54
Kroll Opera House 85

Lacey, Sgt James Harry ix, xi, 11, 13, 16–17, 29–32, 47, 64, 87–8, 90, 93–4, 105–108, 146–7, 153–4, 168–9, 177, 191, 201, 205
Lammermuir Hills 41
Leather, Flt Lt William Johnson 57, 179
Lee, F/O Kenneth Norman Thomson 'Hawkeye' 86–7, 89–91, 139–40
Lewis gun 126
Lincolnshire 41, 44
Little, F/O Thomas Donald 59, 96
Liverpool 14, 57–60, 178–9
Lock, P/O Eric Stanley xiv, 197–8
London xix, 5, 13, 27, 36, 101, 139, 142–4, 150, 161–5, 168, 170, 172–5, 178, 187–8, 199
Lord Gort, General 41
Low Countries 44, 100
Luftflotte 5 126
Luftwaffe xiii, xx, xxii, 40, 52, 66, 68, 75–6, 84–5, 91, 104–105, 109, 111–12, 117, 124, 134–5, 138, 158, 160–1, 163, 168, 178, 182, 188, 202–203, 210
Lyme Regis 97

INDEX

Macfie, P/O Colin 58–9
Mackenzie, P/O Kenneth William 191–3, 205
Maclean, Wg Cdr Hector 180
Mae West 139, 143, 156, 171–2
Maidstone 163, 170–1, 189–90, 198, 201, 206
Mayers, P/O Howard Clive 115–17
McClintock, P/O John Arthur Peter 108
McComb, Sqn Ldr James Ellis 34, 56, 168
McDowall, Sgt Andrew 93, 137, 149, 151, 181, 186, 206
McGrath, P/O John Keswick Ulick Blake 99–100, 103–104, 113–14, 118, 130, 207
McKay, Sgt Donald Alistair Stewart 46, 64, 95, 140
McKellar, Sqn Ldr Archibald Ashmore ix, xi, 35–6, 38, 41, 64, 126–9, 154, 163–4, 170–1, 188–91, 194, 201–203
Me 109 47, 49–51, 53–4, 57–60, 64, 82, 87–8, 91–2, 95–7, 99–100, 102, 104–109, 111, 113–14, 119, 121–3, 130–1, 136–7, 140, 146–9, 151, 154–5, 157, 164–5, 167, 170, 175, 177, 179–82, 184–6, 188–96, 198–207
Me 110 xv–xvi, 47, 49, 50, 52, 55, 57, 60, 78, 81, 96, 99–101, 103–104, 107, 110–11, 114–19, 122, 125, 131, 138, 151, 153–4, 163, 166–7, 175–6, 181–2, 185–6, 195–6, 198–199
Medcalf, F/O Albert Rupert John 54
Medway, Sgt William Thomas 52, 54
Melbourne 93
Merlin, Rolls Royce 31, 172
Merville 42, 49, 55, 69, 101
Moberley, F/O George 53, 74, 148
Mohawk, HMS 37, 39
Montgomery, Maj-Gen Bernard 123
Morton, F/O James Storrs 36–7, 39, 85, 184–5, 208
Mudie, P/O Michael 82
Muirhead, P/O Ian James 43, 51–3, 128, 188
Munich 18, 20–21, 24, 54, 124
Mussolini, Benito 19

Nazi Germany 17, 20, 23, 25, 41, 152
Nazi–Soviet Pact 27
Newcastle 48, 127–8, 130
Norfolk 41
Norrent-Fontes 49–50
North Foreland 105, 153
North Sea 41, 54, 74, 85
Norway 43, 46, 126, 182, 209
Nowierski, P/O Tadeusz 96

Operation *Aerial* 63
Operation *Dynamo* 51

Orkneys 43
Orwell, George 75
Ostazsewski, P/O Piotr 96
Overstrand 41
Overton, F/O Charles Nevil 'Teeny' 81, 111

Paris 55, 63, 158
Park, Air Vice Marshal Keith 68, 81, 162, 167, 210
Parliament 1, 26, 46
Parsons, Sgt Claude Arthur 49, 91–2, 138
Peake, Harald 19
Peel, Sqn Ldr John 123
Peterhead 74
Phoney War 209
Pile, Lt-Gen Sir Frederick 123–4
Pohle, Hauptmann Helmuth 38
Poland 21, 24, 27–8, 71, 162
Poling 135–6
Portland 76, 79–81, 98–9, 103, 115, 117–18, 122, 124, 178, 195
Portland Bill 80, 87
Portobello 39
Portsmouth 100, 109, 111, 146, 182–3, 201
Prestwick 14–15, 73

Radford, Flight Lieutenant Dudley 16
RAF Stations:
  Abbotsinch 24, 35–6, 69
  Acklington 39, 42, 127, 208
  Bentley Priory 68
  Biggin Hill 45, 76, 91, 93, 106, 109, 135, 137–8, 189–90, 194
  Bircham Newton 41
  Catterick 171, 198
  Coltishall 149
  Croydon 42, 64, 80, 93, 138, 140, 163–4, 170, 188, 190, 192
  Debden 69, 142, 206
  Digby 44, 54, 59–60, 167
  Drem 35, 39, 54, 64, 93, 127, 163, 166
  Exeter 15, 157, 197, 208
  Finningley 33
  Gravesend 68, 87, 92–4, 106–107, 138, 147
  Halton 11
  Hawkinge 45, 51–2, 68, 76, 81–2, 87, 92, 94–5, 101, 104–108, 138, 147
  Hendon 4–5, 9, 50, 55, 100, 171–5, 199
  Hornchurch xviii–xix, 68, 104, 135, 150–1, 198, 206
  Kenley 45, 64, 135, 140–3, 168–9, 205
  Lympne 104–105, 147
  Manston 24–6, 44–5, 49, 68, 73, 100, 104–105, 107, 125, 147, 206
  Martlesham Heath 54, 56, 60
  Middle Wallop 76, 80, 93, 97–8, 103, 105, 113, 120, 124, 132

INDEX

Mildenhall 93
North Weald 60, 135, 172, 209
Northolt 3, 60, 69, 81
Redhill 201
Rochford 52, 68
Shawbury 30
Speke 9, 58–9, 69, 179
Tangmere 24, 50, 99–101, 103, 115, 126, 134–5, 164, 166
Turnhouse 3, 35–6, 73, 85, 149–50, 208
Usworth 72, 129–30, 164
Westhampnett 123, 134–7, 149–50, 166, 179–81
Wick 43–4, 172
Ramsgate 84, 107, 147
Reich 18
Reichstag 85
Rhodes-Moorhouse, Flt Lt William Henry 41, 101–103, 158
Richmond 166, 181
Ritchie, P/O Ian Small 74, 85
River Dee 33
Rolls-Royce 6, 31, 85, 206
Rome 19
Romney Marsh 138
Rosyth 35, 37
Rotte 71
Rotterdam 44
Royce, Flt Lt William Barrington 47–8, 175
Runciman, Viscount Leslie 6, 18

Russia 25–6, 30
Rye 194

Salisbury 125, 131
Sample, Sqn Ldr John 39–40, 72, 172
Sassoon, Sir Philip 4
Scapa Flow 43–4
Schöpfel, Gerhard 140
Schwarme 71
Scone 13, 15
Sealion, Operation 83, 160, 170, 177–8, 187
Selsey Bill 118, 130, 149, 151, 166, 181
Shields, Douglas 14–16
Sinclair, Archibald 63, 202
Skua, Blackburn 91
Smith, Sqn Ldr Andrew Thomas 41
Smith, Flt Lt Edward Brian Bretherton 52, 91–2, 109, 155
Smithers, P/O Julian Langley 102–103
Sorbonne 19
Southampton, HMS 37
Southampton 27, 108, 118, 131, 178–9, 182, 195
Soviet Union 24–6
Spitfire, Supermarine xv–xvi, xviii, 22, 31–6, 38, 42, 52–4, 56–7, 60, 71, 73–4, 76, 79, 81, 91–2, 96, 98, 105, 109–11, 113, 120, 122, 125, 132–4, 135–8,

142, 144–5, 149, 152, 155, 158–9, 166–8, 179, 181, 183, 189, 195, 198–9, 200
St Aubyn, Flt Lt Edward Fitzroy 'Teddy' 7, 26, 141, 148
Staples, Sgt Michael 111, 120
Stewart-Clark, P/O Dudley 74, 85
Stoddart, Flt Lt Kenneth Stoddart 59–60
Störangriffe 67, 76
Stowe School 6, 16, 19
Sudetenland 17–18
Sunderland 6
Swanage xv, 81, 97, 114, 195
Sylvester, P/O Edmund John Hilary 90–1

Tedder, Air Chief Marshal Lord 10
The Needles 96, 180–2
Tranent 38
Trenchard, Air Marshal Sir Hugh xix, 2–3, 8–9
Tutor, Avro 16, 30, 60
Tyneside 126–7, 129

University Air Squadron 22, 29, 32, 37, 58, 100, 116
Urie, Sqn Ldr John Dunlop 135–6

Villecoublay 55
Vitry-en-Artois 42, 46
Vouziers 46

Waalhaven 44
Watkins, F/O Douglas 57
Webb, F/O Paul Clifford 36, 38, 73
Wells 41
Westerham 189–90
Weygand, General 63, 65
Weymouth 76–7, 97–9, 116, 119, 196
Weymouth Bay 96, 98, 116
Willoughby de Broke, Lord 4
Wright, Sgt Eric William 51, 170, 188, 194

Yorkshire 13, 16, 19, 27, 132, 141, 148
Yorkshire Post 19, 124, 204

Zeebrugge 45